9th
BLUE
BOOK

DOLLS &
VALUES

by Jan Foulke

photographs
by Howard Foulke

Hobby House Press

Published by

Cumberland,
Maryland 21502

Other Titles by Author:
Blue Book of Dolls & Values®
2nd Blue Book of Dolls & Values®
3rd Blue Book of Dolls & Values®
4th Blue Book of Dolls & Values®
5th Blue Book of Dolls & Values®
6th Blue Book of Dolls & Values®
7th Blue Book of Dolls & Values®
8th Blue Book of Dolls & Values®
Focusing on Effanbee Composition Dolls
Focusing on Treasury of Mme. Alexander Dolls
Focusing on Gebrüder Heubach Dolls
Kestner: King of Dollmakers
Simon & Halbig Dolls: The Artful Aspect
Doll Classics
Focusing on Dolls

TITLE PAGE: 32in (81cm) *Tête Jumeau* with check marks. *Kay & Wayne Jensen Collection.*

Blue Book Dolls & Values is a registered trademark of Hobby House Press, Inc.

ADDITIONAL COPIES AVAILABLE @ $15.95 PLUS $2.25 POSTAGE FROM
HOBBY HOUSE PRESS, INC.
900 FREDERICK STREET
CUMBERLAND, MARYLAND 21502

Using This Book

Doll collecting is increasing in popularity every year. The great number of collectors entering the field has prompted more and larger doll shows, more dealers in dolls, more books on dolls, thicker doll magazines and more doll conventions and seminars, as well as an overwhelming offering of new dolls by mass-production companies as well as individual artists. This explosion has also increased the demand for old dolls and caused prices to rise as more collectors are vying for the same number of dolls which remains relatively static.

20½in (52cm) S.F.B.J. mold #237 character boy. For further information, see page 344. *Private Collection.*

With the average old doll representing a purchase of at least several hundred dollars, today's collectors must be as well-informed as possible about the dolls they are considering as additions to their collections. Since the first *BLUE BOOK OF DOLLS & VALUES*, published in 1974, our objectives have remained the same:

• To present a book which will help collectors to identify dolls and learn more about them.

• To provide retail prices as a guide for buyers and sellers of dolls.

Since every edition of the *BLUE BOOK* has sold more than the previous one, we can only conclude that these objectives are in line with the needs of doll lovers, collectors, dealers and appraisers who keep buying the latest editions of our book.

The dolls presented in this book are listed alphabetically by maker, material or the trade name of the individual doll. An extensive index has been provided to help in locating a specific doll. Of course, in a book this size, not every doll ever made can be discussed, but we have tried to include a broad spectrum of dolls which are available, desirable, interesting, popular and even some that are rare.

For each doll we have provided historical information, a description of the doll, a copy of the mark or label, the retail selling price and a photograph or picture reference to a previous edition of the *BLUE BOOK* as there is not enough space to show a photograph of each doll in each edition.

The price for a doll which is listed in this price guide is the retail value of a doll fulfilling all of the criteria discussed in the following chapter if it is purchased from a dealer.

In some cases the doll sizes given are the only ones known to have been made, but in the cases of the French and German bisque, china, papier-mâché, wood and most cloth dolls, sizes priced are chosen at random and listed sizes must not be interpreted as definitive.

The historical information given for some of the dolls would have been much more difficult to compile were it not for the original research already published by Dorothy S., Elizabeth A. and Evelyn J. Coleman; Johana G. Anderton; and Jürgen and Marianne Cieslik.

The data for the retail prices was gathered during 1988 from antique shops and shows, auctions, doll shops and shows, advertisements in collectors' periodicals, lists from doll dealers, and purchases and sales reported by both collectors and dealers. This information, along with our own valuations and judgments, was computed into the range of prices shown in this book. If we could not find a sufficient number of dolls to be sure of giving a reliable range, we reported the information we could find and marked those prices "**."

In setting a price for each doll, we use a range to allow for the variables of originality, quality and condition which must be reflected in the price. As collectors become more sophisticated in their purchases, fine examples of a doll especially those which are all original or with period clothing, can bring a premium of up to 50% more than prices quoted for ordinary examples. Sometimes a doll will bring a premium price because it is particularly cute, sweet, pretty or visually appealing, making an outstanding presentation. There is no way to factor this appeal into a price guide.

The international market has been more of an influence on domestic doll prices during the past year than previously because of the low value of the American dollar compared with foreign currency which is rising in value. The international interest has added a whole new dimension to the American doll market as increasing awareness of dolls in Japan, Germany, France and Switzerland among other countries is causing a great exodus and depletion of supply of our antique dolls.

Of particular interest in the international arena are French bisque bébés (except Steiners), French fashion ladies, German bisque character children, German bisque closed-mouth shoulder heads, German bisque "dolly" faces by Kestner, Kämmer & Reinhardt, and Handwerck, Lenci dolls, and Käthe Kruse dolls. This interest has caused dramatic price increases in some of these categories.

Although this outward flow of dolls has occurred several times during the past 25 years with the fluctuating international monetary rate, it has never before occurred to such an alarming extent. The Japanese market has been developing for some time and it is unpredictable how long this surge in dolls will continue. In various other areas of the arts, the Japanese swell has come and gone, but it shows no diminishing in the doll area as yet.

In the meantime, those doll categories of special interest to the Japanese will continue to rise in price.

All prices given for antique dolls are for those of good quality and condition, but showing normal wear, and appropriately dressed in new or old clothing, unless other specifications are given in the description accompanying that particular doll. Bisque or china heads should not be cracked, broken or repaired, but may have slight making imperfections, such as speckling, surface lines, darkened mold lines and uneven coloring. Bodies may have repairs or be nicely repainted, but should be old and appropriate to the head. A doll with old dress, shoes and wig will generally be higher than quoted prices as these items are in scarce supply and can easily cost over $50 each if purchased separately.

Prices given for modern dolls are for those in overall very good to excellent condition with original hair and clothing, except as noted. Composition may be lightly crazed, but should be colorful. Hard plastic and vinyl must be perfect. A never-played-with doll in original box with labels would bring a premium price.

The users of this book must keep in mind that no price guide is the final word. It cannot provide the absolute answer of what to pay. It should be used only as an aid in purchasing a doll. The final decision must be yours, for only you are on the scene, actually examining the specific doll in question. No book can take the place of actual field experience. Doll popularity can cycle; prices can fluctuate; regional variations can occur. Before you buy, do a lot of looking. Ask questions. Most dealers and collectors are glad to talk about their dolls and pleased to share their information with you.

19in (48cm) composition and cloth "Mama" doll with original *Happy Ann* label, all original. Unknown maker. For further information, see page 133. *H & J Foulke, Inc.*

Acknowledgements

Again, I want to thank our friends, associates, customers, fellow dealers, acquaintances and readers in the doll world for their encouragement, support and help in the preparation of this *9th BLUE BOOK OF DOLLS & VALUES.*

Those who allowed us to use photographs of their dolls or who provided special information for use in this edition are indispensable: Miriam Blankman, Roberta Roberts, Betty Harms, Emily Manning, Jean Hess, Kerra Davis, Mary Lou Rubright, Joanna Ott, Vern & Cathy Kiefer, Esther Schwartz, Lesley Hurford, Leone McMullen, Yvonne Baird, Nancy Smith, Dolly Valk, Carole Stoessel Zvonar, Nancy Permacoff, Kay & Wayne Jensen, Shirley Cummins, Mary Lu Trowbridge, Jackie Kaner, Richard Wright, Richard Saxman, Jimmy & Faye Rodolfos, Carolyn Tracz Guzzio, Mary Pat Houston, Judy Newell, Sylvia Whatley, Sandy Coons, Mike White, Dr. and Mrs. R. L. Terhune, Regina Steele, Paula Ryscik, Billie Nelson Tyrrell, Joe Jackson & Joel Pearson, Rosemary Dent, Betty Lunz, Richard W. Withington, Inc., Eleonora Miller, Margie Ann Yocum and H & J Foulke, Inc.

Also much appreciation to several collectors who shared their wonderful dolls, but wish their contribution to remain anonymous and to the Colemans who allowed some marks to be reproduced from their book, *The Collector's Encyclopedia of Dolls.*

Thanks to my editor, Donna H. Felger, not only for the nitty-gritty details, but also the wonderful comprehensive index.

And, of course, to Howard, for without his beautiful photographs there would be no book.

Jan Foulke
January 1989

Investing in Dolls

With the price of the average old doll representing a purchase of at least several hundred dollars in today's doll market, the assembling of a doll collection becomes rather costly. Actually, very few people buy dolls strictly as an investment; most collectors buy a doll because they like it. It has appeal to them for some reason: perhaps as an object of artistic beauty, perhaps because it evokes some kind of sentiment, perhaps it fills some need that they feel or speaks to something inside them. It is this personal feeling toward the doll which makes it of value to the collector.

However, most collectors expect to at least break even when they eventually sell their dolls. Unfortunately, there is no guarantee that any particular doll will appreciate consistently year after year; however, the track record for old or antique dolls is fairly good. If you are thinking of the future sale of your collection, be wary of buying expensive new or reproduction dolls. They have no track record and little resale value.

Because most collectors have only limited funds for purchasing dolls, they must be sure they are spending their dollars to the best advantage. There are many factors to consider when buying a doll, and this chapter will give some suggestions about what to look for and what to consider. It follows also that if a collector is not particularly well-informed about the doll in question, he should not purchase it unless he has confidence in the person selling it to him.

MARKS

Fortunately for collectors, most of the antique bisque, some of the papier-mâché, cloth and other types of antique dolls are marked or la-

12in (31cm) Norah Wellings Dutch character boy, all original felt clothing. For further information, see page 389. *H & J Foulke, Inc.*

beled. Marks and labels give the buyer confidence because they identify the trade name, the maker, the country of origin, the style or mold number, or perhaps even the patent date.

Most composition and modern dolls are marked with the maker's name and sometimes also the trade name of the doll and the date. Some dolls have tags sewn on or into their clothing to identify them; many still retain original hang tags.

Of course, many dolls are unmarked but after you have seen quite a few dolls, you begin to notice their individual characteristics so that you can often determine what a doll possibly is. When you have had some experience buying dolls, you begin to recognize an unusual face or an especially fine quality doll. Then

32in (81cm) papier-mâché head with 1858 Greiner label, original cloth body with leather arms, all original. For further information, see page 203. *H & J Foulke, Inc.*

there should be no hesitation about buying a doll marked only with a mold number or no mark at all. The doll has to speak for itself and the price must be based upon the collector's frame of doll reference. That is, one must relate the face and quality to those of a known doll maker and make price judgments from that point.

QUALITY

The mark does not tell all about a doll. Two examples from the same mold could look entirely different and carry vastly different prices because of the quality of the work done on the doll, which can vary from head to head, even with dolls made from the same mold by one firm. To command top price, a bisque doll should have lovely bisque, decoration, eyes and hair. Before purchasing a doll, the collector should determine whether the example is the best available of that type. Even the molding of one head can be much sharper with more delineation of details such as dimples or locks of hair. The molding detail is especially important to notice when purchasing dolls with character faces or molded hair.

The quality of the bisque should be smooth; dolls with bisque which is pimply, peppered with tiny black specks or unevenly colored would be second choices at a lower price. However, collectors must keep in mind porcelain factories sold many heads with small manufacturing defects as companies were in business for profit and were producing expendable play

OPPOSITE PAGE: 24½in (62cm) Simon & Halbig mold #939 child with open mouth and jointed composition body. For further information, see page 360. *H & J Foulke, Inc.*

items, not works of art. The absolutely perfect bisque head is a rarity; small manufacturing defects do not devalue a doll.

Since doll heads are hand-painted, the artistry of the decoration should be examined. The tinting of the complexion should be subdued and even, not harsh and splotchy. Artistic skill should be evident in the portrayal of the expression on the face and in details, such as the lips, eyebrows and eyelashes and particularly the eyes which should show highlights and shading when they are painted. On a doll with molded hair, individual brush marks to give the hair a more

11in (28cm) Alexander cloth *Little Shaver*, all original. For further information, see page 21. *H & J Foulke, Inc.*

realistic look would be a desirable detail.

If a doll has a wig, the hair should be appropriate if not old. Dynel or synthetic wigs are not appropriate for antique dolls; a human hair or good quality mohair wig should be used. If a doll has glass eyes, they should have natural color and threading in the irises to give a lifelike appearance.

If a doll does not meet all of these standards, it should be priced lower than one that does. Furthermore, an especially fine example will bring a premium over an ordinary but nice model.

CONDITION

Another factor which is important when pricing a doll is the condition. A bisque doll with a crack on the face or extensive professional repair involving the face would sell for one quarter or less than a doll with only normal wear. An inconspicuous hairline would decrease the value somewhat but in a rare doll, it would not be as great a detriment as in a common doll. As the so-called better dolls are becoming more difficult to find, a hairline is more acceptable to collectors if there is a price adjustment. The same is true for a doll which has a spectacular face — a hairline would be less important to price in that doll than in one with an ordinary face.

Sometimes a head will have a factory flaw which occurred in the making such as a firing crack, scratch, piece of kiln debris, dark specks, small bubbles, a ridge not smoothed out or light surface lines. Since the factory was producing toys for a profit and not creating works of art, all heads with slight flaws were not discarded, especially if they were inconspicuous or could be covered. If these factory defects are not detracting, they have little or no affect on the value of the doll.

It is to be expected that an old doll will show some wear: perhaps there is a rub on the nose or cheek, a few small "wig pulls" or maybe a chipped earring hole; a Schoenhut doll or a Käthe Kruse may have some scuffs; an old papier-mâché may have a few age cracks; a china head may show wear on the hair; an old composition body may have scuffed toes or missing fingers. These are to be expected and do not necessarily affect the value of the doll. However, a doll in exceptional condition will bring more than "book price."

Unless an antique doll is rare or you particularly want that specific doll, do not pay top price for a doll which needs extensive work: restringing, setting eyes, repairing fingers, replacing body parts, new wig or dressing. All of these repairs add up to a considerable sum at the doll hospital, possibly making the total cost of the doll more than it is really worth.

Composition dolls in perfect condition are becoming harder to find. As their material is so susceptible to the atmosphere, their condition can deteriorate literally overnight. Even in excellent condition, a composition doll nearly always has some fine crazing or slight fading. It is very difficult to find a composition doll in mint condition and even harder to be sure that it will stay that way. However, if a composition doll is a top price, they should have little or no crazing, excellent coloring, original uncombed hair and original clothes in excellent condi-

tion; the doll should be unplayed with. Pay less for a doll which does not have original clothes and hair or one which may be all original but shows extensive play wear. Pay even less for one which has heavy crazing and cracking or other damages.

Hard plastic and vinyl dolls must be in mint condition if they are at top price. The hair should be perfect in the original set; clothes should be completely original, fresh and unfaded. Skin tones should be natural with good cheek color.

BODY

In order to command top price, an

16in (41cm) *Terri Lee* with rare hair style, all original. For further information, see page 377. *H & J Foulke, Inc.*

old doll must have the original or an appropriate old body in good condition. If a doll does not have the correct type of body, the buyer ends up not with a complete doll, but with parts probably not worth as much as one whole doll. As dolls are becoming more difficult to find, more are turning up with "put together" bodies; therefore, all parts of the body should be checked to make sure that they are appropriate to each other. A body which has mixed parts from several makers or types of bodies is not worth as much as one which has correct parts.

Minor damage or repair to an old body does not affect the value of an antique doll. An original body carefully repaired, recovered or even, if necessary, completely repainted is preferable to a new one. An antique head on a new body would be worth only the value of its parts, whatever the price of the head and new body, not the full price of an antique doll. It is just a rule of thumb that an antique head is worth about 40-50% of the price of the complete doll. A very rare head could be worth up to 80%.

If there is a choice of body types for the same bisque head, a good quality ball-jointed composition body is more desirable that a crudely made five-piece body or stick-type body with just pieces of turned wood for upper arms and legs. Collectors prefer jointed composition bodies over kid ones for dolly-faced dolls, and pay more for the same face on a composition body.

Occasionally, the body adds value to the doll. In the case of bisque heads, a small doll with a completely jointed body, a French fashion-type with a wood-jointed body, a *Tête Jumeau* head on an adult body or a character baby head on a jointed toddler-type body would all be higher in price because of their special bodies.

As for the later modern dolls, a composition doll on the wrong body or a body in poor condition which is cracked and peeling would have a greatly reduced value. The same is true of a vinyl doll with replaced parts, body stains or chewed-off fingers.

CLOTHING

It is becoming increasingly difficult to find dolls in old clothing because as the years go by, fabrics continue to deteriorate. Consequently, collectors are paying more than "book price" for an antique doll if it has appropriate old clothes, shoes and hair. Even faded, somewhat worn or carefully mended original or appropriate old clothes are preferable to new ones. As collectors become more sophisticated and selective, they realize the value of old doll clothing and accessories. Some dealers are now specializing in these areas. Good old leather doll shoes will bring over $75 per pair; a lovely Victorian whitework doll dress can easily cost $75; an old dress for a French fashion lady $300. Good old doll wigs can bring from $25 to $250.

However, when the clothing must be replaced and appropriate old clothing cannot be obtained, the new clothes should be authentically styled for the age of the doll and constructed in fabrics which would have been available when the doll was produced. There are many reference books and catalog reprints which show dolls in

24in (61cm) *Queen Louise* by Armand Marseille. For further information, see page 299. *H & J Foulke, Inc.*

original clothing and doll supply companies offer patterns for dressing old dolls.

To bring top price, a modern doll must have original clothes. It is usually fairly simple to determine whether or not the clothing is original and factory made. Some makers even placed tags in the doll's clothing. Replaced clothing greatly reduces the price of modern dolls. Without the original clothing, it is often impossible to identify a modern doll as so many were made using the same face mold.

TOTAL ORIGINALITY

Totally original dolls nowadays are becoming rare. It is often difficult to determine whether the head and body and all other parts of the doll,

including wig, eyes and clothes have always been together. Many parts of a doll could be changed and clothing and accessories could be added over the years. Many dolls labeled "all original" are simply wearing contemporary clothing and wigs. Some collectors and dealers are "embellishing" the more expensive dolls by taking original clothing and wigs from cheaper dolls to further enhance the value of the more costly ones. Dolls with trunks of clothing and in boxed sets are particularly vulnerable to this type of raiding. Collectors should examine such items carefully before they pay ultra high prices for such ensembles. Of course, when these ensembles are genuine, they are the ultimate in doll collecting.

AGE

The oldest dolls do not necessarily command the highest prices, although a circa 1690 "William & Mary" wooden doll holds the world's second highest price at $107,900. A lovely old china head with exquisite decoration and very unusual hairdo would bring a price of several thousand dollars, but not as much as a 20th century S.F.B.J. 252 pouty. Many desirable composition dolls of the 1930s and fairly recent but discontinued Alexander plastic dolls are selling at prices higher than older bisque dolls of 1890 to 1920. So in determining price, the age of the doll may or may not be significant.

SIZE

The size of a doll is usually taken into account when determining a price. Generally, the size and price for a certain doll are related: a smaller size is lower, a larger size is higher.

However, there are a few exceptions on the small size. The 10in (25cm) #1 Jumeau, the 11in (28cm) *Shirley Temple*, the tiny German dolly-faced dolls on fully-jointed bodies and the 6in (9cm) *Wee Patsy* are examples of small dolls which bring higher prices than dolls in their series which may be larger.

AVAILABILITY

The price of a doll is directly related to its availability in most cases. The harder a doll is to find, the higher will be its price. Each year brings more new doll collectors than it brings newly discovered desirable old dolls; hence, the supply of old dolls is diminished. As long as the demand for certain antique and collectible dolls is greater than the supply, prices will rise. This explains the great increase in prices of less common dolls such as the K & R and other German character children, early French dolls, early china heads and papier-mâchés, composition personality dolls, Sasha dolls and some Alexander dolls which were made for only a limited period of time. Dolls which are fairly common, primarily the German dolly-faces and the later china head dolls, which covered a long period of production, show a more gentle increase in price.

POPULARITY

There are fads in dolls just like in clothes, food and other aspects of life. Dolls which have recently risen in price because of their popularity are the Brus and the lady French fashion dolls, as well as American cloth dolls and the 8in (20cm) Alexander *Wendy* series dolls. Some dolls are popular enough to tempt collectors to pay prices higher than the availability factor warrants. Although *Shirley Temples*, Jumeaus, *Bye-Los*, K & R 101 and 114, and some plastic Alexander dolls are not rare, the high prices they bring are due to their popularity.

DESIRABILITY

Some dolls may be very rare, but they do not bring a high price because they are not particularly desirable. There are not many collectors looking for them. Falling into this category are the dolls with shoulder heads made of rubber or rawhide. While an especially outstanding example will bring a high price, most examples bring very low prices in relationship to their rarity.

UNIQUENESS

Sometimes the uniqueness of a doll makes price determination very difficult. If a collector has never seen a doll exactly like it before, and it is not given in a price guide or even shown in any books, deciding what to pay can be a problem. In this case, the buyer has to use all of his available knowledge as a frame of reference in which to place the unknown doll. Perhaps a doll marked "A.M. 2000" or "S & H 1289" has been found, but is not listed in the price guide and no other examples can be found. The price is 25% higher than for the more commonly found numbers by that maker. Or perhaps a black *Kamkins* is offered for twice the price of a white one. In cases such as these, a collector must use his own judgment to determine what the doll is worth to him.

VISUAL APPEAL

Perhaps the most elusive aspect in

pricing a doll is its visual appeal. Sometimes, particularly at auction, we have seen dolls bring well over their "book value" simply because of their look. Often this is nothing more than the handiwork of someone who had the ability to choose just the right wig, clothing and accessories to enhance the doll's visual appeal and make it look particularly cute, stunning, beautiful or otherwise especially outstanding.

Sometimes, though, the visual appeal comes from the face of the doll itself. It may be the way the teeth are put in, the placement of the eyes, the tinting on the face or the sharpness of the molding. Or it may not be any of these specific things; it may just be what some collectors refer to as the "presence" of the doll, an elusive undefinable quality which makes it just the best example known!

14in (36cm) Bähr & Pröschild mold #585 character baby, all original. For further information, see page 91. *H & J Foulke, Inc.*

Selling A Doll

So many times we are asked by people, "How do I go about selling a doll?" that it seems a few paragraphs on the topic would be in order. The first logical step would be to look through the *BLUE BOOK* to identify the doll that you have and to ascertain a retail price. Work from there to decide what you might ask for your doll. It is very difficult for a private person to get a retail price for a doll.

Be realistic about the condition. If you have a marked 18in (46cm) *Shirley Temple* doll with combed hair, no clothing, faded face with crazing and a piece off of her nose, do not expect to get book price of $600 for her because that would be a retail price for an excellent doll, all original, in pristine unplayed-with condition if purchased from a dealer. Your very used doll is probably worth only $50 to $75 as it will have to be purchased by someone who would want to restore it.

If you have an antique doll with a perfect bisque head but no wig, no clothes and unstrung, but having all of its body parts, you can probably expect to get about half its retail value, depending upon how desirable that particular doll is. If your doll has perfect bisque head with original wig, clothing, and shoes, you can probably get up to 75% of its retail value.

As to actually selling the doll, there are several possibilities. Possibly the easiest is to advertise in your local paper. You may not think there are any doll collectors in your area but there probably are. You might also check your local paper to see if anyone is advertising to purchase dolls; many dealers and collectors do so. Check the paper to find out about antique shows in your area. If anyone has dolls, ask if they would be interested in buying your doll. Also, you could inquire at antique shops in your area for dealers who specialize in dolls. You will probably get a higher price from a specialist than a general antique dealer as the former are more familiar with the market for specific dolls. A roster of doll specialists is available from The National Antique Doll Dealers Association, Inc., P.O. Box 143, Wellesley Hills, MA 02181.

You could consign your doll to an auction. If it is a common doll, it will probably do quite well at a local sale. If it is a more rare doll, consider sending it to one of the auction houses which specialize in selling dolls; most of them will accept one doll if it is a good one and they will probably get the best price for you. It would probably be worth your while to purchase a doll magazine (*Doll Reader*, 900 Frederick St., Cumberland, MD 21502) in which you will find ads from auction houses, doll shows and leading dealers. You could advertise in doll magazines, but you might have to ship the doll and guarantee return privileges if the buyer does not like it.

If you cannot find your doll in the *BLUE BOOK*, it might be a good idea to have it professionally appraised. This will involve your paying a fee to have the doll evaluated. We provide this service and can be contacted through *Doll Reader* for which we write a regular column. Many museums and auction houses also appraise dolls.

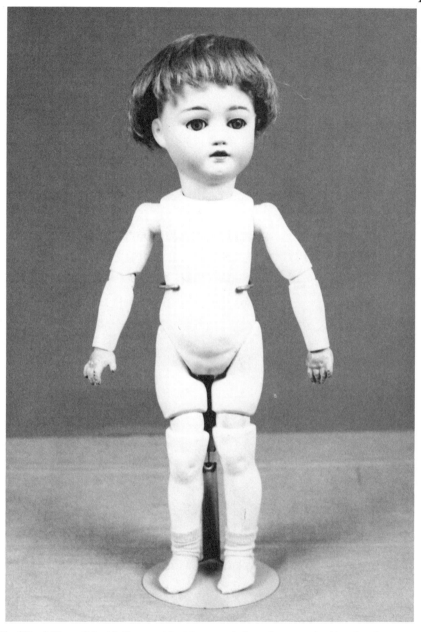

18in (46cm) Franz Schmidt flapper girl with unusual pierced nose and rubber hands, teenage body. For further information, see page 348. *H & J Foulke, Inc.*

A.T.

Maker: Possibly by A. Thuillier, Paris, France. Some heads by F. Gaultier.
Date: 1875—1893
Material: Bisque socket head on wooden, kid or composition body
Size: Size 1 is usually 9in (23cm); size 10 is 19—21in (48—54cm); size 15 with closed mouth is 36in (91cm).

Mark:

AT·N° 8 ———— A. 8 . T

Marked A. T. Child: Perfect bisque head, cork pate, good wig, paperweight eyes, pierced ears, closed mouth; body of wood, kid or composition in good condition; appropriate clothes.

16—18in (41—46cm)	**$38,000—42,000**
24in (61cm)	**55,000**
Open mouth, 2 rows teeth, 16in (41cm)	**12,000****

**Not enough price samples to compute a reliable range.

See cover for color photograph.

15½in (39cm) A. 7 T. *Private Collection.*

Alabama Indestructible Doll

Maker: Ella Smith Doll Co., Roanoke, Ala., U.S.A.
Date: 1900—1925
Material: All-cloth
Size: 11½—27in (29—69cm); 38in (96cm) black one known
Mark: On torso or leg, sometimes both:

PAT. NOV. 9, 1912

NO. 2

ELLA SMITH DOLL CO.

Alabama Baby: All-cloth painted with oils, tab-jointed shoulders and hips, flat derriere for sitting; painted hair (or rarely a wig), molded face with painted facial features, applied ears, (a few with molded ears); painted stockings and shoes (a few with bare feet); appropriate clothes; all in good condition, some wear acceptable.

or
"MRS. S. S. SMITH
Manufacturer and Dealer to
The Alabama Indestructible Doll
Roanoke, Ala.
PATENTED Sept. 26, 1905"
(also 1907 on some)

12—13in (31—33cm)	**$1600—1700**
16—18in (41—46cm)	**1800—2100**
22in (56cm)	**2500—2900**
Black, 23in (58cm)	**3000****

**Not enough price samples to compute a reliable range.

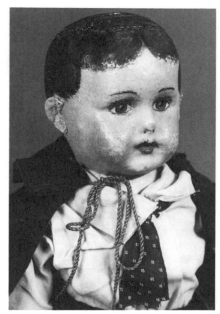

22in (56cm) *Alabama Baby.* See color photograph on page 65. *H & J Foulke, Inc.*

Madame Alexander

Maker: Alexander Doll Co. Inc., New York, N.Y., U.S.A.
Date: 1923—on, but as early as 1912 the Alexander sisters were designing doll clothes and dressing dolls commercially.
Mark: Dolls themselves marked in various ways, usually "ALEXANDER". Clothing has a white cloth label with blue lettering sewn into a seam which says "MADAME ALEXANDER" and usually the name of the specific doll. Cloth and other early dolls are unmarked and identifiable only by the clothing label.

Cloth Character Dolls: Ca. 1933 through the 1930s. All-cloth with one-piece arms and legs sewn on; mohair wig, molded mask face of felt or flocked fabric, painted eyes to the side, original clothes tagged with name of particular doll. Produced characters from *Little Women,* Charles Dickens, Longfellow and other literary works as well as storybook characters. (For photograph see *8th Blue Book,* page 21.)

16in (41cm) only

Fair	**$175—225**
Good	**325—375**
Mint	**550—650**

20in (51cm) *Alice*

Fair	**175—225**
Good	**325—375**
Mint	**550—650**

20in (51cm) *Alice in Wonderland*, yellow yarn hair, all original. *H & J Foulke, Inc.*

Madame Alexander continued

Cloth Baby: Ca. 1936. All-cloth with molded felt or flocked mask face, soft-stuffed stockinette body with flexible arms and legs; yarn or hair wig, painted eyes with long upper and lower eyelashes; original tagged clothes; all in excellent condition. (For photograph see *7th Blue Book*, page 20.)
17in (43cm)   **$375—425**

Dionne Quintuplet: Brown hair and eyes, gold-colored name pin or necklace. (For photograph see *6th Blue Book*, page 18.)
17in (43cm)   **$650—750**

Susie Q. & Bobby Q.: Ca. 1938. All-cloth with turning head, yellow or red yarn braids, mask face, large side-painted googly eyes, button nose, tiny closed mouth; striped stocking legs, white felt spats; original tagged clothes including hat, coat and cardboard suitcase. (For photograph see *6th Blue Book*, page 19.) Came in sizes 12—13in (31—33cm) and 15—16in (38—41cm).
All Sizes:

Fair	$ 250—300
Good	450—500
Mint and boxed, at auction	3200 pair

Little Shaver: 1942. Stuffed pink stocking body, curved arms, tiny waist; floss wig glued on; mask face with large painted eyes to the side, tiny mouth; original clothes; all in excellent condition. (For photograph see page 10.)
Mark: Cloth dress tag:
"Little Shaver
Madame Alexander
New York
All Rights Reserved."

7in (18cm)	$225—275
10—12in (25—31cm)	250—300
16in (41cm)	375—425
20in (51cm)	450—500

Madame Alexander continued

Dionne Quintuplets: 1935. All-composition with swivel head, jointed hips and shoulders, toddler or bent-limb legs; wigs or molded hair, sleep or painted eyes; original clothing, all in excellent condition.
Mark: "ALEXANDER" sometimes "DIONNE"
Clothing label:
"GENUINE
DIONNE QUINTUPLET DOLLS
ALL RIGHTS RESERVED
MADAME ALEXANDER, N.Y."
or
"DIONNE QUINTUPLET
(her name)
EXCLUSIVE LICENSEE
MADAM [sic] ALEXANDER
DOLL CO."

8in (20cm) Dionne Quintuplet *Emelie* toddler, all original. *H & J Foulke, Inc.*

7—8in (18-20cm)	$ 225—250
matched set	1250—1500
10in (25cm) baby	300—350
11—12in (28—31cm)	
toddler	375—425
14in (36cm)	
toddler	475—525
16in (41cm)	
toddler	575—625
16in (41cm) baby	
with cloth body	400—450
Pins, each	85—95

Each Quint has her own color for clothing:
  Yvonne — pink
  Annette — yellow
  Cecile — green
  Emelie — lavender
  Marie — blue

16in (41cm) Dionne Quintuplet *Annette* baby, all original. *H & J Foulke, Inc.*

Topsy Turvy: Ca. 1936. Composition double torso, each with head and movable arms, molded and painted hair, painted eyes, closed mouth; one side white, the other brown; cotton shift with double lines skirt. All in good condition. Unmarked, but dress may have label.
7½in (19cm) **$175—200**

7½in (19cm) *Topsy Turvy*, all original. *H & J Foulke, Inc.*

Composition Girl: Ca. 1935. All-composition with jointed neck, shoulders and hips; mohair wig, painted or sleep eyes, closed mouth; original clothes; all in good condition.
Mark: On head:
   "ALEXANDER"
13in (33cm)   **$225—275**

13in (33cm) Alexander girl. Clothes are not tagged but appear to be contemporary to doll. *H & J Foulke, Inc.*

Madame Alexander continued

Little Colonel: 1935. All-composition with swivel head, jointed hips and shoulders; mohair wig, sleep eyes, closed mouth, dimples; original clothes; all in excellent condition. *Betty* face. (For photograph see *6th Blue Book*, page 22.)
Mark: On head: "ALEXANDER" or none
On dress tag: "Madame Alexander"
13—14in (33—36cm) **$500—600**

Foreign and Storyland: Ca. 1935 to mid 1940s. All-composition with one-piece head and body on smaller ones and separate head on larger ones, jointed shoulders and hips; mohair wig, painted eyes; original tagged clothes; all in excellent condition. Made children to represent foreign lands as well as storybook characters.
Mark: On back: "Mme. Alexander"
7—9in (18—23cm)

Foreign Countries	**$175—225**
Storybook Characters	**225—275**
Birthday Dolls and other special outfits	**250 up**

7in (18cm) Birthday Doll *July*, all original. *H & J Foulke, Inc.*

Madame Alexander continued

Dr. Dafoe: 1936. All-composition with swivel head, jointed hips and shoulders; gray wig, painted eyes, smiling face; original tagged doctor's outfit; all in excellent condition; doll unmarked. (For photograph see *8th Blue Book*, page 24.)
14in (36cm) **$750—800**

Babies: 1936—on. Composition head, hands and legs, cloth bodies; molded hair or wigged, sleep eyes, open or closed mouth; original clothes; all in excellent condition.
Mark: On dolls:
"ALEXANDER"
On clothing: "Little Genius," "Baby McGuffey," "Pinky," "Precious," "Butch," "Bitsey."
11—12in (28—31cm)   **$185—210**
16—18in (41—46cm)   **250—300**
24in (61cm)   **350—400**
*Allow extra for ***Pinky***.

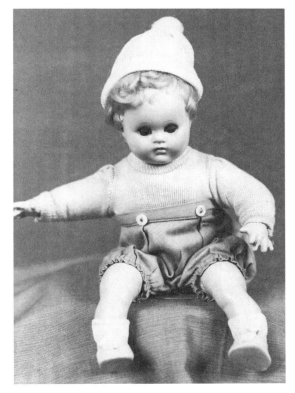

12in (31cm) ***Butch***, all original.
H & J Foulke, Inc.

Madame Alexander continued

Jane Withers: 1937. All-composition with swivel head, jointed shoulders and hips; dark mohair wig, sleep eyes, open smiling mouth; original clothes; all in excellent condition. (For photograph see *5th Blue Book*, page 11.)
Mark: On dress:

"Jane Withers
All Rights Reserved
Madame Alexander, N.Y."

12—13in (31—33cm) closed mouth	$ 700—750
15—16in (38—41cm)	800—850
21in (53cm)	1000—1200
19in (48cm) with trunk and extra clothes, at auction	1300

Princess Elizabeth Face: All-composition, jointed at neck, shoulders and hips; mohair or human hair wig, sleeping eyes, open mouth; original clothes; all in excellent condition.
Mark: On head:

"PRINCESS ELIZABETH
ALEXANDER DOLL CO."

Clothing tagged with individual name of doll
Princess Elizabeth, 1937:

13in (33cm) **Betty** face	$275—300
14—16in (36—41cm)	350—375
20—22in (51—56cm)	450—475
24in (61cm)	525—575
27in (69cm)	650

17in (43cm) *Princess Elizabeth*, all original. *H & J Foulke, Inc.*

Madame Alexander continued

McGuffey Ana, 1937 (braids)

9in (23cm) painted eyes, "Wendy" face	$250—275
11in (28cm) closed mouth	325—350
13—15in (33—38cm)	375—425
18—20in (46—51cm)	475—525
24in (61cm)	625—675

Snow White, 1937 (closed mouth, black hair) (For photograph see *6th Blue Book*, page 23.)

13in (33cm)	325—375
16—18in (41—46cm)	425—475

Flora McFlimsey, 1938 (red hair, freckles) (For photograph see *7th Blue Book*, page 27.)

15in (38cm)	600—650

Kate Greenaway, 1938 (For photograph see *4th Blue Book* page 15.)

16—18in (41—46cm)	525—575

Wendy Ann Face: All-composition, jointed at neck, shoulders and hips; human hair or mohair wig, sleeping eyes, closed mouth; original clothes tagged with name of individual doll; all in excellent condition.

Mark:

"WENDY-ANN
MME ALEXANDER"

or

"ALEXANDER"

Wendy-Ann, 1936:

9in (23cm) painted eyes	$250—275
14in (36cm) swivel waist	350—375
21in (53cm)	525—575

Scarlet O'Hara, 1937 (black hair, blue or green eyes (For photograph see *8th Blue Book*, page 27.)

11in (28cm)	375—425
14in (36cm)	475—500
18in (46cm)	625—675
21in (53cm)	825—875

Note: Sometimes the name is spelled "Scarlet;" other times "Scarlett."

13in (33cm) *McGuffey Ana*, all original. *H & J Foulke, Inc.*

Madame Alexander continued

14in (36cm) **Wendy Ann**, all original. *H & J Foulke, Inc.*

Bride & Bridesmaids, 1940

14in (36cm)	**250—275**
18in (46cm)	**350—400**
21in (53cm)	**425—475**

Portraits, 1940s

21in (53cm)	**825—875 up**

Carmen (Miranda), 1942 (For photograph see *7th Blue Book*, page 30.) (black hair):

9in (23cm) painted eyes	**225—250**
14—15in (36—38cm)	**325—375**

Fairy Princess, 1942 (For photograph see *8th Blue Book*, page 26.)

14in (36cm)	**275—325**

Fairy Queen, 1942 See color photograph on page 65.

18in (46cm)	**450—475**

Armed Forces Dolls, 1942 (For photograph see *7th Blue Book*, page 29.) WAAC, WAVE, WAAF and Soldier

14in (36cm)	**425—450**

14in (36cm) Bridesmaid, all original. *Miriam Blankman Collection.*

Madame Alexander continued

Sonja Henie: 1939. All-composition, jointed at neck, shoulders and hips, human hair or mohair wig, sleep eyes, smiling open mouth with teeth; original clothes; all in excellent condition. 14in (35.6cm) can be found on the WENDY-ANN body with swivel waist. (For photograph see *8th Blue Book*, page 28.)

Mark: On back of neck:

"MADAME ALEXANDER-
SONJA HENIE"

On dress: "Sonja Henie"

14in (36cm)	**$350—375**
18in (46cm)	**475—525**
21in (53cm)	**550—600**

Jeannie Walker: 1941. Composition, jointed at neck, shoulders and hips, with walking mechanism; human hair or mohair wig, sleep eyes, closed mouth; original clothes; all in excellent condition. See color photograph on page 66.

Mark: On body:

"ALEXANDER/PAT. NO.
2171281"

On dress:

"Jeannie Walker —
Madame Alexander — N.Y.,
U.S.A.
All rights reserved"

13—14in (33—36cm)	**$400—425**
18in (46cm)	**575**

Margaret Face: All-composition, jointed at neck, shoulders and hips; human hair, mohair, or floss wig, sleeping eyes, closed mouth; original clothes tagged with name of individual doll; all in excellent condition.

Mark: "ALEXANDER"

Margaret O'Brien, 1946
(dark braided wig):

14in (36cm)	**$475—525**
18in (46cm)	**650—700**
21in (53cm)	**800**

21in (53cm) *Margaret O'Brien*, all original. *H & J Foulke, Inc.*

Karen Ballerina, 1946 (For photograph see *8th Blue Book*, page 29.) (blonde wig in coiled braids):

18in (46cm)	**500—550**

Alice-in-Wonderland, 1947 (For photograph see *5th Blue Book*, page 11.)

14in (36cm)	**325—375**
18in (46cm)	**425—475**

Margaret Face: 1948—on. All-hard plastic, jointed at neck, shoulders and hips; lovely wig, sleep eyes, closed mouth; original clothes tagged with name of doll; all in excellent condition.

Mark: "ALEXANDER"

Nina Ballerina, 1949—1951*

14in (36cm)	**$325—350**
18in (46cm)	**400—425**

Fairy Queen, 1947—1948*

14in (36cm)	**300**

Babs, 1948—1949*

14in (36cm)	**$350—375**

Margaret Rose, 1948—1953*

14in (36cm)	**300—325**

Margaret O'Brien, 1948*

14in (36cm)	**500—600**

Wendy-Ann, 1947—1948

18in (46cm)	**375—400**

Wendy Bride, 1950*

14in (36cm)	**300—325**

Cinderella, 1950*

14in (36cm)	**550—600**

Prince Charming, 1950*

14in (36cm)	**500—600**

Cynthia (black), 1952—1953 (See color photograph on page 66.)

14in (36cm)	**550**

Story Princess, 1954—1956

14in (36cm)	**350—375**

Wendy (from Peter Pan set), 1953:

14in (36cm)	**450**

*For photographs see *Treasury of Mme. Alexander Dolls.*

Madame Alexander continued

Prince Philip, Ca. 1950*
18in (46cm)   500—600
Snow White, 1952
14in (36cm)   500
Bride, 1952:
18in (46cm)   375—400
Margot Ballerina, 1953
18in (46cm)   400—425
Glamour Girls, 1953*
18in (46cm)   700
Queen Elizabeth, 1953
18in (46cm)   700
Godey Ladies, 1950
14in (36cm)   700—750
Me and My Shadow, 1954
18in (46cm)   600—700
*For photographs see *Treasury of Mme. Alexander Dolls.*

14in (36cm) unidentified tagged Alexander girl, all original. *H & J Foulke, Inc.*

Maggie Face: 1948—1956. All-hard plastic, jointed at neck, shoulders and hips; good quality wig, sleep eyes, closed mouth; original clothes tagged with the name of the doll; all in excellent condition.
Mark: "ALEXANDER"
Maggie, 1948—1953*
14in (36cm) $275—325
17in (43cm)   375—425
Polly Pigtails, 1949
14in (36cm)   325—350
Kathy, 1951*
14in (36cm)   375—400
Alice in Wonderland, 1950—1951*
14in (36cm)   325—350
17in (43cm)   400—425
Annabelle, 1952*
17in (43cm)   400—425
Peter Pan, 1953*   450—475
Rosamund Bridesmaid, 1953*
15in (38cm)   325—350
Glamour Girls, 1953*
18in (46cm)   700

14in (36cm) **Poor Cinderella**, all original. *Private Collection.*

Madame Alexander continued

14in (36cm) *Polly Pigtails*, all original. *H & J Foulke, Inc.*

14in (36cm) *Beth*, Maggie face, all original. *H & J Foulke, Inc.*

Me and My Shadow, 1954
18in (46cm)   600—700
Godey Man, 1950*
14in (36cm)   700—750

Little Women: 1948—1956. All-hard plastic, jointed at neck, shoulders and hips; synthetic wig, sleep eyes, closed mouth; original clothes; all in excellent condition. Some models have jointed knees. "Maggie" and "Margaret" faces.
Mark: On head:
    "ALEXANDER."
On clothes tag:
    "Meg", "Jo", "Beth",
    "Amy" and "Marme"
14—15in (36—38cm)
Floss hair,
    1948—1950   **$300—350 each**
Amy
    loop curls   **375—400 each**
    Dynel   **250—275 each**
Little Men: Tommy,
Nat and *Stuffy*,
1952. (For photograph
see *Treasury of Mme.*
Alexander Dolls,
page 42.)   **750 up each**

Little Genius: Ca. 1950. Hard plastic head, sleeping eyes, mohair wig; cloth body with hard plastic hands and legs; original tagged clothes; all in excellent condition. (For photographs see *8th Blue Book*, page 32.)
12in (28cm)   **$165—185**
16—18in (41—46cm)   **225—275**
24in (61cm)   **300—350**

Madame Alexander continued

Winnie and Binnie: 1953—1955. All-hard plastic, walking body, later with jointed knees and vinyl arms; lovely wig, sleep eyes, closed mouth; original clothes; all in excellent condition. (For photograph see *5th Blue Book*, page 16.)

15in (38cm)	**$250—275**
18in (46cm)	**275—300**
24in (61cm)	**350—400**

Cissy: 1955—1959. Head, torso and jointed legs of hard plastic, jointed vinyl arms; synthetic wig, sleep eyes, closed mouth, pierced ears; original clothes; all in excellent condition.
Mark: On head:

"ALEXANDER"

On dress tag:

"Cissy"

21in (53cm)

Street clothes	**$325—375**
Gowns	**400 up***
Elaborate fashion gowns	**600 up***

*Depending upon costume.

21in (53cm) *Cissy* bride, very rare model using "Scarlett" portrait head with applied eyelashes, all original. *H & J Foulke, Inc.*

Madame Alexander continued

Lissy: 1956—1958. All-hard plastic, jointed at neck, shoulders, hips, elbows and knees; synthetic wig, sleep eyes, closed mouth; original clothes; all in excellent condition. (For photograph see *8th Blue Book*, page 33.)

Mark: None on doll
On dress tag:
"Lissy" or name of character

12in (31cm)	**$350—400**
Kelly, 1959*	**400—450**
Little Women, 1957—1967	**225—250**
Southern Belle, 1963*	**1000 up**
McGuffey Ana, 1963*	**1200 up**
Laurie, 1967*	**450—500**
Pamela, 1962—1963*	**650**

*For photographs see *Treasury of Mme. Alexander Dolls*, pages 74—78.

Little Genius: 1956—1962. Hard plastic head with short curly wig, sleep eyes, drinks and wets; vinyl torso, arms and legs; original clothes; all in excellent condition. (For photograph see *7th Blue Book*, page 34.)
8in (20cm) **$185—210**

16½in (42cm) 1963 *Elise* ballerina #1720, all original. *H & J Foulke, Inc.*

Elise: 1957—1964. All-hard plastic with vinyl arms, completely jointed; synthetic wig, sleep eyes, closed mouth; original clothes; all in excellent condition.

16½—17in (42—43cm)	
Street clothes	**$275—325**
Bride, Ballerina	**350—400**
Gowns	**350 up***

*Depending upon costume.

Madame Alexander continued

Cissette: 1957—1963. All-hard plastic, jointed at neck, shoulders, hips and knees; synthetic wig, sleep eyes, closed mouth, pierced ears; original clothes; all in excellent condition. (For photographs see *Treasury of Mme. Alexander Dolls*, pages 79—84.)

Mark: None on doll
On dress tag: "Cissette"

10in (25cm) *Cissette*	**$165* up**
Basic *Cissette*, mint	
and boxed	**190—210**
Margot, 1961	**400—450**
Sleeping Beauty, 1960s	**375—425**
Jacqueline, 1962	**550—600**
Gibson Girl, 1963	**1000—1200**
Gold Rush, 1963	**1250—1400**
Portrettes,	
1968—1973	**450—550**
Jenny Lind, 1969—1970	**600**

*Depending upon costume.

10in (25cm) Portrette *Queen*, all original. *H & J Foulke, Inc.*

Alexander-Kins: All-hard plastic, jointed at neck, shoulders and hips; synthetic wig, sleep eyes, closed mouth; original clothes; all in excellent condition.
7½—8in (19—20cm)
1953, straight leg non-walker
1954—1955, straight-leg walker
1956—1964, bent-knee walker
1965—1972, bent knee
1973—current, straight leg
Mark: On back of torso:
"ALEX"
After 1978:
"MADAME ALEXANDER"
On dress tag:
"Madame Alexander"
"Alexander-Kins" or
specific name of doll

Wendy, in dresses	
1953—1972	**$325 up**

Wendy Ballerina,	
1956—1973	
pink	**250 up**
blue	**300 up**
yellow	**350 up**
Wendy, in	
riding habit	**400—450**
Wendy Nurse	**550 up**
Quizkin, 1953	**400—500**
Bent-knee	
Internationals	**100—125**
Storybooks	**125—150**
Little Women	**125—150**

Madame Alexander continued

8in (20cm) *Wendy*, all original. *H & J Foulke, Inc.*

7½in (19cm) *Quizkin* with "yes" and "no" buttons in back, all original. *H & J Foulke, Inc.*

Special Outfits:

Scarlett O'Hara, 1965—1972	
print dress	**400—500**
McGuffey Ana	**500**
English Guard	**450**
Korea, Africa, Hawaii,	
Vietnam, Eskimo,	
Morocco, Equador,	
Bolivia	**400—450**

Amish Boy and Girl	**500—525**
Cowboy, Cowgirl,	**500—600**
Pocahontas, Hiawatha	**500**
Colonial	**450**
Spanish, Greek,	
Argentinean and	
Peruvian boys	**450**

Madame Alexander continued

Kelly Face: 1958—on. Vinyl character face with rooted hair, vinyl arms, hard plastic torso and legs, jointed waist; original clothes; all in excellent condition.

Mark: On head:

Kelly, 1958—1959 15in (38cm)	$225—250
Pollyana, 1960—1961 15in (38cm)	225—250
Marybel, 1959—1965 15in (38cm), in case	250—275
Edith, 1958—1959 15in (38cm) (For photograph see *7th Blue Book*, page 37.)	225—250

Shari Lewis: 1959. All-hard plastic with slim fashion body; auburn hair, brown eyes, closed mouth; original clothes; all in excellent condition. (For photograph see *5th Blue Book*, page 17.)

14in (36cm)	$350
21in (53cm)	450—475

Maggie Mixup: 1960—1961. All-hard plastic, fully-jointed; red straight hair, green eyes, closed mouth, freckles; original clothes; all in excellent condition. (For photographs see *6th Blue Book*, page 32.)

16½—17in (42—43cm)	$325—375
8in (20cm)	450 up
8in (20cm) angel	1150

20in (51cm) ***Kelly***, all original. *Miriam Blankman Collection.*

Betty: 1960. Vinyl and hard plastic with rooted hair, smiling face; walking body; original tagged clothes; all in good condition. (For photograph see *8th Blue Book*, page 36.)

30in (76cm)   **$350—400**

Madame Alexander continued

21in (53cm) *Jacqueline*, all original. *H & J Foulke, Inc.*

Jacqueline: 1961—1962. Vinyl and hard plastic; rooted dark hair, sleep eyes, closed mouth; original clothes; all in excellent condition.

21in (53cm)	**$700—750**
Portrait Dolls, 1965 to present	**450 up**
Scarlett, green velvet or taffeta 1975—1982	**350—375**
satin print dress, 1978 only	**500—600**
Melanie, 1967—1974	**500**

Caroline: 1961—1962. Hard plastic and vinyl; rooted blonde hair, smiling character face; original clothes; in excellent condition.

15in (38cm)	**$300—350**

Janie: 1964—1966. Vinyl and hard plastic with rooted hair, impish face, pigeon-toed and knock-kneed; original tagged clothes; all in excellent condition.

12in (31cm)	**$225—275**
Lucinda, 1969—1970	**300—350**
Rozy, 1969 See color photograph on page 66.	**350—400**
Suzy, 1970	**350—400**

Smarty: 1962—1963. Hard plastic and vinyl, smiling character face with rooted hair, knock-kneed and pigeon-toed; original clothes; in excellent condition.

12in (31cm)	**$200—250**
Katie (black), 1965	**350—400**

21in (53cm) 1968 *Melanie*, all original. *Private Collection.*

Madame Alexander continued

21in (53cm) **Coco**, 1966 Portrait, all original. *Private Collection.*

Coco: 1966. Vinyl and hard plastic, rooted blonde hair, jointed waist, right leg bent slightly at knee; original clothes; all in excellent condition. This face was also used for the 1966 portrait dolls.
21in (53cm) **$1800—2000**

Elise: 1966 to present. Vinyl face, rooted hair; original tagged clothes; all in excellent condition.

17in (43cm)	**$125—150***
Portrait Elise, 1973	**200—250**
Marlo, 1967	**400—500**
Maggie, 1972—1973	**250—300**

*Discontinued styles only.

Mary Ann Face: Introduced in 1965 and used widely to present a variety of dolls. Only discontinued dolls are listed here. Vinyl head and arms, hard plastic torso and legs; appropriate synthetic wig, sleep eyes; original clothes; all in excellent condition.
Mark: On head:
"ALEXANDER
19©65"
14in (35cm) only:

Madame, 1967—1975	**$ 200**
Mary Ann, 1965	**250**
Orphant Annie, 1965—1966	**250**
Gidget, 1966	**250**
Little Granny, 1966	**200**
Riley's Little Annie, 1967	**250**
Renoir Girl, 1967—1971	**200**
Easter Girl, 1968	**1200—1500**
Scarlett #1495, 1968	**500**

Jenny Lind & Cat, 1969—1971	**300**
Jenny Lind, 1970	**400**
Grandma Jane, 1970—1972	**200**
Disney Snow White, to 1977	**400**
Goldilocks, 1978—1982	**100**

14in (35cm) **Goldilocks**, taffeta dress, all original. *H & J Foulke, Inc.*

Madame Alexander continued

17in (43cm) *Polly*, all original. *H & J Foulke, Inc.*

11in (28cm) *Gretl*, all original. *H & J Foulke, Inc.*

Polly Face: All-vinyl with rooted hair, jointed at neck, shoulders and hips; original tagged clothes; all in excellent condition. (For photograph see *8th Blue Book*, page 66.)
17in (43cm):

Polly, 1965	**$225—250***
Leslie (black), 1965—1971	**300—350***

*Allow extra for ballgowns.

Sound of Music: Large set 1965—1970; small set 1971—1973. All dolls of hard plastic and vinyl with appropriate synthetic wigs and sleep eyes; original clothes; all in excellent condition.

Mark: Each doll tagged as to character.

Small set

8in (20cm) *Friedrich*	$225
8in (20cm) *Gretl*	200
8in (20cm) *Marta*	200
10in (25cm) *Brigitta*	225
12in (31cm) *Maria*	300
10in (25cm) *Louisa*	350
10in (25cm) *Liesl*	300

Large set*

11in (28cm) *Friedrich*	250
11in (28cm) *Gretl*	200
11in (28cm) *Marta*	200
14in (36cm) *Brigitta*	200
17in (43cm) *Maria*	300
14in (36cm) *Louisa*	250
14in (36cm) *Liesl*	250

*Allow considerably more for sailor outfits.

Madame Alexander continued

Nancy Drew Face: Introduced in 1967 and used widely to present a variety of dolls. Only discontinued dolls are listed here. Vinyl head and arms, hard plastic torso and legs; appropriate synthetic wig, sleep eyes; original clothes; all in excellent condition.
12in (31cm) only:

Nancy Drew, 1967	**$200**
Renoir Child, 1967	**200**
Pamela with wigs, 1962—1963	**350—400**

Peter Pan Set: 1969. Vinyl and hard plastic with appropriate wigs and sleep eyes; original clothes; all in excellent condition.

14in (36cm) ***Peter Pan*** ("Mary Ann" face)	**$225—250**
14in (36cm) ***Wendy*** ("Mary Ann" face)	**225—250**
12in (31cm) ***Michael*** ("Janie" face)	**300**
11in (28cm) ***Tinker Bell*** ("Cissette")	**350**

First Ladies: Hard plastic and vinyl with rooted synthetic hair individually styled and sleep eyes; original tagged clothes; in mint condition. "Martha" and "Mary Ann" faces.
14in (36cm)

Series I: 1976—1978
Martha Washington, Abigail Adams, Martha Randolph, Dolley Madison, Elizabeth Monroe and *Louisa Adams.*

Set:	**$950**
Individual:	**150**
Martha Washington	**250**

Series II: 1979—1981
Sarah Jackson, Angelica Van Buren, Jane Findlay, Julia Tyler, Sarah Polk and *Betty Taylor Bliss.*

Set:	**650**
Individual:	**110**

Series III: 1982—1984
Jane Pierce, Abigail Fillmore, Mary Todd Lincoln, Martha Johnson Patterson, Harriet Lane and *Julia Grant.*

Set:	**550**
Individual:	**90**
Mary Todd Lincoln:	**125**

14in (36cm) ***Angelica Van Buren***, Martha face, all original. *H & J Foulke, Inc.*

Henri Alexandre

Maker: Henri Alexandre, Paris, France, 1888—1892; Tourrel 1892—1895; Jules Steiner and successors 1895—1901
Material: Bisque head, jointed composition body
Designer: Henri Alexandre
Trademark: Bébé Phénix

H.A. Bébé: 1889—1891. Perfect bisque socket head, closed mouth, paperweight eyes, pierced ears, good wig; jointed composition and wood body; lovely clothes; all in good condition.
Mark: H 𝔄 A
17—19in (43—48cm)   **$5000****
See color photograph on page 67.
**Not enough price samples to compute a reliable range.

Bébé Phénix: 1889—1900. Perfect bisque head, closed mouth, paperweight eyes, pierced ears, good wig; composition body sometimes with one-piece arms and legs; well dressed; all in good condition.
Mark: Red Stamp   PHÉNIX
Incised   ★95

Approximate Size Chart:
*81 = 10in
*85 = 14in
*88 = 17in
*90 = 18in
*92 = 19—21in
*93 = 22in
*94 = 23—24in
*95 = 23—25in

10in (25cm)	**$2800—3000**
14—16in (36—41cm)	**3000—3300**
19—21in (48—53cm)	**3700—4000**
23—25in (58—64cm)	**4300—4800**
Open mouth	
19—21in (48—53cm)	**2200—2400**

19in (48cm) ***Bébé Phénix*** incised "*92." *Private Collection.*

All-Bisque Dolls
(So-Called French)

Maker: Various French and/or German firms
Date: Ca. 1880—on
Material: All-bisque
Size: Various small sizes, under 12in (31cm)
Mark: None, sometimes numbers

All-Bisque French Doll: Jointed at shoulders and hips, swivel neck, slender arms and legs; good wig, glass eyes, closed mouth; molded shoes or boots and stockings; appropriately dressed; all in good condition, with proper parts.

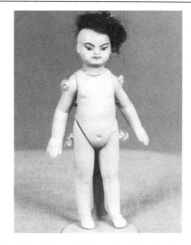

5—6in (12—15cm) $ 750—850*
With bare feet,
5—6in (13—15cm) 750—850*
With jointed elbows and knees,
5—6in (13—15cm) 2200—2500**
With jointed elbows,
5—6in (13—15cm) 1900—2100**
Oriental,
5in (13cm) 900—950**
Pierced-in ears,
6in (15cm) 1100—1200*

5in (13cm) French Oriental. *H & J Foulke, Inc.*

*Allow extra for original clothes.
**Not enough price samples to compute a reliable range.

6in (15cm) French girl with yellow stockings. *Roberts Collection.*

All-Bisque Dolls
(German)

Maker: Various German firms
Date: Ca. 1880—on
Material: Bisque
Size: Various small sizes, most under 12in (31cm)
Mark: Some with "Germany" and/or numbers; some with paper labels on stomachs

All-Bisque French-type: Ca. 1880—on. Jointed usually by wire or pegging at shoulders and hips, stationary neck, slender arms and legs; good wig, glass eyes, closed mouth; molded shoes or boots and stockings; dressed or undressed; many in regional costumes; all in good condition, with proper parts.

3—3½in (8—9cm)	$200—225
3¾—4in (10cm)	185—210
5in (13cm)	275—300
6in (15cm)	325—350
7in (18cm)	400—450
Swivel neck:	
4in (10cm)	300—350
6—6½in (15—17cm)	450—500
Black or Mulatto:	
4—4½in (10—12cm)	275—325

LEFT: 3¾in (10cm) French-type all-bisque boy, all original, regional costume. *H & J Foulke, Inc.*

RIGHT: 4½in (12cm) fine early all-bisque girl with stiff legs, shirred blue hose and brown strap shoes. *H & J Foulke, Inc.*

All-Bisque with painted eyes: Ca. 1880—on. Jointed at shoulders, stiff or jointed hips, stationary neck; molded and painted hair or mohair wig, painted eyes, closed mouth; molded and painted shoes and stockings; fine quality work; dressed or undressed; all in good condition, with proper parts.

1¼in (3cm)	$ 65—75
1½—2in (4—5cm)	75—85
4—5in (10—13cm)	140—175
6—7in (15—18cm)	200—225
Swivel neck:	
2½in (9cm)	150
4—5in (10—13cm)	200—250
Early round face, bootines:	
6—7in (15—18cm)	350—450
8½in (22cm)	550—600
Early face as pictured, pink or blue shirred hose:	
4½in (12cm)	175—200
6in (15cm)	350—375
8in (20cm)	525—575

All-Bisque Dolls (German) continued

All-Bisque with molded clothes: Ca. 1890—on. Many by Hertwig & Co. Jointed at shoulders (sometimes hips), molded and painted clothes or underwear; molded and painted hair, sometimes with molded hat, painted eyes, closed mouth; molded shoes and socks (if in underwear often barefoot); good quality work; all in good condition, with proper parts.

Children:

3¼in (8cm)	$ 95—110
4—5in (10—13cm)	135—160
6—7in (15—18cm)	200—250

Glass Eyes, molded underwear,
  5½in (14cm)   350

Punch, Judy and other
  white bisque characters,
  3—4in (8—10cm)   95—110

LEFT: 3¼in (8cm) all-bisque boy with molded and flocked gray suit, white molded yoke. *H & J Foulke, Inc.*

RIGHT: 6¾in (17cm) all-bisque girl 130, white stockings, brown two-strap shoes, sleep eyes. *H & J Foulke, Inc.*

All-Bisque with glass eyes: Ca. 1890—on. Very good quality bisque, jointed at shoulders, stiff or jointed hips; good wig, glass eyes, closed mouth (sometimes open); molded and painted shoes and stockings; dressed or undressed; all in good condition, with proper parts.

3in (8cm)	$225—250*
4—5in (10—13cm)	225—250*
6in (15cm)	300—325*
7in (18cm)	350—375*
8in (20cm)	475—525*
9in (23cm)	600—700
11in (28cm)	850—950

Early style model, stiff hips, shirred
  hose:

4½in (12cm)	250—275
6in (15cm)	400—425

*Allow $25—50 extra for yellow boots (Kestners).

4½in (12cm) all-bisque girl with stiff hips, stationary glass eyes, pink shirred hose, brown strap shoes. *H & J Foulke, Inc.*

All-Bisque Dolls (German) continued

All-Bisque with swivel neck and glass eyes: Ca. 1880—on. Swivel neck, pegged shoulders and hips; good wig, glass eyes, closed mouth; molded and painted shoes or boots and stockings; dressed or undressed; all in good condition, with proper parts.

4—4½in (10—12cm)	**$ 300—325**
5—6in (13—15cm)	**350—400**
7in (18cm)	**475—525**
8in (20cm)	**700—750**
10in (25cm)	**1000—1100**

Early Kestner or S&H type:
(For photograph see *8th Blue Book*, page 44.)

5in (13cm)	**700—750**
6—7in (15—18cm)	**850—950**
8in (20cm)	**1200—1300**
11in (28cm)	**2000—2200**

With jointed knee:

5½in (14cm)	**1800**

So-called "Wrestler" (**#102**):

6½in (16cm)	**900—950**
8½in (22cm)	**1100—1200**
9½in (24cm)	**1300—1400**

Bare feet: (For photograph see *Doll Reader®* Aug/Sept 1988 page 98.)

5—6in (13—15cm)	**900—1100**
8—9in (20—23cm)	**1500—1800**
11—12in (28—31cm)	**2500—3000**

Round face, Bootines:

6in (15cm)	**550**
8in (20cm)	**950**

See color photograph on page 67.

8½in (22cm) 102, so-called "Wrestler" with swivel neck, yellow boots. *Betty Harms Collection.*

7in (18cm) 190 with swivel neck, all original. *H & J Foulke, Inc.*

5½in (14cm) all-bisque girl with long black stockings, brown strap shoes. *H & J Foulke, Inc.*

All-Bisque Dolls (German) continued

All-Bisque with long black or blue stockings: Ca. 1890—on. Jointed at neck, shoulders and hips; good wig, glass sleep eyes, open mouth with teeth; molded brown shoes and molded long black or blue stockings; dressed or undressed; all in good condition, with proper parts. Sometimes marked "S & H 886" or "890."
4½in (12cm),

closed mouth	**$450—500**
5½—6in (14—15cm)	**550—600**
7—7½in (18—19cm)	**700—750**

4in (10cm) 144 baby with molded shoes and socks. *H & J Foulke, Inc.*

All-Bisque Baby: 1900—on. Jointed at shoulders and hips with curved arms and legs; molded and painted hair, painted eyes; not dressed; all in good condition, with proper parts.

2½—3½in (6—9cm)	**$ 75—85**
4—5in (10—13cm)	**125—150**

Fine early quality, blonde molded hair: (For photograph see *8th Blue Book*, page 45.)

4½in (12cm)	**150—165**
6—7in (15—18cm)	**200—250**
13in (33cm)	**750—850**

8¼in (21cm) all-bisque character baby. *H & J Foulke, Inc.*

All-Bisque Character Baby: Ca. 1910. Jointed at shoulders and hips, curved arms and legs; molded hair, painted eyes, character face; undressed; all in good condition, with proper parts.

4in (10cm)	**$ 150—175**
6in (15cm)	**225—250**
8in (20cm)	**400—450**

With glass eyes,

4—5in (10—13cm)	**260—285**

Swivel neck, glass eyes:

6in (15cm)	**400—450**
8in (20cm)	**550—600**
10in (25cm)	**750—800**

Toddler, swivel neck, glass eyes, (Kestner quality):

6in (15cm)	**500—550**
8in (20cm)	**850**

Mildred, the Prize Baby #880:

6-1/2in (17cm)	
at auction	**1600**

All-Bisque Dolls (German) continued

7½in (19cm) all-bisque 178 toddler by Kestner. *Jan Foulke Collection.*

5in (13cm) **Orsini MiMi**. See color photograph on page 68. *H & J Foulke, Inc.*

All-Bisque Character Dolls: 1913—on. Character faces with well-painted features and molded hair; usually jointed only at arms. Also see individual listings.

Chin Chin (Heubach),	
4in (10cm)	**$225—250**
Small pink bisque characters	
(many by Hertwig & Co.),	
up to 3in (8cm)	**45**
3in (8cm) glass eyes	**85**
Peterkin,	
6in (13cm)	**200**
Orsini: MiMi or DiDi,	
5in (13cm)	
glass eyes	**1000—1100**
ViVi, 5in (13cm)	
glass eyes	**1200—1300**
HEbee SHEbee	
4½in (12cm)	**300—325**
8½in (22cm)	**850**
Buster Brown,	
4in (10cm)	**175—200**
Max and **Moritz** (Kestner),	
5-1/2in (14cm)	**2500 pair**

6in (15cm) "Germany" pink bisque character. *H & J Foulke, Inc.*

Oscar Hitt Snowflake	**150**
Little Annie Roonie,	
4in (10cm)	**225—250**
Scootles,	
7in (18cm)	**700**

All-Bisque Dolls (German) continued

Later All-Bisque with glass eyes: Ca. 1915. Many of pretinted pink bisque. Jointed at shoulders and hips; good wig, glass eyes, closed or open mouth; molded and painted black one-strap shoes and stockings; undressed or dressed; all in good condition, with proper parts.
Good smooth bisque:

4—5in (10—13cm)	**$135—165**
6in (15cm)	**200—225**
7in (18cm)	**265—285**

Grainy bisque:

4½in (12cm)	**95**
6in (15cm)	**150**

All-Bisque with character face: Ca. 1915. Jointed at shoulders and hips; smiling character face, closed or open mouth; molded and painted black one-strap shoes and stockings; dressed or undressed; all in good condition, with proper parts. Very good quality.

8in (20cm) all-bisque 545 girl, good smooth quality pretinted pink bisque, open mouth, brown strap shoes. *H & J Foulke, Inc.*

#167 Painted eyes, molded hair, (For photograph see *6th Blue Book,* page 48.)

5in (13cm)	**$160—185**

#150 open/closed mouth with two painted teeth,

4½in (12cm) glass eyes	**250—275**
6in (15cm) glass eyes	**325—350**
5—5½in (13—14cm) painted eyes	**200—225**

Kestner type, swivel neck glass eyes, (For photograph see *8th Blue Book,* page 68.)

4½—5½in (12—14cm)	**450—500**

#155, smiling face, (For photograph see *8th Blue Book,* page 48.)

5½in (14cm)	**350—375**

7in (18cm) all-bisque 150 character girl with dimples and two upper teeth. *H & J Foulke, Inc.*

All-Bisque Dolls (German) continued

Later All-Bisque with painted eyes: Ca. 1920. Some of pretinted bisque. Jointed at shoulders and hips, stationary neck; mohair wig or molded hair, painted eyes, closed mouth; molded and painted one-strap shoes and white stockings; dressed or undressed; all in good condition, with proper parts.

3½in (9cm)	**$ 65—75**
4½—5in (12—13cm)	**90—100**
6—7in (15—18cm)	**140—175**

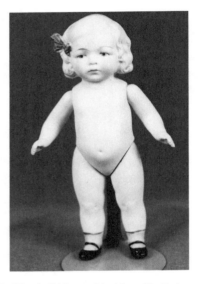

7in (18cm) all-bisque girl with molded hair and painted eyes. *H & J Foulke, Inc.*

3in (8cm) all-bisque flappers with molded hair in original box. *Jan Foulke Collection.*

All-Bisque "Flapper" (tinted bisque): Ca. 1920. Jointed at shoulders and hips; molded bobbed hair with loop for bow, painted features; long yellow stockings, one-strap shoes with heels; undressed or dressed; all in good condition, with proper parts, very good quality. (For photograph see *6th Blue Book*, page 49.)

5in (13cm)	**$225—275**
6—7in (15—18cm)	**325—375**
Standard quality,	
5in (13cm)	**150—175**

All-Bisque Baby: Ca. 1920. Pink bisque, so-called "Candy Baby," jointed at shoulders and hips, curved arms and legs; painted hair, painted eyes; original factory clothes; all in good condition, with proper parts. (For photograph see *8th Blue Book*, page 50.)

2½—3in (6—8cm)	**$ 60—65**
8in (20cm)	**135—165**

All-Bisque "Flapper:" Ca. 1920. Pink bisque with wire joints at shoulders and hips; molded bobbed hair and painted features; painted shoes and socks; original factory clothes; all in good condition, with proper parts.

3in (8cm)	**$ 45—55**
Molded hats	**165—185**

All-Bisque Dolls (German) continued

Bathing Beauty: 1920s. All-bisque lady, either nude or partially dressed in painted-on clothing; modeled in various sitting, lying or standing positions; painted features; molded hair; possibly with bathing cap or bald head with mohair wig; may be dressed in bits of lace.

Common type,	
3—4in (8—10cm)	**$ 65—85**
Fine quality,	
5in (13cm)	**425—475**
seated nude	**500**
7in (18cm)	**550—600**

All-Bisque Nodder Characters: Ca. 1920. Many made by Hertwig & Co. Nodding heads, elastic strung, molded clothes; all in good condition. Decoration is usually not fired so it wears and washes off very easily. Marked "Germany."

3—4in (8—10cm)	**$ 50—60**
German Comic Characters,	
3—4in (8—10cm)	**100 up***

*Depending upon rarity.

3—4in (8—10cm) bathing beauties in painted bathing suits. *H & J Foulke, Inc.*

All-Bisque Immobiles: Ca. 1920. All-bisque figures with molded clothes, molded hair and painted features. Decoration is not fired, so it wears and washes off very easily. Marked "Germany."

Tinies: adults and children,	
1½—2¼in (4—6cm)	**$ 35—45**
Children,	
3¼in (8cm)	**40—45**
Bride & Groom,	
4—5in (10—13cm)	**75—85**
Santa,	
3in (8cm)	**100**
Children with animals on string,	
3in (8cm)	**85**

1½—2¼in (4—6cm) tiny immobile colonial family. *H & J Foulke, Inc.*

All-Bisque Dolls
(Made in Japan)

Maker: Various Japanese firms
Date: Ca. 1915—on
Material: Bisque
Size: Various small sizes
Mark: "Made in Japan" or "NIPPON"

Baby Doll with bent limbs: Jointed shoulders and sometimes hips; molded and painted hair and eyes; not dressed; all in good condition.

White, 4in (10cm)	**$25**	*Nodders,*	
Black,		4in (10cm)	**25—30**
4—5in (10—13cm)	**50—60**	*Orientals,*	
Betty Boop-type,		3—4in (8—10cm)	**20—25**
4—5in (10—13cm)	**15—20**	*Queue San,*	
6—7in (15—18cm)	**25—30**	4in (10cm)	**65—75**
Child,		*Marked "Nippon" Characters,*	
4—5in (10—13cm)	**25**	4—5in (10—13cm)	**45**
6—7in (15—18cm)	**35—40**	*Three Bears*	
Comic Characters,		boxed set	**125—150**
3—4in (8—10cm)	**25 up***	*Snow White*	
Stiff Characters,		boxed set	**350**
3—4in (8—10cm)	**5—8**	*Depending upon rarity.	
6—7in (15—18cm)	**20—25**		
Cho-Cho San,			
4½in (12cm)	**65—75**		

3in (8cm) and 3½in (9cm) comic characters. *H & J Foulke, Inc.*

Alma

Maker: Unknown manufacturer, Turin, Italy
Date: 1929—on
Material: All-felt
Mark: Cloth label, cardboard tag; sometimes stamp on foot

Alma Doll: All-felt with swivel head, jointed shoulders and hips; painted features, eyes usually side-glancing, mohair sewn on head, distinctive curled felt ear; original intricate clothing; in excellent condition.
16in (41cm)   **$600—700**

16in (41cm) Alma girl, all original. *H & J Foulke, Inc.*

Alt, Beck & Gottschalck

Maker: Alt, Beck & Gottschalck, porcelain factory, Nauendorf near Ohrdruf, Thüringia, Germany. Made heads for many producers including Wagner & Zetzsche.

Date: 1854—on

Material: China and bisque heads for use on composition, kid or cloth bodies; all-bisque or all-china dolls.

China Shoulder Head: Ca. 1880. Black or blonde-haired china head; old cloth body with china limbs or kid body; dressed; all in good condition. Mold numbers, such as *784, 1000, 1008, 1028, 1046, 1142, 1210,* etc.

Mark: 1008×9

Also $\times$ or $\overline{}$ in place of $\times$

10in (25cm)	**$185—210**
15—18in (38—46cm)	**300—325**
20—22in (51—56cm)	**375—425**
25—26in (64—66cm)	**500—600**

16in (41cm) #1046 china shoulder head. *H&J Foulke, Inc.*

24in (61cm) #990 bisque shoulder head with molded pink bonnet. *H&J Foulke, Inc.*

Bisque Shoulder Head: Ca. 1880. Molded hair, painted or glass eyes, closed mouth; cloth body with bisque lower limbs; dressed; all in good condition. Mold numbers, such as *890, 990, 1000, 1008, 1028, 1064, 1142, 1254, 1288, 1304.*

Mark: See above

Painted eyes,

15—18in (38—46cm)	**$375—450***
23—25in (58—64cm)	**550—600***

Glass eyes,

16in (41cm)	**700***
18—20in (46—51cm)	**575—675***

Blue Scarf Lady, glass eyes,

20in (51cm)	**1300—1500**

*Allow extra for unusual or elaborate hairdo or molded hat.

Alt, Beck & Gottschalck continued

Bisque Shoulder Head: Ca. 1885—
on. Turned shoulder head, mohair
or human hair wig, plaster dome or
bald head, glass sleeping or set
eyes, closed mouth; kid body with
gusseted joints and bisque lower
arms, dressed; all in good condition. Mold numbers, such as ***639,
698, 1123, 1235.***

Mark: 639 ⚹ 6

26in (66cm) #1123½ shoulder head with open
mouth. *H&J Foulke, Inc.*

with DEP after 1888

15—17in (38—43cm)	$ 550—650
20—22in (51—56cm)	750—850
26in (66cm)	1000—1100

#911, 916, swivel neck:

20in (51cm)	2000

With open mouth:
Mark:

698 ½ *Germany Dep No. 10*

14—16in (36—41cm)	400—425
20—22in (51—56cm)	450—500
25in (64cm)	550—600

Child Doll: Perfect bisque head, good wig, sleep eyes, open mouth; ball-
jointed body in good condition; appropriate clothes. Mold ***#1362.*** (For
photograph see *8th Blue Book*, page 56.)

Mark:

2 ½

A B & G

Made in Germany

11—12in (28—31cm)	$ 350—375
16—18in (41—46cm)	425—475
21—24in (53—61cm)	500—600
29—31in (74—79cm)	900—950
36in (91cm)	1500—1600
39—42in (99—107cm)	2300—2500

#630, closed mouth:

23in (68cm)	1800—2000**

**Not enough price samples to compute a reliable range.

Alt, Beck & Gottschalck continued

All-Bisque Girl: 1911. Chubby body, loop strung shoulders and hips, inset glass eyes, open/closed mouth, painted eyelashes, full mohair or silky wig; molded white stockings, blue garters, black Mary Janes.

Mark:
$$\frac{83}{225}$$
$$24$$

Also **#100, 125** or **150** in place of **225**. Bottom number is centimeter size.

5in (13cm)	**$185—200**
7in (18cm)	**275—325**
8in (20cm)	**375—400**
10in (25cm)	**550—600**

5in (13cm) all-bisque girl #100. *H&J Foulke, Inc.*

19in (48cm) #1361 character baby. *H&J Foulke, Inc.*

Character: 1910—on. Perfect bisque head, good wig, sleep eyes, open mouth; some with open nostrils; composition body; all in good condition; suitable clothes.

Mark:

#1322, 1352, 1361:
10—12in (25—31cm)	**$325—375***
15—17in (38—43cm)	**475—525***
23—24in (58—61cm)	**800—850***

#1357:
(For photograph, see *7th Blue Book,* page 55.)
18—20in (46—51cm)   **800—850*** toddler

#1358:
(For photograph, see *7th Blue Book,* page 180.)
18—20in (46—51cm)
2800—3000*

*Allow $50 extra for flirty eyes or toddler body.
**Not enough price samples to compute a reliable average.

Louis Amberg & Son

Maker: Louis Amberg & Son, New York, N.Y., U.S.A.
Date: 1907—on (although Amberg had been in the doll business under other names since 1878)

Jointed Girl: 1912. Composition dolly face head, sleeping eyes, open mouth, human hair wig; jointed composition body; all in good condition with appropriate clothes. (For photograph see *7th Blue Book*, page 56.)
Mark: Body:

"AMBERG
VICTORY

Head: "L.A. &S"
22—24in (56—61cm)

DOLL"

$250—300

New Born Babe: 1914, reissued 1924. Designed by Jeno Juszko. Bisque head of an infant with painted hair, sleep eyes, closed mouth; soft cloth body with celluloid, rubber or composition hands; appropriate clothes; all in good condition.
Mark: "© L.A.&S. 1914, G 45520 Germany #4", also
"Heads copyrighted by LOUIS AMBERG and Son", also
"© L. Amberg & Son Germany 886/2"

Length:
8in (20cm)	**$325—350**
10—11in (25—28cm)	**425—450**
14—15in (36—41cm)	**550—650**

Charlie Chaplin: 1915. Composition portrait head with molded and painted hair, painted eyes to the side, closed full mouth, molded mustache; straw-filled cloth body with composition hands; original clothes; all in good condition with wear. (For photograph see *8th Blue Book*, page 57.)
Mark: cloth label on sleeve:
"CHARLIE CHAPLIN DOLL
World's Greatest Comedian
Made exclusively by Louis Amberg
& Son, N.Y.
by Special Arrangement with
Essamay Film Co."
14in (36cm) **$450**

13in (33cm) *New Born Babe. H&J Foulke, Inc.*

Louis Amberg & Son continued

Composition Character Child: Ca. 1916. Composition character head, flange neck, molded and painted hair, painted eyes, open mouth with painted teeth; cloth body with composition hands: original clothes; all in good condition.
Mark: "L. A. & S."
16½ (42cm) **$150**

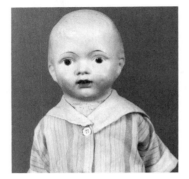

16½in (42cm) composition character child, all original. See color photograph on page 68. *H & J Foulke, Inc.*

Composition Mibs: 1921. Composition shoulder head designed by Hazel Drucker with wistful expression, molded and painted blonde or reddish hair, blue painted eyes, closed mouth; cloth body with composition arms and legs with painted shoes and socks; appropriate old clothes; all in good condition. (For photograph see *5th Blue Book*, page 57.)
Mark: None on doll; paper label only:

"Amberg Dolls
Please Love Me
16in (41cm)   I'm Mibs"   **$750 up****

Baby Peggy: 1923. Composition head, arms and legs, cloth body; molded brown bobbed hair, painted eyes, smiling closed mouth; appropriately dressed; all in good condition. (For photograph see *6th Blue Book*, page 57.)
20in (51cm)   **$550—600****

Baby Peggy: 1924. Perfect bisque head with character face; brown bobbed mohair wig, brown sleep eyes, closed mouth; composition or kid body, fully-jointed; dressed or undressed; all in very good condition.
Mark:

"19 © 24
LA & S NY
Germany
—50—
also: 982/2"
973 (smiling socket head)
972 (pensive socket head)
983 (smiling shoulder head)
982 (pensive shoulder head)
18—22in (46—56cm)   **$2500—2850**
See color photograph on page 68.

**Not enough price samples to compute a reliable range.

Louis Amberg & Son continued

All-Bisque Character Children: 1920s. Made by a German porcelain factory. Pink pretinted bisque with molded and painted features, molded hair; jointed at shoulders and hips; molded stockings with blue garters, brown strap shoes, white stockings.

4in (10cm)	**$125**
5—6in (13—15cm)	**160—185**
girl with molded bow	
6in (15cm)	**225—250**

5¾in (15cm) all-bisque character girl with blue molded bow. *H&J Foulke, Inc.*

Mibs
(For photograph see *8th Blue Book*, page 58.)

4¾in (12cm)	**$300—325**
3in (8cm)	**225**

Baby Peggy
(For photograph see *8th Blue Book*, page 59.)

5½in (14cm)	**$350**
3in (8cm)	**225**

3½in (9cm) all-bisque character girl with molded flowers in her hair. *H&J Foulke, Inc.*

Vanta Baby: 1927. A tie-in with Vanta baby garments. Composition or bisque head with molded and painted hair, sleep eyes, open mouth with two teeth (closed mouth and painted eyes in all-composition small dolls); muslin body jointed at hips and shoulders, curved composition arms and legs; suitably dressed; all in good condition.

Mark:

"VANTA BABY -- AMBERG"

20in (51cm):

Composition head	**$225—250**
Bisque head	**650—750****

**Not enough price samples to compute a reliable range.

22in (56cm) *Vanta Baby* with composition head, redressed. *Emily Manning Collection.*

Louis Amberg & Son continued

Sue, Edwina or It: 1928. All-composition with molded and painted hair, painted eyes; jointed neck, shoulders and hips, a large round ball joint at waist; dressed; all in very good condition. (For photograph see *7th Blue Book*, page 59).
Mark:

> "AMBERG
> PAT. PEND.
> L.A. & S. © 1928"

14in (36cm)   **$375—425**

Peter Pan, distinctive face as pictured.
14in (36cm)   **$400—500****
**Not enough price samples to compute a reliable range.

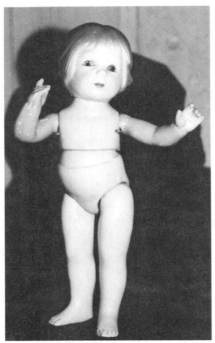

Tiny Tots Body Twists: 1928. All-composition with jointed shoulders and a large round ball joint at the waist; molded and painted hair in both boy and girl styles, painted eyes; painted shoes and socks; dressed; all in good condition. (For photograph see *8th Blue Book*, page 60.)
Mark: tag on clothes:
"An Amberg Doll with
BODY TWIST
all its own
PAT. PEND. SER. NO.
32018"
8in (20cm)   **$165—185**

14in (36cm) *Peter Pan. Courtesy of Jean Hess.*

American Character

Maker: American Character Doll Co., New York, N.Y., U.S.A.
Date: 1919—on
Trademark: Petite

Sally: 1930. All-composition jointed at neck, shoulders and hips; molded and painted hair, painted side-glancing eyes, closed mouth; original or appropriate old clothes; all in good condition.
Mark:

> "PETITE
> SALLY"

12in (31cm)	**$160—185**
16in (41cm) sleeping eyes	**225—250**

Marked Petite or American Character Mama Dolls: 1923—on. Composition head, arms and legs, cloth torso; mohair or human hair wig, sleep eyes, closed or open mouth; original clothes; all in good condition.

16—18in (41—46cm)	**$175—200**
24in (61cm)	**250—275**

13in (33cm) *Sally*, appropriate clothes. *H&J Foulke, Inc.*

17in (43cm) American Character mama dolls, all original with "Petite-Chuckles" tag. *Courtesy of Kerra Davis.*

Marked Petite Girl Dolls: 1930s. All-composition jointed at neck, shoulders and hips; human hair or mohair wig, lashed sleeping eyes, open mouth with teeth; original or appropriate old clothes; all in good condition. (For photograph see *8th Blue Book*, page 62.)

16—18in (41—46cm)   **$200—225**
24in (61cm)   **250—300**

Puggy: 1928. All-composition chubby body jointed at neck, shoulders and hips; molded and painted hair, painted eyes to the side, closed mouth, pug nose, frowning face; original clothes; all in good condition. (For photograph see *7th Blue Book*, page 61.)

Mark: "A PETITE DOLL"
12in (31cm)   **$450—500**

Sweet Sue: 1953. All-hard plastic or hard plastic and vinyl, some with walking mechanism, some fully-jointed including elbows, knees and ankles; original clothes; all in excellent condition.

Marks: Various, including: "A.C.," "Amer. Char. Doll," "American Character" in a circle.

14in (36cm)   **$125—150**
18—20in (46—51cm)   **175—200**
24in (61cm)   **225—250**
30in (76cm)   **300—350**

14in (36cm) *Sweet Sue* bride, all original. *H&J Foulke, Inc.*

Eloise: Ca. 1955. All-cloth with molded face, painted side-glancing eyes, smiling mouth, yellow yarn hair; flexible arms and legs; original clothing; in excellent condition. Designed by Bette Gould from the fictional little girl "Eloise" who lived at the Plaza Hotel in New York City. (For photograph see *8th Blue Book*, page 63.)

Mark: Cardboard tag
21in (53cm)   **$225—250**

American Character continued

Betsy McCall: 1957. All-hard plastic with legs jointed at knees; rooted Saran hair on a wig cap, round face with sleep eyes, plastic eyelashes; original clothes; all in excellent condition.

Mark:

8in (20cm) $100—125

Betsy McCall: 1960. All-vinyl with rooted hair, lashed sleep eyes, round face, turned-up mouth; slender arms and legs; original clothes; all in excellent condition.

Mark:

McCALL
19©56
CORP.

13—14in (33—36cm)	$150—175
18—20in (46—51cm)	175—225
30—36in (76—91cm)	300—325

8in (20cm) ***Betsy McCall***, all-hard plastic, all original. *H&J Foulke, Inc.*

13in (33cm) ***Betsy McCall***, all vinyl, all original. *Mary Lou Rubright Collection.*

Max Oscar Arnold

Maker: Max Oscar Arnold (doll and porcelain factory), Neustadt, Thüringia, Germany.

Date: 1877—on for dolls; 1919—1931 for porcelain heads (Some made for Welsch & Co., Sonneberg.)

Mark:

Made in Germany

Marked M.O.A. Child Doll: Perfect bisque socket head, original or appropriate wig, set or sleep eyes, open mouth; ball-jointed composition body; dressed; entire doll in good condition. Mold *#150* or *#200*.

14—15in (64—66cm)	**$275—300***
18—20in (46—51cm)	**400—425***
25—26in (64—66cm)	**525—550***

*Do not pay as much for a doll with poor bisque.

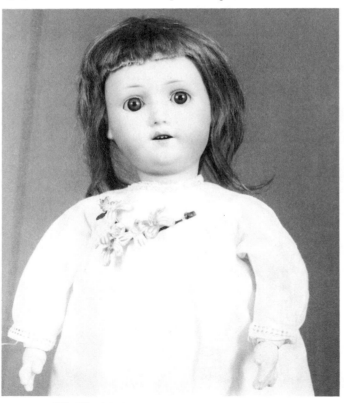

20in (51cm) *MOA* Welsch child. *H&J Foulke, Inc.*

22in (56cm) *Alabama Indestructible Doll* by Ella Smith Doll Co., all-cloth with oil painted face. For further information see page 19. *H & J Foulke, Inc.*

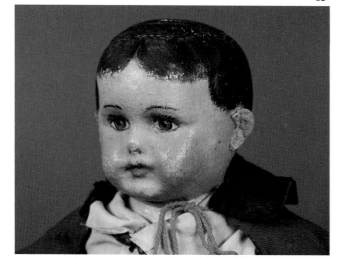

18in (46cm) Alexander composition *Fairy Queen*, all original. For further information see page 28. *H & J Foulke, Inc.*

ABOVE: 12in (31cm) Alexander vinyl **Rozy**, all original. For further information see page 38. *H & J Foulke, Inc.*

18in (46cm) Alexander hard plastic **Cynthia** in original clothes. For further information see page 30. *Private Collection.*

14in (36cm) Alexander composition **Jeannie Walker**, all original. For further information see page 29. *H & J Foukle, Inc.*

17in (43cm) H.A. bébé by Henri Alexandre. For further information see page 42. *Private Collection*

5½in (14cm) early all-bisque with swivel neck, all original. For further information see page 46. *Kay & Wayne Jensen Collection.*

5in (13cm) all-bisque *MiMi* by J. Orsini. For further information see page 48. *H & J Foulke, Inc,*

16½in (42cm) doll with composition head marked "L.A. & S." by Amberg. For further information see page 59. *H & J Foulke, Inc.*

BELOW: *Baby Peggy* by Amberg. For further information see page 58. *Billie Nelson Tyrrell.*

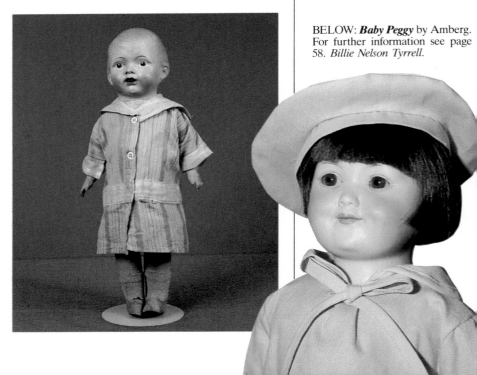

16in (41cm) French fashion lady by E. Barrois, stockinette body with bisque hands, bisque legs with black molded shoes. For further information see page 92. *Private Collection.*

6½in (17cm) **Bing** cloth doll, signed on bottom of shoe, all original. For further information see page 96. *Kay & Wayne Jensen Collection.*

BELOW: 14in (36cm) composition **Nancy Lee** by Arranbee, all original. For further information see page 82. *H & J Foulke, Inc.*

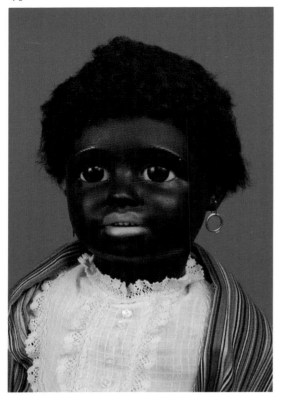

ABOVE: 13½in (34cm) *Tête Jumeau* (red stamp mark). For further information see page 97. *Kiefer Collection.*

14in (36cm) Simon & Halbig 1358 character child. For further information see page 99. *Private Collection.*

22½in (61cm) Simon & Halbig 739 child. For further information see page 97. *Kiefer Collection.*

17in (43cm) Bru fashion lady with smiling face, kid body with wood arms. For further information see page 105. *Private Collection.*

12in (31cm) head circum-ference **Bye-Lo Baby** by Grace Storey Putnam, all original with labeled gown and metal button. For further information see page 109. *H & J Foulke, Inc.*

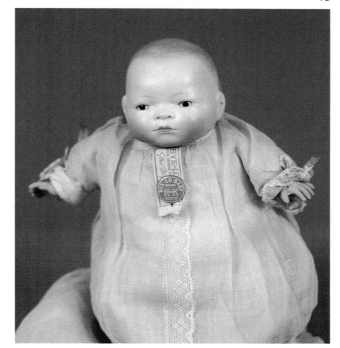

17in (43cm) Chad Valley **Golliwog**, all original. For further information see page 120. *Kiefer Collection.*

LEFT: 26in (66cm) Bru Jne 10 bébé. For further information see page 107. *Kay & Wayne Jensen Collection.*

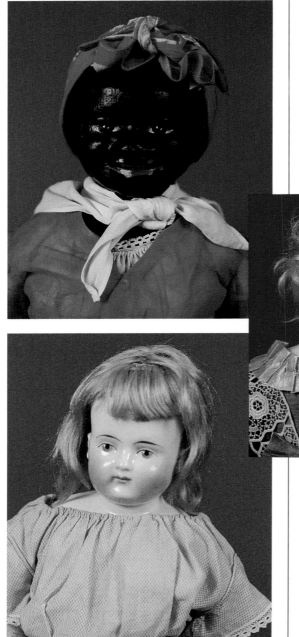

24in (61cm) black lady by Martha Chase, all original. For further information see page 121. *Kiefer Collection.*

19½in (50cm) French-type china head lady with glass eyes. For further information see page 122. *Kay & Wayne Jensen Collection.*

19in (48cm) china with bald head and wig. For further information see page 123. *Kay & Wayne Jensen Collection.*

24in (61cm) early china lady with molded brown hair, marked "T.P.M." For further information see page 123. *Private Collection*

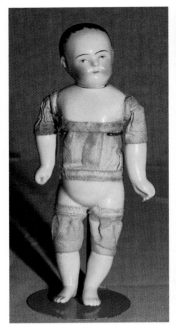

ABOVE: 9in (23cm) china child with swivel neck, china shoulder plate, hips and lower limbs, cloth midsection and upper limbs. For further information see page 124. *H & J Foulke, Inc.*

ABOVE LEFT: 10in (25cm) china with painted brown eyes, Greiner-style hairdo, all original. For further information see page 124. *H & J Foulke, Inc.*

LEFT: 19in (48cm) china with glass eyes, Greiner-style hairdo. For further information see page 124. *Private Collection.*

23½in (60cm) china with braids encircling head, known as "Young Victoria." For further information see page 125. *Joe Jackson & Joel Pearson.*

21in (53cm) china with pierced ears, brushmarks and curls hanging free from neck. For further information see page 125. *Joe Jackson & Joel Pearson.*

19in (48cm) *Columbian doll*, unmarked. For further information see page 131. *Private Collection.*

14in (36cm) printed cloth pair of unidentified characters. For further information see page 128. *H & J Foulke.*

RIGHT: 21in (53cm) *Paris Bébé* by Danel & Cie. For further information see page 79. *Private Collection.*

12in (31cm) Effanbee composition *Candy Kid,* all original. For further information see page 160. *H & J Foulke.*

21in (53cm) Effanbee composition Historical doll *1840 Covered Wagon Days,* all original. For further information see page 158. *Private Collection.*

Arranbee

Maker: Arranbee Doll Co., New York, N.Y., U.S.A.
Date: 1922—1960
Mark: "ARRANBEE" or "R & B"

Baby: 1924. Perfect solid dome bisque head with molded and painted hair, sleep eyes, open mouth with teeth, dimples; cloth body with celluloid or composition hands, may have a molded celluloid bottle in hand, "Nursing Bottle Baby;" dressed; all in good condition. (For photograph see *6th Blue Book*, page 61.)
Head circumference: 12—13in (31—33cm)   **$375—425**

My Dream Baby: 1924. Perfect bisque head with solid dome and painted hair, sleep eyes, closed or open mouth; all-composition or cloth body with composition hands; dressed; all in good condition. Some heads incised "A.M.," *"341"* or *"351"*; some incised "AR-RANBEE."
Head circumference:

10in (25cm)	**$275**
12—13in (31—33cm)	**350—425**
15in (38cm)	**600—650**

11in (28cm) *My Dream Baby* with A.M. 351 head. *H&J Foulke, Inc.*

Storybook Dolls: 1930s. All-composition with swivel neck, jointed arms and legs; molded and painted hair, painted eyes; all original storybook costumes; all in good condition.
9—10in (25cm)   **$150**

9in (23cm) Storybook Doll, all original. *H&J Foulke, Inc.*

Arranbee continued

14in (36cm) unmarked **Nancy**, all original.
Joanna Ott Collection.

Nancy: 1930. All-composition, jointed at neck, shoulders and hips, molded hair, painted eyes and closed mouth; original or appropriate old clothes; all in good condition. (For photograph see *8th Blue Book*, page 81.)

Mark: "ARRANBEE" or "NANCY"

12in (31cm)	**$160—185**
16in (41cm) sleep eyes, wig, open mouth	**225—250**

Debu' Teen and Nancy Lee: 1938—on. All-composition or composition swivel shoulder head and limbs on cloth torso; mohair or human hair wig, sleep eyes, closed mouth, original clothes; all in good condition.

Mark: "R & B"

14in (36cm)	**$160—185**
18in (46cm)	**200—215**
21in (53cm)	**235—265**
Skating doll, 14in (36cm)	**175—200**

15in (38cm) **Nancy Lee**, all-composition, all original. For color photograph see page 69. *H&J Foulke, Inc.*

Nanette and Nancy Lee: 1950s. All-hard plastic, jointed at neck, shoulders and hips; synthetic wig, sleep eyes, closed mouth; original clothes; all in excellent condition. This face mold was also used for dolls which were given other names.

Mark: "R & B"

14in (36cm)	**$150—175**
18in (46cm)	**200—225**

Georgene Averill
(Madame Hendren)

Maker: Averill Mfg. Co. and Georgene Novelties, Inc., New York, N.Y., U.S.A.
Date: 1915—on
Designer: Georgene Averill (See also Maud Tousey Fangel and Grace Drayton)
Trademarks: Madame Hendren, Georgene Novelties

Tagged Mme. Hendren Character: Ca. 1915—on. Composition character face, usually with painted features, molded hair or wig (sometimes yarn); hard-stuffed cloth body with composition hands; original clothes often of felt, included Dutch children, Indians, sailors, cowboys, blacks; all in good condition.
10—14in (25—36cm) **$110—135**

Mama & Baby Dolls: Ca. 1918—on. Composition shoulder head, lower arms and legs, cloth torso with cry box; mohair wig or molded hair, sleep eyes, open mouth with teeth or closed mouth; appropriately dressed; all in good condition. Names such as ***Baby Hendren, Baby Georgene*** and others.
15—18in (38—46cm) **$150—175**
22—24in (56—61cm) **210—265**

Dolly Reckord: 1922. Composition shoulder head, lower arms and legs, cloth torso with record player; nice human hair wig, sleep eyes, open mouth with upper teeth; appropriate clothes; all in good condition with records. (For photograph see *6th Blue Book*, page 193.)
26in (66cm) **$450—500**

10in (25cm) tagged Mme. Hendren Dutch child. *H&J Foulke, Inc.*

Georgene Averill (Madame Hendren) continued

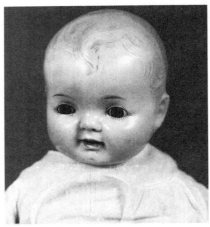

24in (61cm) *Baby Hendren*. *H&J Foulke, Inc.*

Infant Baby Dolls: Ca. 1924. Composition infant head with flange neck, painted hair, sleeping eyes, closed mouth; soft cloth body with composition hands; appropriately dressed. Good condition with light crazing. Sometimes stamped on body. (For photograph see *8th Blue Book*, page 83.)

Mark:

Genuine
Madame Hendren
Doll
522
Made in U.S.A.

16in (41cm)	**$135—150**
22in (56cm)	**200—215**

14in (36cm) black *Rufus*, all original. *Kiefer Collection.*

Whistling Doll: 1925—1929. Composition head with molded hair, side-glancing eyes, mouth pursed to whistle through round opening; composition arms, cloth torso; legs are coiled spring bellows covered with cloth; when head is pushed down or feet are pushed up, the doll whistles. Original or appropriate clothes; all in good condition. (For additional photograph see *7th Blue Book*, page 198.)

Mark: None

Original Cardboard Tag:
"I whistle when you dance me on one
foot and then the other.
Patented Feb. 2, 1926
Genuine Madame Hendren Doll."

14—15in (36—38cm) sailor, cowboy, cop or boy	
(*Dan*)	**$165—185**
Black *Rufus* or	
Dolly Dingle	**300—350****

**Not enough price samples to compute a reliable range.

Georgene Averill (Madame Hendren) continued

Bonnie Babe: 1926. Bisque heads by Alt, Beck & Gottschalck; cloth bodies by K & K Toy Co.; distributed by George Borgfeldt, New York. Perfect bisque head with smiling face, molded hair, glass sleep eyes, open mouth with two lower teeth; cloth body with composition arms (sometimes celluloid) and legs often of poor quality; all in good condition. Mold **#1368** or **1402**.

Mark:

Head circumference:

Copr. by Georgene Averill Germany 1005/3652 1368

9—10in (23—25cm)	$ 625—675
12—13in (31—33cm)	800—900
15in (38cm)	1100—1300
Composition body, 8in (20cm)	1250**

All-Bisque Bonnie Babe: 1926. Jointed at neck, shoulders and hips; smiling face with glass sleeping eyes, open mouth with two lower teeth; pink or blue molded slippers. Unmarked except for round paper label on stomach.

5in (13cm)	$ 675—725
7in (18cm)	850—950
With molded clothes, 5in (13cm)	1250**

Body Twists: 1927. All-composition, jointed at neck, shoulders and hips, with a large round ball joint at waist; molded and painted hair, painted eyes, closed mouth; dressed; all in good condition. Advertised as **Dimmie** and **Jimmie**. (For photographs see *5th Blue Book*, page 170 and *4th Blue Book*, page 161.)

14½in (37cm)	$300—325

**Not enough price samples to compute a reliable range.

13in (33cm) *Bonnie Babe*, all original with tag. *Esther Schwartz Collection.*

Georgene Averill (Madame Hendren) continued

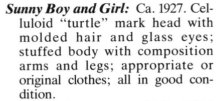

Sunny Boy and Girl: Ca. 1927. Celluloid "turtle" mark head with molded hair and glass eyes; stuffed body with composition arms and legs; appropriate or original clothes; all in good condition.

15in (38cm)   **$275—325****

**Not enough price samples to compute a reliable range.

15in (38cm) **Sunny Boy**, replaced clothes. *H&J Foulke, Inc.*

Snookums: 1927. Composition shoulder head, molded and painted hair with hole for one tuft of hair, painted eyes, smiling face with open/closed mouth; composition yoke and arms; cloth body and legs; dressed; all in good condition. From the comic strip "The Newlyweds" by George McManus. (For photograph see *5th Blue Book*, page 169.)

14in (36cm)   **$275—325**

Patsy-Type Girl: 1928. All-composition, jointed at neck, shoulders, and hips; molded hair, sleeping eyes, tiny closed mouth; bent right arm; original or appropriate old clothing; good condition with light crazing.

Mark: A.D. Co.

14in (36cm)   **$185—210**

14in (36cm) Averill girl, all original. *H&J Foulke, Inc.*

Georgene Averill (Madame Hendren) continued

Harriet Flanders: 1937. All-composition with jointed neck, shoulders and hips; chubby toddler body; solid dome head with tufts of molded blonde hair, lashed sleeping eyes, closed mouth; original clothes. Very good condition. Designed by Harriet Flanders. (For photograph see *7th Blue Book*, page 167.)

Mark: HARRIET ©
     FLANDERS

16in (41cm)	**$250**
Painted eyes, 12in (31cm)	**150**

13in (33cm)*Uncle Wiggily*, all original. *Esther Schwartz Collection.*

Cloth Dolls: Ca. 1930s—on. Mask face with painted features, yarn hair, painted and/or real eyelashes; cloth body with movable arms and legs; attractive original clothes; all in excellent condition.

Children or Babies:
12in (31cm)	**$ 85—125**
24—26in (61—66cm)	**175—225**

Topsy & Eva
10in (25cm)	**125—135**

International and Costume Dolls:
12in (31cm)	**65—75**
Mint in box with wrist tag	**85—95**

Uncle Wiggily,
13in (33cm)	**300**

Characters, 14in (36cm):
Little Lulu, 1944	**300—400******
40in (100cm)	**750**
Nancy, 1944	**350—400******
Sluggo, 1944	**350—400******
Tubby Tom, 1951	**350—400******

**Not enough price samples to compute a reliable range.

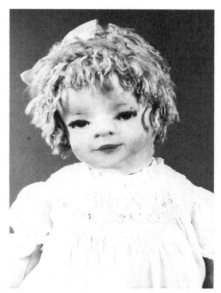

25in (63cm) child, replaced dress. *Betty Harms Collection.*

Baby Bo Kaye

Maker: Composition heads by Cameo Doll Company; bisque heads made in Germany, by Alt, Beck & Gottschalck; bodies by K & K Toy Co., New York, N.Y., U.S.A.

Date: 1925

Material: Bisque, composition or celluloid head with flange neck; composition or celluloid limbs, cloth body

Designer: J. L. Kallus

Mark:

> "Copr. by
> J. L. Kallus
> Germany
> 1394/30"

Baby Bo Kaye: Perfect bisque head marked as above, molded hair, glass eyes, open mouth with two lower teeth; body as above; dressed; all in good condition.

17—19in (43—48cm)   **$2500—2800**

All-Bisque Baby Bo Kaye: Molded hair, glass sleep eyes, open mouth with two teeth; swivel neck, jointed shoulders and hips; molded shoes and socks; unmarked. (For photograph see *8th Blue Book*, page 87.)

Mark:

5in (13cm)   **$1250**

6in (15cm)   **1500—1600**

Baby Bo Kaye, all original.
Courtesy Lesley Harford.

Babyland Rag

Maker: E. I. Horsman, New York, N.Y., U.S.A
Date: 1904—1920
Material: All-cloth
Size: 12—30in (31—76cm)
Mark: None

Babyland Rag: Cloth face with hand-painted features, later with printed features, sometimes mohair wig; cloth body jointed at shoulders and hips; original clothes.

Early hand-painted face:

13—15in (33—38cm)	
very good	$ 750—850*
fair	350—400
22in (56cm) fair	450—500
30in (76cm)	
very good	1600—1800**

Life-like face:

13—15in (33—38cm)	
very good	600—650*

Topsy Turvy,

13—15in (33—38cm)	
good	650—750*

Black,

20in (51cm)	1000—1100*

*Allow more for mint condition doll.
**Not enough price samples to compute a reliable range.

14in (36cm) Babyland Rag with brown hand-painted face. *H&J Foulke, Inc.*

15in (38cm) Babyland Rag Dutch Girl with life-like face of 1907. *H&J Foulke, Inc.*

Bähr & Pröschild

Maker: Bähr & Pröschild, porcelain factory, Ohrdruf, Thüringia, Germany. Made heads for Bruno Schmidt, Heinrich Stier, Kley & Hahn and others.

Date: 1871—on

Material: Bisque heads for use on composition or kid bodies, all-bisque dolls

---

Marked Belton-type Child Doll: Ca. 1880. Perfect bisque head, solid dome with flat top having two or three small holes, paperweight eyes, closed mouth with pierced ears; wood and composition jointed body with straight wrists; dressed; all in good condition. Mold numbers in *200* series, usually *204* or *224.*

Mark: 204

10—12in (25—31cm)	**$1250—1350**
15—17in (38—43cm)	**1600—1800**
19—21in (48—53cm)	**2200—2400**
24in (61cm)	**2800—3000**

11in (28cm) 224 child, closed mouth. *H&J Foulke, Inc.*

Marked Child Doll: 1888—on. Perfect bisque shoulder or socket head, sleeping eyes, open mouth with four or six upper teeth, good human hair or mohair wig; gusseted kid or jointed composition body (many of French-type); dressed; all in good condition. Mold numbers in *200* and *300* series.

Mark: 224
dep

#224, 239, 273, 275, 277, 297, 325, 379, 394 and other socket heads:

15—17in (38—43cm)	**$ 650—700**
20—22in (51—56cm)	**800—850**
25in (64cm)	**1100**

#246, 309 and other shoulder heads:

16—18in (41—46cm)	**$ 400—450**
22—24in (56—61cm)	**550—600**
29in (74cm)	**900—1000**
35in (89cm)	**1700**

16in (41cm) 309 shoulder head child. *H&J Foulke, Inc.*

Bähr & Pröschild continued

Marked B. P. Character Child: Ca. 1910. Perfect bisque socket head, good wig, sleep or painted eyes, closed mouth; toddler or jointed composition body; dressed; all in good condition. Mold *#2072, 536* and other child *500* series. Models made for Kley & Hahn and Bruno Schmidt.

Mark:

15—16in (36—38cm)	**$3000—3200**
19—21in (48—53cm)	**4000—4500**

16in (38cm) character child 520 made for Kley & Hahn. *Betty Harms Collection.*

12in (31cm) character baby 585. *H&J Foulke, Inc.*

Marked B. P. Character Baby: Ca. 1910—on. Perfect bisque socket head, solid dome or good wig, sleep eyes, open mouth; composition bent-limb baby body; dressed; all in good condition. Mold *#585, 604, 624, 678, 619, 641* and *587.*

Mark:

12—14in (31—36cm)	**$ 450—500***
16—18in (41—46cm)	**550—650***
22—24in (56—61cm)	**800—900***
26in (66cm)	**1100—1200***

*Allow extra for a toddler body.

E. Barrois

Maker: E. Barrois, doll factory, Paris, France. Heads purchased from an unidentified French or German porcelain factory.
Date: 1844—1877
Material: Bisque or china head, cloth or kid body
Mark:

E. (DÉPOSÉ B.

E.B. Fashion Lady: Perfect bisque shoulder head (may have a swivel neck), glass eyes (may be painted with long painted eyelashes), closed mouth; appropriate wig; kid body, some with jointed wood arms or wood and bisque arms; appropriate clothing. All in good condition.
16—19in (41—48cm)   **$3000—3500***
*Allow $500 extra for wood or bisque arms.

See color photograph on page 69.

16in (41cm) French fashion lady. Stockinette body with bisque hands, bisque legs with black molded shoes.

Bawo & Dotter

Maker: Bawo & Dotter, Bavaria, France and New York, N.Y., U.S.A.
Date: 1880s
Material: China head, cloth body, china lower limbs
Mark: On back shoulders:

7
Pat. Dec. 7/80

Marked Bawo & Dotter China Head: Perfect china shoulder head with
black or blonde molded hair (several styles with a high forehead exposed and
one with soft curly bangs), small painted eyes, closed mouth, rosy cheeks;
cloth body with patented printed corset, china lower arms and lower legs with
molded boots (limbs often marked with same size number as head).

16—18in (41—46cm)   **$225—250**
20—22in (51—56cm)   **275—325**
24in (61cm)   **350—375**

21in (53cm) china head with black molded hair marked "Pat. Dec. 7/80." *H&J Foulke, Inc.*

Belton-type
(So-called)

Maker: Various French and German firms such as Bähr & Pröschild
Date: 1875—on
Material: Bisque socket head, ball-jointed wood and composition body with straight wrists
Mark: None, except sometimes numbers

7½in (19cm) Belton-type child, five-piece body. *H&J Foulke, Inc.*

Belton-type Child Doll: Perfect bisque socket head, solid but flat on top with two or three small holes for stringing; paperweight eyes, closed mouth, pierced ears; wood and composition ball-jointed body with straight wrists; dressed; all in good condition.

Fine early quality
  (French-type face):
    13—15in (33—38cm) **$1700—2000**
    18—20in (46—51cm) **2400—2700**
    23—25in (58—64cm) **2900—3300**
Standard quality
  (German-type face):
    10—12in (25—31cm) **1250—1350**
    14—16in (36—41cm) **1500—1700**
    18—20in (46—51cm) **2100—2300**
    24in (61cm) **2800—3000**
Tiny with five-piece body:
    8—9in (20—23cm) **650—750**
#137:
    14—16in (36—41cm) **1800—2100**

16in (41cm) Belton-type child 137, standard quality. *Private Collection.*

C. M. Bergmann

Maker: C. M. Bergmann doll factory of Waltershausen, Thüringia, Germany; heads manufactured for this company by Armand Marseille, Simon & Halbig, Alt, Beck & Gottschalck and perhaps others.
Date: 1888—on
Material: Bisque head, composition ball-jointed body
Trademarks: Cinderella Baby (1897), Columbia (1904), My Gold Star (1926)
Mark:

C.M. BERGMANN   C. M. Bergmann
A-H ½-M: Waltershausen
Made in Germany   Germany
                        1916
                        6½ a

Distributor: Louis Wolfe & Co., New York, N.Y., U.S.A.

Bergmann Child Doll: Ca. 1889—on. Marked bisque head, composition ball-jointed body, good wig, sleep or set eyes, open mouth; dressed; all in nice condition.

Heads by A.M. and unknown makers:

18—21in (46—53cm)	$ 400—450
24—26in (61—66cm)	500—550
30in (76cm)	800
35in (89cm)	1100—1150
39in (99cm)	1800
10in (25cm)	400—425

Heads by Simon & Halbig:

10in (25cm)	$ 475—500
18—21in (46—53cm)	450—500
24—26in (61—66cm)	550—600
30in (76cm)	850—950
35in (89cm)	1250—1350
39in (99cm)	2000

Eleonore:

25in (64cm)	$ 700

25in (64cm) C.M. Bergmann Simon & Halbig child. *H&J Foulke, Inc.*

Bergmann Character Baby: 1909—on. Marked bisque socket head, mohair wig, sleep eyes, composition bent-limb baby body; dressed; all in good condition.
#612: (open/closed mouth)

16in (41cm)	$850**

**Not enough price samples to compute a reliable range.

Bing Art Dolls

Maker: Bing Werke (Bing Kunstlerpuppen) Nürnberg, Germany
Date: 1921—1932
Material: All-cloth or composition head and cloth body
Size: 6—17½in (15—45cm)
Designer: Prof. Vogt of Nürnberg & Emil Wagner of Sonneberg
Mark: "Bing" on sole of shoe or unmarked

Bing Art Doll: Cloth or composition head, molded face, hand-painted features, painted hair or wigged; cloth body with pin jointed shoulders and hips; original clothing; very good condition.

10—12in (25—31cm)
cloth head, painted hair **$625—675**
14in (36cm)
cloth head, painted hair **775—825**
12in (31cm)
wigged, cloth head **400**

**Not enough price samples to compute a reliable range.

See color photograph on page 69.

10½in Bing-type child, all original. *H&J Foulke, Inc.*

Black Dolls*

Black Bisque Doll: Ca. 1880—on. Various French and German manufacturers from their regular molds or specially designed ones with Negroid features. Perfect bisque socket head either painted dark or with dark coloring mixed in the slip, this runs from light brown to very dark; composition or sometimes kid body in a matching color, cloth bodies on some baby dolls; appropriate clothes; all in good condition.

FRENCH Makers:

Bru, Circle Dot, 13—15in
(33—38cm)   **$23,000—26,000**
Jumeau, closed mouth
17in (43cm)   **4000**
open mouth, 14—16in
(36—41cm)   **2300—2400**
SFBJ/Unis 60,
12—14in (31—36cm) **375**
16½in (42cm)   **550**
SFBJ 226,
17in (43cm)   **2200—2300**
Steiner, open mouth, 14—16in
(36—41cm)   **2200—2500**

GERMAN Makers (Child Dolls):

AM 1894,
15in (38cm)   **750—800**
B.P., 12—14in
(31—36cm)   **1100—1200**
K★R,
19in (48cm)   **1450**
Simon & Halbig 1249,
21in (53cm)   **1600—1700**
739, 17—18in
(43—46cm)   **1200—1400**
1039,
21in (53cm)   **1200—1400**
949 OM,
15in (38cm)   **1700**
Unmarked, good quality
10—13in (25—33cm),
jointed body   **350—400**
8—9in (20—23cm),
5-piece body   **265—285**
5in (13cm),
closed mouth   **225—275**
Kestner 134,
13in (33cm)   **800—850**

14½in (37cm) Steiner, Figure A, size 7, open mouth. *Private Collection.*

*Also see entries for specific doll makers.

Black Dolls continued

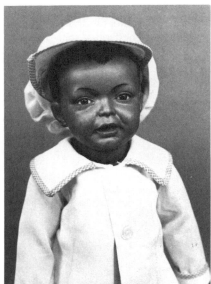

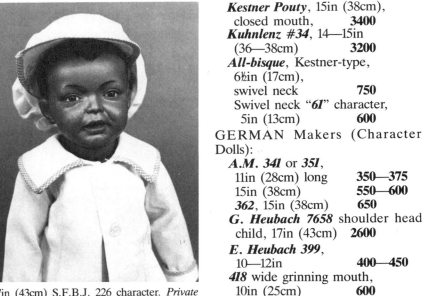

Kestner Pouty, 15in (38cm),
closed mouth, **3400**
Kuhnlenz #34, 14—15in
(36—38cm) **3200**
All-bisque, Kestner-type,
6½in (17cm),
swivel neck **750**
Swivel neck "**61**" character,
5in (13cm) **600**

GERMAN Makers (Character
Dolls):
A.M. 341 or **351**,
11in (28cm) long **350—375**
15in (38cm) **550—600**
362, 15in (38cm) **650**
G. Heubach 7658 shoulder head
child, 17in (43cm) **2600**
E. Heubach 399,
10—12in **400—450**
418 wide grinning mouth,
10in (25cm) **600**

17in (43cm) S.F.B.J. 226 character. *Private Collection.*

16½in (42cm) 1907 Jumeau child. *Kiefer Collection.*

21in (53cm) Simon & Halbig 1039 child. *Private Collection.*

Black Dolls continued

E. Heubach,
463 or **444**,
14in (36cm)   **700—750**
300, 18—19in
(46—48cm)   **1000—1200**
JDK Hilda, 13—14in
(33—36cm)   **3000—3500**
SPBH Hanna, 8—10in
(20—25cm)   **275—325**
S&H 1358, 18in (46cm)
     5,000
S&H 1301,
19in (48cm)   **15,000**
S&H 1294,
21in (53cm)   **1350**
Bye-Lo Baby,
10in (25cm)   **2100**

See color photographs on page 70.

Papier-Mâché Black Doll: Ca. 1890. By various German manufacturers. Papier-mâché character face, arms and legs, cloth body; glass eyes; original or appropriate clothes; all in good condition.
10—12in (25—31cm)   **$275—300**
Hottentots
7½—8½in (19—24cm)   **110—140**

Tony Sarg's Mammy Doll: Composition character face with wide smiling mouth, painted features; large composition hands and molded shoes; cloth body; original clothes, carrying a white baby; all in good condition. (For photograph see *6th Blue Book*, page 74.)
18in (46cm)   **$450—500**

22in (56cm) Simon & Halbig 1358 character. See color photograph on page 70. *Private Collection.*

18½in (47cm) E. Heubach 300 character baby. *Kiefer Collection.*

Black Dolls continued

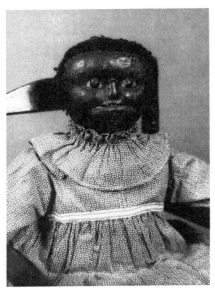

18in (46cm) black painted-over stockinette doll. *Betty Harms Collection.*

21in (53cm) black cloth face, embroidered features. *Betty Harms Collection.*

Cloth Black Doll: Ca. 1910. American-made cloth doll with black face, painted, printed or embroidered features; jointed arms and legs; original clothes; all in good condition.

Mammy-type, 18—22in
(46—56cm) **$350 up***

Babyland Rag-type,
13—15in (33—38cm),
painted face **800—850**

Stockinette
(so-called Beecher-type)
2000—2500

1930s Mammy, 14—16in
(36—41cm) **150 up***

WPA, molded cloth face,
(For photograph see *7th Blue Book*, page 83.)
22in (56cm) **1250—1350**

Paint over molded stockinette
(Chase-type),
18in (46cm) **1800—2000**

Black cloth, embroidered face,
18—21in (46—53cm)
1000—1100 up*

*Greatly depending upon appeal.

Black Dolls continued

Black Composition Doll: Ca. 1920 on. German made character doll, all-composition, jointed at neck, shoulders and hips; molded hair or wig, glass eyes (sometimes flirty); appropriate clothes; all in good condition.

15—17in (38—43cm)   **$500—600**

Black Composition Doll: Ca. 1930. American-made bent-limb baby or mama-type body, jointed at hips, shoulders and perhaps neck; molded hair, painted or sleep eyes; original or appropriate clothes; some have three yarn tufts of hair on either side and on top of the head; all in good condition.

13in (33cm) composition with molded hair (***Snow White*** head), all original. *H&J Foulke, Inc.*

Baby,
10—12in (25—31cm)	**$ 85—100**	
16—17in (41—43cm)	**165—185**	

Mama Doll,
20—22in (51—56cm)	**200**

Patsy-type,
12—14in (31—36cm)	**165—185**

Toddler,
18in (46cm)	**250**

27in (69cm) composition "mama" doll, all original. *Leone McMullen Collection.*

18in (46cm) composition ***Topsy*** toddler, appropriate clothes. *Leone McMullen Collection.*

George Borgfeldt & Co.

Maker: George Borgfeldt, New York, N.Y., U.S.A., importer, assembler and distributor contracted with various doll factories, particularly in Germany and Japan, to make dolls and doll parts of all types and materials.

G.B. Character Baby: Ca. 1910. Perfect bisque head with smiling face, dimples, sleeping eyes, open mouth with teeth, human hair or mohair wig; composition baby body; appropriate clothing. All in good condition.

Mark:

Germany

G. B.

11—12in (28—31cm)	$400—450
19—21in (48—53cm)	750—850

G.B./A.M. Character Baby: 1913. Perfect bisque socket head, molded hair or mohair wig, sleeping eyes, open smiling mouth; composition bent-limb baby body; appropriate clothes. All in good condition. Mold *#327*, *#328* and *#329*.

Mark:

G. 327. B.
Germany
A. 2 M

13—15in (33—38cm)	$375—425
18—20in (46—51cm)	500—550
22in (56cm)	650
24—25in (61—64cm)	750—850

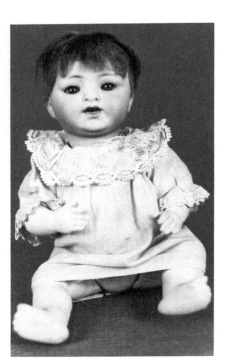

11in (28cm) G.B. baby with dimples. *H&J Foulke, Inc.*

George Borgfeldt & Co. continued

My Girlie & Pansy: 1910—1922. Perfect bisque socket head, sleep eyes, open mouth with teeth, good wig; ball-jointed composition body; nicely dressed; all in good condition.

Mark:

My Girlie
III
Germany

23—25in (58—64cm) $500—550

25in (64cm) ***My Girlie III.*** *H&J Foulke, Inc.*

Boudoir Dolls

Maker: Various French, U.S. and Italian firms
Date: Early 1920s into the 1940s
Material: Heads of composition and other materials; bodies mostly cloth but also of composition and other substances
Size: Many 24—36in (61—91cm); some smaller
Mark: Mostly unmarked

Boudoir Doll: Head of composition, cloth or other material, painted features, mohair wig, composition or cloth stuffed body, unusually long extremities, usually high-heeled shoes; original clothes elaborately designed and trimmed; all in good condition.

1920s Art Doll, exceptional quality, silk hair, 28—30in (71—76cm)	**$ 350—450**
Standard quality, dressed, 28—30in (71—76cm)	**125—150**
undressed	**65—75**
1940s composition head	**75—85**
Lenci, 24—28in (61—71cm)	**1600 up**
Smoking Doll, 25in (64cm)	**300 up**

19in (48cm) boudoir doll with cloth face. *H&J Foulke, Inc.*

Bru

Maker: Bru Jne. & Cie, Paris, and Montreuil-sous-Bois, France
Date: 1866—1899

Fashion Lady: 1866—on. Perfect bisque swivel head on shoulder plate, cork pate, appropriate old wig, closed smiling mouth, paperweight eyes, pierced ears; gusseted kid lady body; original or appropriate old clothes; all in good condition. Incised with letters A through O in sizes 11in (28cm) to 36in (91cm) tall. See color photograph on page 71.

12—13in (31—33cm)	**$2200—2500***
15in (38cm)	**2800—3200***
17—18in (43—46cm)	**3400—3800***

Double face, asleep and awake,
13in (33cm)	**23,000****

Wood body,
14in (36cm), naked	**4600**

*Allow $800 extra for wood arms.
**Not enough price samples to compute a reliable average.

Fashion Lady: 1866—on. Perfect bisque swivel head on shoulder plate, cork pate, old mohair wig, closed mouth, paperweight eyes, pierced ears; gusseted or straight kid body; original or appropriate old clothes; all in good condition. Oval face, incised with numbers only. (For photograph see *Doll Classics*, page 14.)

13—14in (33—36cm)	**$2100—2400**
16in (41cm)	**2600—2800**
20in (51cm)	**3500—3800**
Wood body 14in (36cm)	**4000**

14½in (37cm) Bru fashion lady on kid body. *Private Collection.*

Bru continued

Marked Brevete Bébé: Ca. 1870s. Perfect bisque swivel head on shoulder plate, cork pate, skin wig, paperweight eyes with shading on upper lid, closed mouth with white space between lips, full cheeks, pierced ears; gusseted kid body pulled high on shoulder plate and straight cut with bisque lower arms (no rivet joints); dressed; all in good condition. (For photograph see *6th Blue Book*, page 78.)

Mark: Size number only on head.

Oval sticker on body:

> BÉBÉ
> Breveté SoDG
> PARIS

12—13in (31—33cm) $10,000—13,000
17—19in (43—48cm) 16,000—19,000

Marked Crescent or Circle Dot Bébé: Ca. late 1870s. Perfect bisque swivel head on a deep shoulder plate with molded breasts, cork pate, attractive wig, paperweight eyes, closed mouth with slightly parted lips, molded and painted teeth, plump cheeks, pierced ears; gusseted kid body with bisque lower arms (no rivet joints); dressed; all in good condition. (For photograph see *8th Blue Book*, page 103.)

Mark: ⌒ ☉
Sometimes with "BRU Jne"
16—17in (41—43cm) $19,000—21,000
21—23in (53—58cm) 24,000—26,000

Marked Nursing Bru (Bébé Teteur): 1878—1898. Perfect bisque head, shoulder plate and lower arms, kid body; upper arms and upper legs of metal covered with kid, lower legs of carved wood, or jointed composition body; attractive wig, lovely glass eyes, open mouth with hole for nipple, mechanism in head sucks up liquid, operates by turning key; nicely clothed; all in good condition.

13—15in (33—38cm) $5500—6500

14in (36cm) ***Bébé Teteur*** marked "Bru Jne//4", composition body. *Private Collection.*

Bru continued

Marked Bru Jne Bébé: Ca. 1880s. Perfect bisque swivel head on deep shoulder plate with molded breasts, cork pate, attractive wig, paperweight eyes, closed mouth, pierced ears; gusseted kid body with scalloped edge at shoulder plate, bisque lower arms with lovely hands, kid over wood upper arms, hinged elbow, all kid or wood lower legs (sometimes on a jointed composition body); dressed; all in good condition. (For body photograph see *6th Blue Book*, page 79.) Size "0" is 11in (28in); 8 = 21—22in (53—56cm); 11 = 25in (64cm).

Mark: "BRU Jne"

Body Label:

BÉBÉ BRU ᴮᵀᴱ S.G.D.G.
Tout Contrefacteur sera saisiet poursuivi conformement ala Loi

11in (28cm) at auction	**$31,000**
14—16in (36—41cm)	**15,000—16,000**
21—23in (53—58cm)	**22,000—24,000**
28—30in (71—76cm)	**28,000—32,000**

See color photograph on page 72.

Marked Bru Jne R Bébé: Ca. Early 1890s. Perfect bisque head on a jointed composition body; attractive wig, paperweight eyes, closed mouth, pierced ears; dressed all in good condition.

Mark: BRU Jⁿᵉ R
11

Body Stamp: "Bebe Bru" with size number

14—16in (36—41cm)	**$4000—4500***
23—24in (58—61cm)	**6000—6500***
Open mouth	
22—24in (56—61cm)	**4000—4500***

*Allow more for an especially pretty model.

21in (53cm) Bru Jne R. *Private Collection.*

18½in (46cm) Bru Jne, all original. *Private Collection.*

Brückner Rag Doll

Maker: Albert Brückner, Jersey City, N.J., U.S.A.
Date: 1901—on
Material: All-cloth with stiffened mask face
Size: 12—14in (31—36cm)
Mark: On right front shoulder: PAT'D. JULY 8ᵀᴴ 1901

Marked Brückner: Cloth head with printed features on stiffened mask face, cloth body flexible at shoulders and hips; appropriate clothes; all in good condition. These dolls were sold by Horsman as part of their "Babyland Rag" line.

12—14in (31—36cm)

White	$185—210
Black	225—250
Topsy Turvy	400—500
Dollypop	250**

**Not enough price samples to compute a reliable range.

12in (31cm) Brückner *Topsy Turvy*, all original. *H&J Foulke, Inc.*

Bye-Lo Baby

Maker: Bisque heads — J. D. Kestner; Alt, Beck & Gottschalck; Kling & Co.;
Hertel Schwab & Co.; all of Thüringia, Germany.
Composition heads — Cameo Doll Company, New York, N.Y.,
U.S.A.
Celluloid heads — Karl Standfuss, Saxony, Germany
Wooden heads (unauthorized) — Schoenhut of Philadelphia, Pa.,
U.S.A.
All-Bisque Baby — J. D. Kestner
Cloth Bodies and Assembly — K & K Toy Co., New York, N.Y.,
U.S.A.
Composition Bodies — König & Wernicke
Date: 1922—on
Designer: Grace Storey Putnam
Distributor: George Borgfeldt, New York, N.Y., U.S.A.

Bisque Head Bye-Lo Baby: Ca.
1923. Perfect bisque head, cloth
body with curved legs (sometimes
with straight legs), composition or
celluloid hands; sleep eyes;
dressed. Made in seven sizes 9—
20in (23—51cm). (May have purple
"Bye-Lo Baby" stamp on front of
body.) Sometimes Mold *#1373*
(ABG)
Mark: © 1923 *by*
Grace S. Putnam
MADE IN GERMANY

Head circumference:

8—9in (20—23cm)	**$ 350—375***
10in (25cm)	**400—425***
12—13in (31—33cm)	**475—550***
15in (38cm)	**800—850***
17in (43cm)	**1100—1200***
18in (46cm)	**1250—1500***
Black, 13in (33cm)	**2600***

*Allow extra for original tagged gown
and button.

12in (31cm) h.c. *Bye-Lo Baby*, all original with
label and pin. See color photograph on page
73. *H&J Foulke, Inc.*

Bye-Lo Baby continued

Mold **#1369** (ABG) socket head on composition body, some marked "K&W." 13—14in (33—36cm) long
$1300—1500

Mold **#1415**, smiling with painted eyes 13½in (34cm) h.c. at auction.
3250**

Composition head, 1924. 12—13in (31—33cm) h.c.　　**350—375**

Celluloid head,
10in (25cm) h.c.　　**300****

Painted bisque head, late 1920s.
12—13in (31—33cm) h.c.
325**

Wooden head, (Schoenhut), 1925.
1500—1600

**Not enough price samples to compute a reliable range.

15in (38cm) ***Bye-Lo Baby***, composition K&W body. *H&J Foulke, Inc.*

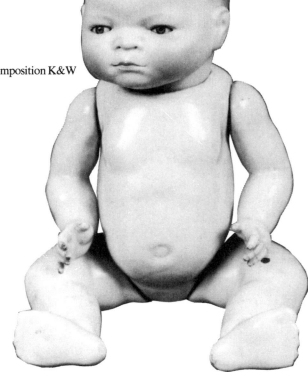

Bye-Lo Baby continued

Marked All-Bisque Bye-Lo Baby: 1925—on. Sizes 10cm (4in) to 20cm (8in).

Mark: Dark green paper label on front torso often missing; incised on back "20-12" (or other stock and size number).
"Copr. by G.S. Putnam"

Solid head with molded hair and painted eyes, jointed shoulders and hips.

4—5in (10—13cm)	$ 275—300
6in (15cm)	400—425
8in (20cm)	600

Solid head with swivel neck, glass eyes, jointed shoulders and hips.

4—5in (10—13cm)	450—550
6in (15cm)	650

Head with wig, glass eyes, jointed shoulders and hips.

4—5in (10—13cm)	550—650
6in (15cm)	750—800
8in (20cm)	1150—1250

Action **Bye-Lo Baby**, immobile in various positions, painted features.

3in (8cm)	325—375
Celluloid, 4in (10cm)	125

Vinyl Bye-Lo Baby: Ca. 1948. Sticky vinyl head with molded hair, painted eyes; cloth body with vinyl arms and legs, appropriate or original clothing; all in good condition.
Mark: ⊕Grace Storey Putnam

16in (41cm)	$150

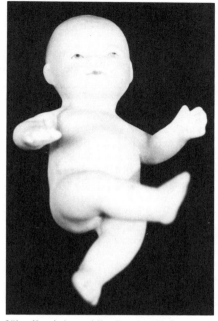

3½in (9cm) immobile **Bye-Lo Baby**. *H&J Foulke, Inc.*

5in (13cm) all-bisque **Bye-Lo** with glass eyes, swivel neck, and molded shoes and socks. *H&J Foulke, Inc.*

Cameo Doll Company

Maker: Cameo Doll Company, New York, N.Y. U.S.A. later Port Allegany, Pa., U.S.A. Original owner: Joseph L. Kallus.
Date: 1922—on
Material: Wood-pulp composition and wood
(See also *Kewpie* and *Baby Bo Kaye*)

Scootles: 1925. Designed by Rose O'Neill. All-composition, un-marked, jointed at neck, shoulders and hips; molded hair, blue or brown painted eyes looking to the side, closed smiling mouth; not dressed; all in very good condition.
Mark: Wrist tag only

7—8in (18—20cm)	$275—300**
12in (31cm)	400—425
15—16in (38—41cm)	500
20in (51cm)	800**
Black, 14in (36cm)	600—675**
All-bisque, 8in (20cm) at auction	900

12in (31cm) *Scootles. H&J Foulke, Inc.*

Composition Little Annie Rooney: 1925. Designed by Jack Collins. All-composition, jointed at neck, shoulders and hips, legs as black stockings, feet with molded shoes; braided yarn wig, painted round eyes, watermelon mouth; original clothes; all in good condition.
Mark: None
16in (41cm) $650**

**Not enough price samples to compute a reliable range.

Cameo Doll Company continued

Wood Segmented Characters: Designed by Joseph L. Kallus. Composition head, molded hair, painted features; segmented wood body; undressed; all in very good condition. (For photographs see *8th Blue Book*, pages 110 and 111.)
Mark: Label with name on chest.

Margie, 1929. 10in (25cm) **$225—250**
Pinkie, 1930. 10in (25cm) **275—325**
Joy, 1932. 10in (5cm) **275—325**
    15in (38cm) **375—425**
Betty Boop, 1932.
    12in (31cm) **450—550**
    With molded bathing suit and composition legs; wearing a cotton print dress, **650**
Pete the Pup, 1932.
    9in (23cm) **200****
Bimbo, 1932.
    9in (23cm) **250****
**Not enough price samples to compute a reliable range.

12in (31cm) *Betty Boop*. *Miriam Blankman Collection.*

Giggles: 1946. Designed by Rose O'Neill. All-composition, unmarked, jointed at neck, shoulders and hips, molded hair with bun in back, large painted side-glancing eyes, closed mouth; original romper; all in very good condition.
Mark: Paper wrist tag only
14in (36cm) **$450—500**

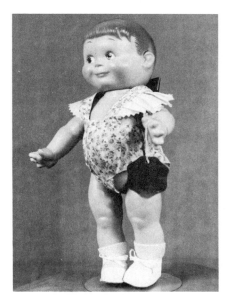

14in (36cm) *Giggles*, all original. *H&J Foulke, Inc.*

Campbell Kid

Maker: E. I. Horsman Co., Inc., New York, N.Y., U.S.A.; American Character Doll Co., New York, N.Y., U.S.A.
Date: 1910—on
Material: Composition head and arms, cloth body and legs; or all-composition
Size: Usually 9—16in (23—41cm)
Designer: Grace G. Drayton

Campbell Kid: 1910-1914. By Horsman. Marked composition head with flange neck, molded and painted bobbed hair, painted round eyes to the side, watermelon mouth; original cloth body, composition arms, cloth legs and feet; all in fair condition.
Mark: On head: E.I.H. © 1910
Cloth label on sleeve:

> The Campbell Kids
> Trademark by
> Joseph Campbell
> Mfg. by E. I. HORSMAN Co.

Indian complexion, all original	**$400**
Brown complexion, all original	**300**
10—13in (25—33cm)	**175—200**

Campbell Kid: 1928. By American Character, sometimes called "Dolly Dingle". All-composition with swivel head, jointed shoulders and hips; molded and painted hair, eyes to the side, watermelon mouth; original clothes; all in good condition. (For photograph see *4th Blue Book*, page 86.)
Mark: On back:
"A PETITE DOLL"
12in (31cm) **$450—500****
**Not enough price samples to compute a reliable range.

Campbell Kid: 1948. By Horsman. Unmarked all-composition, molded painted hair, painted eyes to the side, watermelon mouth; painted white socks and black slippers; original clothes; all in good condition. (For photograph see *8th Blue Book*, page 112.)
12in (31cm) **$250—275**

12in (31cm) 1910 *Campbell Kid*, all original. *H&J Foulke, Inc.*

Catterfelder Puppenfabrik

Maker: Catterfelder Puppenfabrik, Catterfeld, Thüringia, Germany. Heads by J. D. Kestner and other porcelain makers
Date: 1902—on
Material: Bisque head; composition body
Trademark: My Sunshine
Mark:

C. P.
2 0 8
45
N

C.P. Child Doll: Ca. 1902—on. Perfect bisque head, good wig, sleep eyes, open mouth with teeth; composition jointed body; dressed; all in good condition. (For photograph see *6th Blue Book*, page 90.)
#264 (made by Kestner):

17—18in (43—46cm)	**$500—550**
22—24in (56—61cm)	**650—750**

12in (31cm) black C.P. 208 baby. *Kiefer Collection.*

C.P. Character Child: Ca. 1910—on. Perfect bisque character face with wig, painted eyes; composition jointed body; dressed; all in good condition. Sometimes mold *#207* (For photograph see *5th Blue Book*, page 85) or mold *#219*.
15—16in (38cm)   **$2800—3200**
**Not enough price samples to compute a reliable range.

C.P. Character Baby: Ca. 1910—on. Perfect bisque character face with wig or molded hair, painted or glass eyes; jointed baby body; dressed; all in good condition. (For photograph see *8th Blue Book*, page 121.)
#200, 201, 208, 209, 262, 263:

15—17in (38—43cm)	**$475—525**
22—24in (56—61cm)	**800—900**

#208 black baby:

12in (31cm)	**500—600**

Celluloid Dolls

Makers: Germany:
  Rheinische Gummi und Celluloid Fabrik Co. (Turtle symbol)
  Buschow & Beck. *Minerva* trademark. (Helmet symbol)
  E. Maar & Sohn. *Emasco* trademark. (3 M symbol)
  Cellba. (Mermaid symbol)
  Poland:
  P.R. Zask. (ASK in triangle)
  France:
  Petitcolin. (Eagle symbol)
  Société Nobel Francaise. (SNF in diamond)
  Neumann & Marx. (Dragon symbol)
  Société Industrielle de Celluloid (Sicoine)
  United States:
  Parsons-Jackson Co., Cleveland, Ohio and other companies
Date: 1895—1940s
Material: All-celluloid or celluloid head with jointed kid, cloth or composition body.
Marks: Various as indicated above: sometimes also in combination with the marks of J. D. Kestner, Kämmer & Reinhardt, Bruno Schmidt, Käthe Kruse and König & Wernicke

---

13in (33cm) celluloid head child with Minerva mark, cloth body, all original. *H&J Foulke, Inc.*

Celluloid Head Fashion Lady: Ca. 1879. Celluloid socket head on celluloid shoulder plate, cork pate, closed mouth, paperweight eyes; all-kid body or cloth body with kid arms; appropriate clothing; all in good condition. (For photographs see *A Century of Celluloid Dolls* by Shirley Buchholz, pages 15-20.)
15—19in (38—48cm)   **$1625***
*One-time auction price.

Celluloid Dolls continued

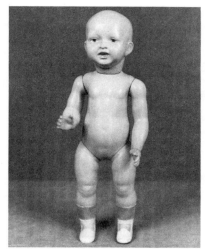

13in (33cm) celluloid shoulder head child, all original. *H&J Foulke, Inc.*

13in (33cm) Parsons-Jackson toddler with molded shoes and socks. *H&J Foulke, Inc.*

Celluloid head Child doll: Ca. 1900—on. Molded hair or wig, painted or glass eyes, open or closed mouth; cloth or kid body, celluloid or composition arms; dressed; all in good condition.

Painted eyes:

13—15in (33—38cm)	**$125—150**

Glass eyes:

13—15in (33—38cm)	**150—175**
18—20in (46—51cm)	**200—225**
22—24in (56—61cm)	**250—275**

All-Celluloid Child Doll: Ca. 1900—on. Jointed at neck, shoulders, and hips; molded hair or wig, painted eyes; dressed; all in good condition.

6—7in (13—15cm)	**$ 45—55**
9—10in (23—25cm)	**80—90**
13—14in (33—36cm)	**135—165**
Tommy Tucker-type character,	
12—13in (31—33cm)	**125—150**

Glass eyes:

12—13in (31—33cm)	**165—185***
15—16in (38—41cm)	**250—275***
18in (46cm)	**325—375***
Parsons-Jackson toddler with stork trademark,	
13in (33cm)	**250—275**

*Allow extra for K★R dolls and character faces.

Celluloid Dolls continued

Celluloid socket head Doll: Ca. 1910—on. Wig, glass eyes, sometimes flirty, open mouth with teeth; ball-jointed or bent-limb composition body; dressed; all in good condition.

15—18in (38—46cm)	**$275—325**
22—24in (56—61cm)	**400—450**

Characters:		***K★R 728,***	
K★R 701,		12—13in (31—33cm)	
12—13in (31—33cm)	**700—750****	baby	**300—350**
K★R 717,		18in (46cm)	**450—475**
16in (41cm) flirty	**375—400**	***K&W toddler,***	
		16in (41cm)	**375—425**

All-Celluloid Baby: Ca. 1910—on. Bent-limb baby, molded hair, painted eyes, closed mouth; jointed arms and/or legs; no clothes; all in good condition.

6—8in (15—20cm)	**$ 60—80**
10—12in (25—31cm)	**100—125**
15in (38cm)	**165**
Japanese, 18—20in (46—51cm)	**200—250**
Black, French SNF, 19in (48cm)	**275—325**
Glass eyes, 14—15in (36—38cm)	**200—250**

Celluloid Head Baby: Ca. 1920s—on. Celluloid baby head with glass eyes, painted hair, open or closed mouth; cloth body sometimes with celluloid hands; appropriate clothes; all in good condition.

12—15in (31—38cm)	**$125—150**

**Not enough price samples to compute a reliable range.

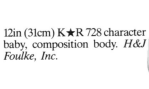

14in (36cm) K★R 701 character boy. *Yvonne Baird Collection.*

12in (31cm) K★R 728 character baby, composition body. *H&J Foulke, Inc.*

Century Doll Co.

Maker: Century Doll Co., New York, N.Y., U.S.A.; bisque heads by J.D. Kestner, Germany
Date: 1909—on
Material: Bisque or composition head, cloth body, composition arms (and legs)
Mark: "Century Doll Co." Sometimes ⟨K⟩ (for Kestner). "Germany"

Marked Century Infant: Ca. 1925. Perfect bisque solid-dome head, molded and painted hair, sleep eyes, open/closed mouth; cloth body, composition hands or limbs; dressed; all in good condition. (For photographs see *Kestner, King of Dollmakers*, pages 193 and 194.)
Head circumference:

10—11in (25—28cm)	**$475—525**
13—14in (33—36cm)	**650—700**

Mama doll, bisque shoulder head #281, (for photograph see *Kestner, King of Dollmakers*, page 194.) 21in (53cm) **650—750****
**Not enough price samples to compute a reliable average.

Marked "Mama" Doll: Ca. 1920s. Composition shoulder head with character face, molded hair, smiling open mouth with two teeth, dimples, tin sleep eyes. Cloth torso with cryer, composition arms and legs; appropriate clothing. All in good condition.
16in (41cm) **$165—185**
"Chuckles" Baby, 1927.
16½in (42cm) **165—185**

16in (41cm) Century "Mama" doll. *H&J Foulke, Inc.*

Chad Valley

Maker: Chad Valley Co. (formerly Johnson Bros., Ltd.), Birmingham, England
Date: 1917—on
Material: All-cloth
Mark: Cloth label usually on foot:
"HYGENIC TOYS
Made in England by
CHAD VALLEY CO. LTD."

20in (51cm)*Long John Silver*, all original with label. *Esther Schwartz Collection.*

Chad Valley Doll: All-cloth, usually felt face and velvet body, jointed neck, shoulders and hips; mohair wig, glass or painted eyes; original clothes; all in excellent condition.

Characters, painted eyes,
10—12in (25cm) $ **80—110**
Children, painted eyes,
9in (23cm)   **135**
13—14in (33—36cm)   **325—375**
16—18in (41—46cm)   **450—500**
Children, glass eyes,
16—18in (41—46cm)   **575—675**
Royal Children, glass eyes,
16—18in (41—46cm)   **1200—1500**
Mabel Lucie Attwell, glass inset side-glancing eyes, smiling watermelon mouth, for photograph (see *6th Blue Book*, page 63.)
14in (36cm)   **525—575**
Snow White and Seven Dwarfs
6in (15cm) and 16in (41cm) complete set, mint and boxed, at auction   **3525**
Golliwog. See color photograph on page 73. 1940s.
17in (43cm)   **95—110**
Long John Silver,
20in (51cm)   **1800—2000**

14in (36cm) child with glass eyes, all original. *H&J Foulke, Inc.*

Martha Chase

Maker: Martha Jenks Chase, Pawtucket, R.I., U.S.A.
Date: 1889 on
Material: Stockinette and cloth, painted in oils; some fully painted washable models; some designed for hospital training use.

Size: 9in (23cm) to life-size
Designer: Martha Jenks Chase

PAWTUCKET, R.I
MADE IN U.S.A.

Mark: "Chase Stockinet Doll" stamp on left leg or under left arm, paper label on back (usually gone)

Chase Doll: Head and limbs of stockinette, treated and painted with oils, large painted eyes with thick upper lashes, rough-stroked hair to provide texture, cloth bodies jointed at shoulders, hips, elbows and knees, later ones only at shoulders and hips; some bodies completely treated; showing wear.

Baby,
13—15in (33—38cm) **$ 450—525**
17—20in (43—51cm) **650—750**
24—26in (61—66cm) **850—900**
37—40in (94—102cm) **1800—2000**

Child, molded bobbed hair. (For photograph see *6th Blue Book*, page 95.) 15in (38cm) **900—1000**
22in (56cm) **2200**

Lady, 13—15in (33—38cm) **1600 up**
14in (36cm) molded blonde braids, at auction **2550**

Black, 24in (61cm) **5500**
See color photograph on page 74.

Hospital Lady,
64in (163cm) **1600—2000**

Mad Hatter, Dutchess, Frogman
at auction **20,000 set**

13in (33cm) Chase character lady with molded bun. *Nancy Smith Collection.*

21in (53cm) Chase boy or baby. *Dolly Valk Collection.*

China Heads*
(French)

Maker: Various French doll firms; some heads may have been made in Germany

Date: 1850s

Material: China head, shapely kid fashion body, some with large china arms

Mark: None

French China Head Lady: China shoulder head, glass or beautifully painted eyes, painted eyelashes, feathered eyebrows, closed mouth, open crown, cork pate, good wig; shapely kid fashion body (may have china arms curved to above elbow); appropriately dressed; all in good condition.

13—16in (33—41cm)   **$3000—4000**
19—21in (48—53cm)   **4500—5000**

See color photograph on page 74.

*For dolls marked "Huret" or "Rohmer," see appropriate entry under those names.

13in (33cm) French fashion lady with china head, painted eyes. *Private Collection.*

China Heads
(German)

Maker: Some early dolls by K.P.M., Meissen and Royal Copenhagen (Denmark), but most by unidentified makers. Later dolls by firms such as Kling & Co., Alt, Beck & Gottschalck, Kestner & Co., Hertwig & Co., and others

Material: China head, cloth or kid body, leather arms or china limbs

Mark: K.P.M., Meissen and Royal Copenhagen usually marked inside the shoulders; later dolls by Kling & Co. and A.B.G. are identifiable by their mold numbers.

1840s Hairstyles: China shoulder head with black molded hair; may have pink tint complexion; old cloth body; (may have china arms); appropriate old clothes; all in good condition.

Hair swept back into bun. See color photograph on page 75.

18—21in (46—53cm)	**$1800—3800***
24in (61cm)	**4500 up***
With Wood Body, china lower limbs	
9in (23cm)	**2500**

Brown hair with bun (For photograph see *5th Blue Book*, page 93.)

18in (46cm)	**3500 up***

Young Man, brown hair

16—18in (41—46cm)	**2500****

Kinderkopf (china head)

15—16in (38—41cm)	**750—850****

Long Curls (For photograph see *6th Blue Book*, page 102.)

10in (25cm)	**900—1000**
16in (41cm)	**2250****

*Depending upon quality, hairdo and rarity.

**Not enough price samples to compute a reliable range.

1850s Hairstyles: China shoulder head (some with pink tint), molded black hair (except bald), painted eyes; old cloth body with leather or china arms; appropriate old clothes; all in good condition.

Bald head, some with black areas on top, proper wig. See color photograph on page 74.

Fine quality:

15—17in (38—43cm)	**$ 900—1000**
22—24in (56—61cm)	**1300—1500**

13in (33cm) china head with covered wagon hairdo. *H&J Foulke, Inc.*

China Heads (German) continued

10in (25cm) china head with Greiner-style hairdo and brown painted eyes, all original. (See color photograph on page 76.) *H&J Foulke, Inc.*

17in (43cm) china head with high brow hairdo. *H&J Foulke, Inc.*

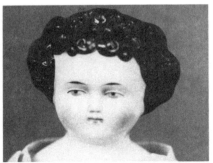

14in (36cm) china head with molded flowers, a *Dolly Madison*-style variant. *H&J Foulke, Inc.*

With Glass eyes, fine quality,
20in (51cm) **2200****
Standard quality:
18—22in (46—56cm) **550—650**
Covered Wagon
13—16in (33—41cm) **425—525**
22—24in (56—61cm) **700—800**
With brown eyes,
18—21in (46—53cm) **1000—1200**
With wood body (For photograph see *5th Blue Book*, page 98.)
6in (15cm) **1200**
10½in (27cm) **2800**
Greiner-style, with brown eyes
17—19in (43—48cm) **900—1100**
11—12in (28—31cm) **500—550**
With glass eyes. For color photograph see page 76.
15—16in (38—41cm) **3250****
18in (46cm) **4000****
Waves framing face, brown eyes. (For photograph see *7th Blue Book*, page 114.)
17—19in (43—48cm) **800—1000**
With glass eyes,
16in (41cm) **2600****

Child or Baby, flange swivel neck; china or papier-mâché shoulder plate and hips, china lower limbs; cloth midsection (may have voice box) and upper limbs. See color photograph on page 76.
10in (25cm) **$1900—2000**
Alice Hairstyle (For photograph see *6th Blue Book*, page 98.)
10in (25cm) **2200—2300**
**Not enough price samples to compute a reliable range.

1860s and 1870s Hairstyles: China shoulder head with black molded hair (a few blondes), painted eyes, closed mouth; old cloth body may

China Heads (German) continued

have leather arms or china lower arms and legs with molded boots; appropriate old clothes; all in good condition.

Plain style with center part (so-called flat top and high brow)

5—6in (13—15cm)	$ 85—95
14—16in (36—41cm)	200—225
20—22in (51—56cm)	275—325
24—26in (61—66cm)	400—500
34in (86cm)	700
Molded necklace, 21in (53cm)	700

Mary Todd Lincoln with snood. (For photograph see *8th Blue Book*, page 130.)
21in (53cm)   **$750—800**

Dolley Madison with molded bow or flowers

21—24in (53—61cm)	500—575
14—16in (36—41cm)	325—375

Adelina Patti (For photograph see *Doll Classics*, page 130.)

15—17in (38—43cm)	$275—325
22—24in (56—61cm)	500—550

Fancy style (only a sampling can be covered because of the wide variety). See color photograph on page 77.

Jenny Lind (For photograph see *Doll Classics*, page 130.)
18in (46cm)   **850**

Curly Top (For photograph see *7th Blue Book*, page 115.)
20—21in (51—53cm)   **600—700**

Grape Lady (For photograph see *8th Blue Book*, page 130.)
19—21in (48—53cm)   **1400—1500**

Countess Dagmar with pierced ears (For photograph see *6th Blue Book*, page 102 top.)
19in (48cm)   **800—850**

Spill Curl (For photograph see *5th Blue Book*, page 98.)
18in (46cm)   **550—600**

7in (18cm) china head with flat top hairdo, all original. *H&J Foulke, Inc.*

18in (46cm) china head man. *Dr. Carole Stoessel Zvonar Collection.*

China Heads (German) continued

15½in (39cm) blonde china head with molded curly bangs and hair band. *H&J Foulke, Inc.*

Young Victoria. See color photograph on page 77.
22—24in (56—61cm) **3200**
Man or Boy
Fine quality 20in (51cm) **1600**
Standard quality
16in (41cm) **425—475**
Molded jester cap and mustache
16in (41cm) **850—950**

Coiled braided bun high in back,
24in (61cm) **900**
Loose bun, gold beads, side "wings,"
16in (41cm) **700**
Blonde "Alice" hairdo with snood,
21in (53cm) **750**
Blonde hair with pink scarf and snood, 12in (31cm) **450**

1880s Hairstyles: China shoulder head with black or blonde molded hair, blue painted eyes, closed mouth; cloth body with china arms and legs or kid body; appropriate old clothes; all in good condition. Many made by Alt, Beck & Gottschalck (see page 54 for mold numbers) or Kling & Co. (see page 281 for mold numbers).
Bangs on forehead,
13—15in (33—38cm) **$225—275**
18—20in (46—51cm) **325—375**
24—25in (61—64cm) **450—500**
Short wavy hair, exposed ears (ABG **#784**) (For photograph see *8th Blue Book*, page 133.)
14—16in (36—41cm) **225—250**
22—23in (56—58cm) **375—400**

15in (38cm) black hair china head similar to A.B.G.'s mold **#1000**. *H&J Foulke, Inc.*

China Heads (German) continued

1890s Hairstyle: China shoulder
head with black or blonde molded
wavy hair, blue painted eyes, closed
mouth; old cloth or kid body with
stub, leather, bisque or china limbs;
appropriate clothes; all in good
condition.

7—8in (18—20cm)	$ 65—75
12—13in (31—33cm)	**110—135**
16—18in (41—46cm)	**185—210**
22—24in (56—61cm)	**250—300**
Open mouth, 16in (41cm)	**400**
Molded poke bonnet,	
13in (33cm)	**185**

22in (56cm) china head with common 1890s
hairstyle. *H&J Foulke, Inc.*

6in (15cm) china head **Ruth** pet name. *H&J
Foulke, Inc.*

Pet Name: Ca. 1905. Made by Hertwig & Co. for Butler Bros., N.Y.
China shoulder head, molded yoke
with name in gold; black or blonde
painted hair (one-third were
blonde), blue painted eyes; old
cloth body (some with alphabet or
other figures printed on cotton material), china limbs; properly
dressed; all in good condition.
Used names such as **Agnes, Bertha,
Daisy, Dorothy, Edith, Esther,
Ethel, Florence, Helen, Mabel,
Marion** and **Pauline.**

9—10in (23—25cm)	**$125—140**
14—16in (36—41cm)	**200—225**
19—21in (48—53cm)	**275—300**

12½in (32cm) china head with molded poke
bonnet. *H&J Foulke, Inc.*

Cloth, Printed

Maker: Various American companies, such as Cocheco Mfg Co., Lawrence & Co., Arnold Print Works, Art Fabric Mills and Selchow & Righter.
Date: 1896—on
Material: All-cloth
Size: 6—30in (15—76cm)
Mark: Mark could be found on fabric part which was discarded after cutting

---

Cloth, Printed Doll: Face, hair, underclothes, shoes and socks printed on cloth; all in good condition, some soil acceptable. Dolls in printed underwear are sometimes found dressed in old petticoats and frocks. Names such as: *Dolly Dear, Merry Marie, Improved Foot Doll, Standish No Break Doll,* and so on.

6—7in (15—18cm)	**$ 85**
16—18in (41—46cm)	**160—175**
24—26in (61—66cm)	**185—225**

Uncut sheet, bright colors
20in (51cm) doll   **225—250**

Brownies: 1892.
Designed by Palmer Cox; marked on foot.

8in (20cm)	**90—95**
15in (38cm)	**200**

Boys and Girls with printed outer clothes, Ca. 1903, 12—13in (31—33cm)   **160—185**
17in (43cm)   **225**

Darkey Doll, made up
16in (41cm)   **250—300**

Aunt Jemima Family, (four dolls) **85—95 each**

Punch & Judy,   **425 pair**
Soldier, 12in (31cm)   **110—125**
Hen and Chicks,
uncut sheet   **75**

Gutsell, 16in (41cm) made up with shirt and jacket   **500—600**

Mother's Congress Doll, Baby Steuart, fading and wear, at auction **1100**

E.T. Gibson, red sailor dress with separate skirt,
at auction   **495**
Black Child, Art Fabric,
18in (46cm)   **400—450**
1930s Characters, see color photograph on page 78,
14in (36cm)   **Pair 150**

12in (31cm) *Soldier Boy. H&J Foulke, Inc.*

17in (43cm) boy in printed blue suit. *H&J Foulke, Inc.*

Cloth, Russian

Maker: Unknown craftsmen
Date: Ca. 1930
Material: All-cloth
Size: 10—15in (25—38cm)
Mark: "Made in Soviet Union" sometimes with identification of doll, such as "Ukranian Woman", "Village Boy", "Smolensk District Woman"

Russian Cloth Doll: All-cloth with stockinette head and hands, molded face with hand-painted features; authentic regional clothes; all in very good condition.

11in (28cm) child	**$ 75—85**
15in (38cm)	**125—150**

10½in Russian cloth child. *H&J Foulke, Inc.*

Dewees Cochran

Maker: Dewees Cochran, Fenton, Calif., U.S.A.
Date: 1940—on
Material: Latex
Size: 9—18in (23—46cm)
Designer: Dewees Cochran
Mark: Signed under arm or behind right ear

Dewees Cochran Doll: Latex with jointed neck, shoulders and hips; human
   hair wig, painted eyes, character face; dressed; all in good condition.
   15—16in (38—41cm) ***Cindy***, 1947-1948.   **$ 650—750**
Grow-up Dolls: Stormy, Angel, Bunnie, J.J. and ***Peter Ponsett*** each at ages 5,
   7, 11, 16 and 20, 1952-1956.   **1000—1200**
Look-Alike Dolls (6 different faces)   **1000—1200**
Baby, 9in (23cm)   **1300**
Individual Portrait Children   **1200—1400 up**
Composition American Children (see Effanbee, page 157).

 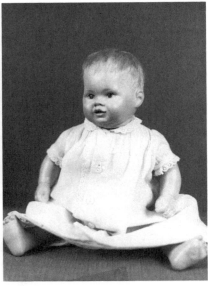

13in (33cm) Portrait child using ***"Stormy"*** face, all original with trunk of clothing. *Esther Schwartz Collection.*

9½in (24cm) Dewees Cochran baby. *Esther Schwartz Collection.*

Columbian Doll

Maker: Emma and Marietta Adams
Date: 1891—1910 or later
Material: All-cloth
Size: 15—29in (38—74cm)
Mark: Stamped on back of body
Before 1900:

"COLUMBIAN DOLL
EMMA E. ADAMS
OSWEGO CENTRE
N.Y."

After 1906:

"THE COLUMBIAN DOLL
MANUFACTURED BY
MARIETTA ADAMS RUTTAN
OSWEGO, N.Y."

Columbian Doll: All-cloth with
hair and features hand-painted on a
flat face; treated limbs; appropriate
clothes; all in fair condition, showing wear.
17—21in (43—53cm)   **$4000**
20in (51cm) excellent,
at auction   **9500**
Columbian type,
18—20in (46—51cm)   **800—1000**
See color photograph on page 78.

Composition
(American)

Maker: Various United States firms, many unidentified
Date: 1912—on
Material: All-composition or composition head and cloth body, some with composition limbs

---

All-Composition Child Doll: 1912—1920. Various firms, such as Bester Doll Co., New Era Novelty Co., New Toy Mfg. Co., Superior Doll Mfg. Co., Artcraft Toy Product Co., Colonial Toy Mfg. Co. Composition with mohair wig, sleep eyes, open mouth; ball-jointed composition body; appropriate clothes; all in good condition. These are patterned after German bisque head dolls.
22—24in (56—61cm) **$250—300**

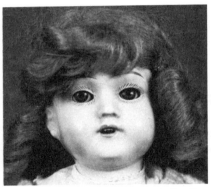

24in (61cm) Artcraft child. *H&J Foulke, Inc.*

Early Composition Character Head: Ca. 1912. Composition head with molded hair and painted features; hard cloth body with composition hands; appropriate clothes; all in good condition.
10—12in (25—31cm) **$100—125**
16—18in (41—46cm) **200—250**
24—26in (61—66cm) **350 up**

Girl-type Mama Dolls: Ca. 1920—on. Made by various American companies. Composition head with hair wig, sleep eyes, open mouth with teeth; composition shoulder plate, arms and legs, cloth body; original clothes; all in good condition, of good quality.
16—18in (41—46cm) **$150—185**
22—25in (56—64cm) **225—250**

15in (38cm) early composition head character boy. *Betty Harms Collection.*

Composition (American) continued

Molded Loop Dolls: Ca. 1930s. All-composition with molded bobbed hair and loop for tying on a ribbon, painted eyes, closed mouth; composition or cloth torso, composition arms and legs; original or appropriate clothing; all in good condition. Quality is generally mediocre. (For photograph see *7th Blue Book*, page 250.)

13—15in (33—38cm)   **$85—110**

Patsy-type Girl: Ca. 1930s. All-composition with molded bobbed hair, sleep or painted eyes, closed mouth; jointed at neck, shoulders and hips; original clothes; all in very good condition, of good quality.

9—10in (23—25cm)	**$100—125**
14—16in (36—41cm)	**175—200**
20in (51cm)	**225—250**

18in (46cm) girl-type "mama" doll. *H&J Foulke, Inc.*

Composition Baby: Ca. 1930. All-composition or composition head, arms and legs, cloth torso; with molded and painted hair, sleep eyes; appropriate or original clothes; all in very good condition, of good quality.

10—12in (25—31cm)	**$ 85—110**
16—18in (41—46cm)	**150—175**
24in (61cm)	**250—275**

12in (31cm) **Patsy**-type girl, all original. *H&J Foulke, Inc.*

Dionne-type Doll: Ca. 1935. All-composition with molded hair or wig, sleep eyes (painted in small dolls), closed or open mouth; jointed at neck, shoulders and hips; original clothes; all in very good condition, of good quality. (For photograph see *6th Blue Book*, page 113.)

7—8in (18—20cm)	**$ 60—70**
18—20in (46—51cm) toddler	**225—250**

Composition (American) continued

Shirley Temple-type Girl: Ca. 1935—on. All-composition, jointed at neck, shoulders and hips; blonde curly mohair wig, sleep eyes, open smiling mouth with teeth; original clothes; all in very good condition, of good quality.
16—18in (41—46cm) **$200—250**

13in (33cm) Alexander-type girl, all original. *H&J Foulke, Inc.*

Alexander-type Girl: Ca. 1935. All-composition, jointed at neck, shoulders and hips; sleeping eyes, mohair wig, closed mouth, dimples. Original or appropriate clothing. All in good condition, of good quality.
13in (33cm) **$150**
17—18in (43—46cm) **200—250**

Costume Doll: Ca. 1940. All-composition, jointed at neck, shoulders and hips, sleep or painted eyes, mohair wig, closed mouth; original costume; all in good condition.
11in (28cm)
Excellent quality **$60—70**
Standard quality **40—45**

11in (28cm) costume doll, all original. *H&J Foulke, Inc.*

Miscellaneous Specific Dolls:
Orphan Annie, 1920s.
12in (31cm) with Sandy, all original with labels, at auction **$450**
Jackie Robinson.
13½in (34cm) **500—525**
Trudy 3 faces, 1946.
14in (36cm) **175—200**
Lone Ranger. 16in (41cm) **350**
Kewpie-type characters,
12in (31cm) **65—75**
Mountie (Reliable)
16in (41cm) **150**
Scrappy, 15in (38cm) **150**
HeBEE, SheBEE,
10½in (27cm) **500**
Buddy Lee, 12in (31cm) **110—135**

14in (36cm) **Trudy**, all original. *H&J Foulke, Inc.*

Composition

(German)

Maker: Various German firms such as König & Wernicke, Kämmer & Reinhardt and others
Date: Ca. 1925
Material: All-composition or composition head and cloth body
Size: Various

All-Composition Child Doll: Socket head with good wig, sleep (sometimes flirty) eyes, open mouth with teeth; jointed composition body; appropriate clothes; all in good condition, of excellent quality. (For photograph see *6th Blue Book*, page 111.)

12—14in (31—36cm)	**$200—225**
18—20in (46—51cm)	**275—325**

Character face, (For photograph see *7th Blue Book*, page 128.)

18—20in (46—51cm)	**325—425**

Character Baby: Composition head with good wig, sleep eyes, open mouth with teeth; bent-limb composition baby body or hard-stuffed cloth body; appropriate clothes; all in good condition, of excellent quality.

All-composition baby, 16—18in (41—46cm)	**$225—275**
Cloth body, 14—16in (36—41cm)	**175—200**
All composition toddler, 16—18in (41—46cm)	**300—350**

14in (36cm) ***Baby Gloria***, Germany. *H&J Foulke, Inc.*

Composition Shoulder Head
(Patent Washable Dolls)

Maker: Various German firms, such as Heinrich Steir, J.D. Kestner, F.M. Schilling and C. & O. Dressel
Date: 1880—1915
Material: Composition shoulder head, cloth body, composition lower limbs
Size: 10—42in (25—107cm)
Mark: None

Composition Shoulder Head: Composition shoulder head with mohair or skin wig, glass eyes, closed or open mouth; cloth body with composition arms and lower legs, sometimes with molded boots; appropriately dressed; all in good condition.

Superior Quality:

13—15in (33—38cm)	$275—325
19—21in (48—53cm)	400—450
24in (61cm)	500—550
30in (76cm)	750

Painted hair, Täufling

9—10in (23—25cm)	150—175

Standard Quality:

11—12in (28—31cm)	125—150
14—16in (36—41cm)	175—200
18—20in (45—51cm)	225—250
22—24in (56—61cm)	275—300
30in (76cm)	425—475
38in (97cm)	600
Lady, 13—16in (33—41cm)	500
Oriental, 12in (31cm)	225

38in (97cm) composition shoulder head, Patent Washable-type, standard quality. *H&J Foulke, Inc.*

14½in (37cm) composition shoulder head lady. *Private Collection.*

11½in (29cm) Oriental composition shoulder head, all original. *H&J Foulke, Inc.*

15in (38cm) composition shoulder head, Patent Washable-type, superior quality. *Private Collection.*

Creche Figures

Maker: Various European craftsmen, primarily Italian
Date: 18th and 19th centuries
Material: Wood and terra-cotta on a wire frame
Size: Various
Mark: None

Creche Figures of various people in a Christmas scene: 18th century. Gesso-over-wood head and limbs, fabric-covered wire frame body; beautifully detailed features with carved hair and glass inset eyes, lovely hands; original or appropriate replacement clothes; all in good condition.

13—14in (33—35cm)	$ 350—400*
18—20in (46—51cm)	750—850*
All-wood, 28in (71cm)	2100*

Mid 19th Century: Later doll with terra-cotta head and limbs, painted eyes; fabric-covered wire frame body; workmanship not as detailed; original or appropriate clothes; all in good condition.

11—13in (28—33cm)	$175—200
15in (38cm)	225
22in (56cm)	400—450

*Price would be higher on "art" and "antiques" market.

11½in (29cm) creche figure with terra-cotta head. *H&J Foulke, Inc.*

Danel

Maker: Danel & Cie., Paris & Montreuil-sous-Bois, France
Date: 1889—1895
Material: Bisque socket head, composition body
Trademarks: Paris Bébé, Bébé Français (Also used by Jumeau)

Marked Paris Bébé: 1889. Perfect bisque socket head, good wig, paperweight eyes, closed mouth, pierced ears; composition jointed body; appropriately dressed; all in good condition.

Mark: On head   TÊTE DÉPOSÉ   On body
PARIS BEBE

24—26in (61—66cm) **$4500—4800**
17—19in (43—48cm) **3900—4100**

PARIS-BEBE
Bréveté

Marked B.F.: Ca. 1891. Perfect bisque head, appropriate wig, paperweight eyes, closed mouth, pierced ears; jointed composition body; appropriate clothes; all in good condition.

Mark: B 9 F

12in (31cm) boxed and all original
$4200
15in (38cm) with trunk, clothes and accessories **4200**
21—24in (53—61cm) **4200—4700**

21in (53cm) *Paris Bébé.* See color photograph on page 79. *Private Collection.*

Dean's Rag Book

Maker: Dean's Rag Book Company, England
Date: 1903—on
Material: Cloth
Size: Various
Mark: Cloth label, black stamp, or printed name

Felt-faced children: 1920s. Mask faces with molded and painted features, wigs, jointed arms and legs; original clothes; in good condition.
14—16in (36—41cm)   **$ 450—500**
Girl in fancy organdy dress, with tag and label, mint,
18in (46cm) at auction   **1250**

Velvet-faced: Late 1920s-on. Mask face with molded and painted features, wig; clothes sometimes an integral part of body.
8—10in (20—25cm)
souvenir doll   **$ 70—80**
12in (31cm) girl   **110—125**

Printed on Cloth: 1903 on. Various children, characters and advertising dolls to cut out, sew and stuff. In good condition.
10in (25cm)   **$ 85**
16—18in (41—46cm)   **150—165**

10in (25cm) printed cloth Dean's rag doll. *H&J Foulke, Inc.*

Henri Delcroix

Maker: Henri Delcroix, Paris and Montreuil-sous-Bois (porcelain factory)
Date: 1865—87
Material: Bisque head, composition body

Marked PAN Bébé: Ca. 1887. Perfect bisque socket head, paperweight eyes, closed mouth, pierced ears, good wig; French-style composition and wood body; appropriate clothes; all in good condition.
Mark: PAN
2
12—14in (31—36cm) $6000—7000**+
**Not enough price samples to compute a reliable range.
+Bisque must be of very good quality to bring this price.

12in (31cm) *PAN Bébé. Private Collection.*

D E P*
(Open Mouth)

Maker: Maison Jumeau, Paris, France; (heads possibly by Simon & Halbig, Gräfenhain, Thüringia, Germany)
Date: Late 1890s
Material: Bisque socket head, French jointed composition body (sometimes marked Jumeau)
Size: About 12—33in (31—84cm)
Mark: "DEP" and size number (up to 16 or so); sometimes stamped in red "Tete Jumeau;" body sometimes with Jumeau stamp or sticker

DEP: Perfect bisque socket head, human hair wig, sleep eyes, painted lower eyelashes only, upper hair eyelashes (sometimes gone), deeply molded eye sockets, open mouth, pierced ears; jointed French composition body; lovely clothes; all in good condition.

13—15in (33—38cm)	$ 650—750
18—20in (46—51cm)	900—1000
23—25in (58—64cm)	1300—1500
29—30in (74—76cm)	2100—2200

*The letters DEP appear in the mark of many dolls, but the particular dolls priced here have only "DEP" and a size number (unless they happen to have the red stamp "Tete Jumeau"). The face is characterized by deeply molded eye sockets and no painted upper eyelashes.

**DEP
8**

18½in (47cm) *DEP* with red stamped *Tête Jumeau*. *Kiefer Collection.*

Doll House Dolls

Maker: Various German firms
Date: Ca. 1890—1920
Material: Bisque shoulder head, cloth body, bisque arms and legs
Size: Under 7in (18cm)
Mark: Sometimes "Germany"

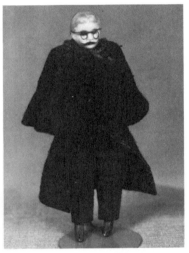

Doll house man with molded mustache and wire glasses, all original. *H&J Foulke, Inc.*

Doll House Doll: Man or lady 5½—7in (14—18cm), as above with molded hair, painted eyes; original clothes or suitably dressed; all in nice condition.

Victorian lady,	**$ 150—165**
Victorian man with mustache	**175—225**
Lady with glass eyes and wig	**325—375**
Man with mustache, original Military uniform	**600—700**
Molded hair, glass eyes,ca. 1870, 6in (15cm)	**375—400**
Swivel neck, French-type head, 6½in (17cm)	**750**
Molded hair, painted eyes. Ca 1870 4—5in (10—13cm)	**250—275**
Man with molded hair, glass eyes, mustache, all original and boxed, at auction	**1675**
1920s man or lady	**100—125**

Doll house lady with molded hair styled in a bun, all original but tattered clothes. *H&J Foulke, Inc.*

Door of Hope

Maker: Door of Hope Mission, China; heads by carvers from Ning-Po
Date: 1901—on
Material: Wooden heads; cloth bodies, sometimes with carved wooden hands
Size: Usually under 13in (33cm)
Mark: Sometimes "Made in China" label

Door of Hope: Carved wooden head with painted and/or carved hair, carved features; cloth body, sometimes carved hands; original handmade clothes, exact costuming for different classes of Chinese people; all in good condition. 25 dolls in the series.

Adult,
    11—13in (28—33cm) **$ 300—350**
Child,
    6—7in (15—18cm) **400—425**
Mother and Baby,
    11in (28cm) **475**
Manchu Lady, at auction **1025**

6in (15cm)*Kindergarten Girl*, all original.
H&J Foulke, Inc.

Grace G. Drayton

Maker: Various companies
Date: 1909—on
Material: All-cloth, or composition and cloth combination, or all-composition
Size: Various
Designer: Grace G. Drayton
Mark: Usually a cloth label or a stamp

g. g. Drayton

Puppy Pippin: 1911. Horsman Co., New York, N.Y., U.S.A. Composition head with puppy dog face, plush body with jointed legs; all in good condition. Cloth label. (For photograph see *7th Blue Book*, page 135.)
8in (20cm) sitting   **$375—400****

TRADE "Puppy Pippin" Nov 24 11 MARK COPYRIGHT 1911 BY E.I. HORSMAN CO.

Campbell Kid: (see page 114).

16in (41cm) cloth **Dolly Dingle.** *H&J Foulke, Inc.*

Peek-a-Boo: 1913—1915. Horsman Co., New York, N.Y., U.S.A. Composition head, arms, legs and lower torso, cloth upper torso; character face with molded hair, painted eyes to the side, watermelon mouth; dressed in striped bathing suit, polka dot dress or ribbons only; cloth label on outfit; all in good condition. (For photograph see *7th Blue Book*, page 136.)
7½in (19cm)   **$135—150**

Hug-Me-Tight: 1916. Colonial Toy Mfg. Co., New York, N.Y., U.S.A. Mother Goose characters and others in one piece, printed on cloth; all in good condition. (For photograph see *8th Blue Book*, page 149.)
11in (28cm)   **$225—250**
**Not enough price samples to compute a reliable range.

Grace G. Drayton continued

Chocolate Drop: 1923. Averill Manufacturing Co., New York, N.Y., U.S.A. Brown cloth doll with movable arms and legs; painted features, three yarn pigtails; appropriate clothes; all in good condition. Stamped on front torso and paper label. (For photograph see *6th Blue Book*, page 120.)

11in (28cm)   **$350—375**
16in (41cm)   **500****

Dolly Dingle: 1923. Averill Manufacturing Co., New York, N.Y., U.S.A. Cloth doll with painted features and movable arms and legs; appropriate clothes; all in good condition. Stamped on front torso and paper label.

DOLLY DINGLE
COPYRIGHT BY
G.G. DRAYTON

11in (28cm)   **$325—350**
16in (41cm)   **450**

Composition Child: Composition shoulder head, arms and legs, cloth torso; molded bobbed hair, watermelon mouth, painted eyes, round nose; original or appropriate clothes; in fair condition. (For photograph see *8th Blue Book*, page 150.)
Mark: *9 . 9 . DRAYTON*
14in (36cm)   **$350—400****

Kitty-Puss: All-cloth with painted cat face, flexible arms and legs, tail; original clothing; all in good condition.
Mark: Cardboard tag   **$400****

**Not enough price samples to compute a reliable range.

Grace Drayton's **Kitty-Puss** by Madame Hendren. *Courtesy of Nancy Permacoff.*

Dressel

Maker: Cuno & Otto Dressel verlager & doll factory of Sonneberg, Thüringia, Germany. Heads by Armand Marseille, Simon & Halbig, Ernst Heubach, Gebrüder Heubach.

Date: 1700—on

Material: Composition wax over or bisque head, kid, cloth body or ball-jointed composition body

Trademarks: Fifth Ave. Dolls (1903), Jutta (1907), Bambina (1909), Poppy Dolls (1912), Holz-Masse (1875)

Mark:

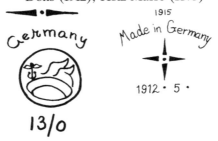

Marked Holz-Masse Heads: 1875—on. Composition shoulder head, molded hair or sometimes mohair wig, usually painted eyes, sometimes pierced ears; cloth body with composition arms and legs with molded boots; old clothes; all in good condition.

Mark:

Molded hair:
16—18in (41—46cm)	**$300—350**
22—24in (56—61cm)	**400—500**

Wigged with glass eyes:
(Patent Washable)
16—18in (41—46cm)	**325—375**
22—24in (56—61cm)	**450—500**

21in (53cm) composition shoulder head of the type made by Dressel. *H&J Foulke, Inc.*

Dressel continued

Child Doll: 1893—on. Perfect bisque head, original jointed kid or composition body; good wig, glass eyes, open mouth; suitable clothes; all in good condition.

Mark: Various including those above and 1896 C.o.D7 DEP

Composition body:

16—18in (41—46cm)	**$325—375***
22—24in (56—61cm)	**425—475***
28—30in (71—76cm)	**650—700***

Kid body:

14—16in (36—41cm)	**250—275***
19—21in (48—53cm)	**325—350***
24in (61cm)	**400—425***

*Allow extra for fine bisque.

Portrait Series: 1896. ***Admiral Dewey*** and his men, ***Uncle Sam*** and perhaps others. Perfect bisque heads with portrait faces, glass eyes, some with molded mustaches and goatees; composition body; original clothes; all in good condition. Sometimes marked with "S" or "D" and a number. Heads by Simon & Halbig. (For photograph see *8th Blue Book*, page 152.)

23in (58cm) 1912//B4 child. *H&J Foulke, Inc.*

Uncle Sam 13in (33cm)	**$1500**
Farmer 11in (28cm)	**1100**
Old Man, 12½in (32cm)	**1100**

Soldiers with molded mustaches, five-piece bodies, all original. Set of three at auction **1300**

Marked Jutta Child: Ca. 1906—1921. Perfect bisque socket head, good wig, sleep eyes, open mouth, pierced ears; ball-jointed composition body; dressed; all in good condition. Head made by Simon & Halbig.

Mold ***1348 or 1349***

Mark: 1349 Jutta S &H 11

13—15in (33—38cm)	**$ 525—550**
18—21in (46—53cm)	**550—600**
24—26in (61—66cm)	**750—850**
30—32in (76—81cm)	**1200—1400**
38in (97cm)	**2500**

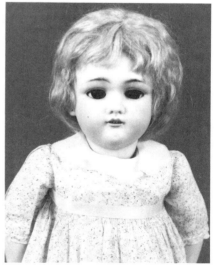

22in (56cm) Jutta 1349 child. *H&J Foulke, Inc.*

Dressel continued

Character Child: 1909—on. Perfect bisque socket head, ball-jointed composition body; mohair wig, painted eyes, closed mouth; suitable clothes; all in good condition. Glazed inside of head. (For photograph see *4th Blue Book*, page 83.)

16—18in (41—46cm) **$2500—2600****

**Not enough price samples to compute a reliable range.

Marked C.O.D. Character Baby: Ca. 1910—on. Perfect bisque character face with marked wig or molded hair, painted or glass eyes; jointed baby body; dressed; all in good condition. (For photograph see *5th Blue Book*, page 117.)

13—15in (33—38cm) **$350—400**
18—20in (46—51cm) **475—525**
22—24in (56—61cm) **650—750**

Marked Jutta Character Baby: Ca. 1910—1922. Perfect bisque socket head, good wig, sleep eyes, open mouth; bent-limb composition baby body; dressed; all in good condition.

Mark:
> Heubach 6½ Koppelsdorf
> Jutta - Baby
> Dressel
> Germany
> 1922
> 10½

> Jutta
> 1914
> 8

12—13in (31—33cm) **$ 425—475**
16—18in (41—46cm) **550—650**
23—24in (58—61cm) **1100—1300**

Toddler:
7—8in (18—20cm) **450—475**
14—16in (36—41cm) **750—800**
19—21in (48—53cm) **1050—1250**

Lady Doll: Ca. 1920s. Mold *#1469*. Bisque socket head with young lady face, good wig, sleep eyes, closed mouth; jointed composition body in adult form with molded bust, slim waist and long arms and legs, feet modeled to wear high-heeled shoes; appropriate clothes; all in good condition. (For photograph see *5th Blue Book*, page 117.)

Mark:
> 1469
> C.O.Dressel
> Germany

14in (36cm) 2. **$2500—4200***

In original box with extra shoes, pristine condition, at auction

6750

*Wide price range usually indicates imminent rise to higher price.

22in (56cm) 1914 Jutta toddler. *H&J Foulke, Inc.*

E. D. Bébé

Maker: Probably Danel & Cie or Etienne Denamur of Paris, France
Date: 1885—1895
Material: Bisque head, wood and composition jointed body
Mark:

E 8 D
DEPOSÉ

Marked E. D. Bébé: Perfect bisque head, wood and composition jointed
body; good wig, beautiful blown glass eyes, pierced ears; nicely dressed;
good condition. Often found on a marked Jumeau body.
Closed mouth:

14—16in (36—41cm)	**$2400—2700***
21—24in (53—61cm)	**3200—3500***
29—30in (74—75cm)	**4200—4500***

Open mouth:

22—24in (56—61cm)	**2200—2500***

*For a pretty face.

21in (53cm) *E.D. Kay & Wayne Jensen Collection.*

Eden Bébé

Maker: Fleischmann & Bloedel, doll factory, of Fürth, Bavaria, and Paris, France
Date: Founded in Bavaria in 1873. Also in Paris by 1890, then on into S.F.B.J. in 1899.
Material: Bisque head, composition jointed body
Trademark: Eden Bébé (1890), Bébé Triomphe (1898)
Mark: "EDEN BÉBÉ, PARIS"

Marked Eden Bebe: Ca. 1890. Perfect bisque head, fully-jointed or five-piece composition jointed body; beautiful wig, large set paperweight eyes, closed or open/closed mouth, pierced ears; lovely clothes; all in nice condition.

Closed mouth, 14—16in (36—41cm) **$2100—2300**
21—24in (53—61cm) **2700—3100**
Open mouth, 18—20in (46—51cm) **1900—2100**

Kissing, Walking, Flirting Doll: 1892. Head from mold 1039 by Simon & Halbig, ball-jointed composition body with mechanism for walking, throwing kisses and flirting eyes. (For photograph see *7th Blue Book*, page 142.)
20—22in (51—56cm) **$ 900—1000**
All original with French label, 22in (56cm) at auction **1450**

26in (66cm) ***Eden Bébé.*** *Private Collection.*

EFFanBEE®

Maker: EFFanBEE Doll Co., New York, N.Y., U.S.A.
Date: 1912—on
Marks: Various, but nearly always marked "EFFanBEE" on torso or head. Wore a metal heart-shaped bracelet; later a gold paper heart label.

EFFANBEE
DURABLE
DOLLS

Metal Heart Bracelet: **$45—50**

Baby Grumpy: 1912—1939. Composition shoulder head with frowning face, molded and painted hair, painted eyes, closed mouth; composition arms and legs, cloth body; original or appropriate old clothes; all in good condition. Came with metal heart bracelet.

Mark:

EFFANBEE
DOLLS
WALK-TALK-SLEEP

12in (31cm), White	**$175—200**
Black	**250—275**

Early model, marked *172, 174* or *176:*
14—15in (36—38cm)   **225—250**

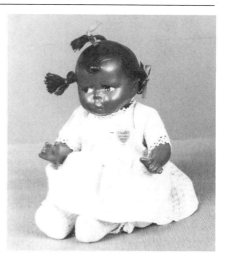

11in (28cm) rare model *Baby Grumpy*, brown complexion, yarn braids, curved legs, all original. *Leone McMullen Collection.*

Buds: 1915—1918. All-composition with character face, smiling mouth, painted eyes, molded hair; chubby torso with molded suit, shoulders, stiff hips. Originally came in a variety of costumes, both brown and white composition. All in good condition.
Mark: *Effanbee*
7in (18cm)   **$165—175**

7in (18cm) *Buds* in Hawaiian outfit. *H&J Foulke, Inc.*

EFFanBEE continued

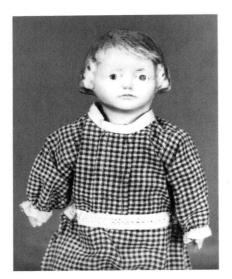

12in (31cm) unmarked **Pouting Bess.** *H&J Foulke, Inc.*

18in (46cm) unmarked boy which appears to be **Katie Kroose** by Effanbee. *Betty Harms Collection.*

Pouting Bess: 1915. Composition character face, molded painted hair with bangs combed to side, closed pouty mouth; cloth stuffed body with disc joints at shoulders and hips, composition lower arms, black sewn-on shoes; appropriate clothes; in fair condition. Some mold **#162** and **#166;** otherwise unmarked.

10—15in (25—38cm)   **$150—175****

Katie Kroose: 1918. Composition head with molded hair combed to side, painted eyes, closed mouth; stuffed cloth body with metal disk joints at shoulders and hips, sewn-on shoes, composition lower arms; appropriate clothes; all in fair condition.

15in (38cm)   **$225—250****

Not enough price samples to compute a reliable range.

Mary Ann and Mary Lee: 1928—on. Composition head on **Lovums** shoulder plate, composition arms and legs, cloth torso; human hair wig, sleep eyes, open smiling mouth; appropriate clothes; in good condition. Later version came on an all-composition body marked "Patsy-Ann" for **Mary Ann** and "Patsy-Joan" for **Mary Lee.** Came with metal heart bracelet. (For photograph see *8th Blue Book,* page 158.) ©

Mark: MARY-ANN

16in (41cm) **Mary Lee** $200—225
19in (48cm) **Mary Ann**   240—265

EFFanBEE continued

Lovums: 1928—1939. Composition swivel head on shoulder plate, arms and legs; molded painted hair or wig, pretty face, sleep eyes, smiling open mouth with teeth; cloth body; original or appropriate clothes; all in good condition. Various sizes. Came with metal heart bracelet. Note: The "Lovums" shoulder plate was used for many other dolls as well. (For photograph see *8th Blue Book*, page 158.)

Mark: EFF AN BEE
LOVUMS
©
PAT. Nº. 1,283,558

16—18in (41—46cm)   **$225—250**
22—24in (56—61cm)   **300—350**

Mary Jane: 1917—1920. Composition "dolly face" head with metal sleeping eyes, painted eyebrows and eyelashes, open mouth with teeth, original human hair or mohair wig; jointed composition body with wood arms; dressed; all in very good condition. (For photograph see *7th Blue Book*, page 144.)

Mark: *Effanbee* back of head and torso in raised letters
20—24in (51—61cm)   **$250—275**

Bubbles: 1924—on. Composition head with blonde molded and painted hair, sleep eyes, open mouth with teeth, smiling face; cloth body, curved composition arms and legs; original or appropriate old clothes; all in good condition. Came with metal heart bracelet or necklace.

Mark:

19 © 24

EFFANBEE
DOLLS
WALK-TALK-SLEEP
MADE IN U.S.A.

EFFANBEE
BUBBLES
COPYR. 1924
MADE IN U.S.A.

16—18in (41—46cm)   **$250—275**
22—24in (56—61cm)   **325—375**

19in (48cm) ***Bubbles***, tagged "Effanbee," pink silk coat and hat. *H&J Foulke, Inc.*

EFFanBEE continued

Marilee and Rosemary: 1924 (***Marilee***), 1925 (***Rosemary***). Composition shoulder head, human hair wig, open mouth, tin sleep eyes; cloth torso, composition arms and legs; original or appropriate old clothes; all in good condition. Various sizes. Came with metal heart bracelet. (For photograph see *8th Blue Book*, page 157)

Mark:

| EFFanBEE ROSEMARY WALK-TALK-SLEEP | EFFanBEE MARILEE COPYR. DOLL |

14in (36cm)   **$190—210**
22in (56cm)   **240—265**
28in (71cm)   **450****

Harmonica Joe: 1924. Black or white composition and cloth doll with attached harmonica at mouth; squeeze the tummy and air blows out of the mouth to activate the harmonica; original clothes; all in good condition.

Mark: *Effanbee*

14½in (37cm)   **$225—275****
**Not enough price samples to compute a reliable range.

14½in (37cm) girl version of **Harmonica Joe**, tagged dress and Effanbee bluebird pin. *Courtesy of Shirley Cummins.*

14in (36cm) sleep-eyed **Patsy** with molded hair. *H&J Foulke, Inc.*

EFFanBEE continued

LEFT: 9in (23cm) *Patsy Babyette* twins with caracul wigs, all original. *H&J Foulke, Inc.*

BELOW: 7in (18cm) *Baby Tinyette*, all original. *H&J Foulke, Inc.*

Patsy Family: 1928—on. All-composition, jointed at neck, shoulders and hips; molded hair (sometimes covered with wig), bent right arm on some members, painted or sleep eyes; original or appropriate old clothes; may have some crazing. Came with metal heart bracelet. (See previous *Blue Books* for *Patsy* dolls not pictured here.)

Mark:

Bracelet

```
EFFANBEE       EFFANBEE      (EFFANBEE
PATSY JR.       PATSY         PATSY
  DOLL          DOLL         BABY KIN)
```

6in (15cm) **Wee Patsy**, all original	**$325**
Black, mint-in-box with pin	**650**
7in (18cm) **Baby Tinyette**	**185—210**
9in (23cm) **Patsy Babyette**	**200—225**
Patsyette	**225—235**
11in (28cm) **Patsy Baby**	**225—250**
Patsy Jr.	**250—275**
Patricia Kin	**250—275**
14in (36cm) **Patsy**	**275—325**
Patricia	**325—375**
16in (41cm) **Patsy Joan**	**325—375**
19in (48cm) **Patsy Ann**	**375—425**
22in (56cm) **Patsy Lou**	**400—450**
26in (66cm) **Patsy Ruth**	**650—700**
30in (76cm) **Patsy Mae**	**650—700**

11in (28cm) *Patsy Jr. H&J Foulke, Inc.*

EFFanBEE continued

Skippy: 1929. All-composition, jointed at neck, hips and shoulders, (later a cloth torso, still later a cloth torso and upper legs with composition molded boots for lower legs); molded hair, painted eyes to the side; original or appropriate clothes; all in good condition. Came with metal heart bracelet.

Mark: EFFANBEE
SKIPPY
©
P. L. Crosby

14in (36cm)   **$375**

14in (36cm) ***Skippy***, all original. *Kay & Wayne Jensen Collection.*

Dy-Dee Baby: 1933—on. First dolls had hard rubber head with soft rubber body, caracul wig or molded hair, open mouth for drinking, soft ears (after 1940). Later dolls had hard plastic heads with rubber bodies. Still later dolls had hard plastic heads with vinyl bodies. Came with paper heart label.
Various sizes from 9—20in (23—51cm). Very good condition.

Mark:
*"EFF-AN-BEE
DY-DEE BABY
US PAT.-1-857-485
ENGLAND-880-060
FRANCE-723-980
GERMANY-585-647
OTHER PAT PENDING"*
Rubber body:
14—16in (36—41cm)   **$125—135**
24in (61cm)   **250—275**

16in (41cm) ***Dy-Dee Baby***, rubber body. *H&J Foulke, Inc.*

EFFanBEE continued

Anne Shirley: 1935—1940. All-composition, jointed at neck, shoulders and hips; human hair wig, sleep eyes, closed mouth; original clothes; all in very good condition. Came with metal heart bracelet. "Anne Shirley" body used on other dolls as well.

Mark: On back: "EFFanBEE/ANNE SHIRLEY."

14—15in (36—38cm)	**$210—235**
17—18in (43—46cm)	**260—285**
21in (53cm)	**325—350**
27in (69cm) unmarked	**450**

American Children: 1936-1939. Composition swivel head on composition *Anne Shirley* body, jointed at shoulders and hips. Four different faces designed by Dewees Cochran with either open or closed mouths, human hair wigs, painted or sleep eyes; original clothes; all in excellent condition. Came with metal heart bracelet and paper heart label. Sizes: 15in (38cm), 17in (43cm), 19in (48cm) and 21in (53cm).

Mark: Head: "EFFANBEE//
AMERICAN//
CHILDREN"
Body: "EFFANBEE//
ANNE SHIRLEY"

The boy and the open-mouth girl are not marked.

Open mouth:
  15in (38cm)

Barbara Joan	**$ 550—600**
17½in (45cm)	
Barbara Ann	**650—700**
21in (53cm)	
Barbara Lou	**750—800**

Closed mouth:

19—21in (48—53cm)	**1100—1200**
17in (43cm) boy	**1200**

21in (53cm) *Anne Shirley* with painted eyes, all original. *H&J Foulke, Inc.*

19in (48cm) *American Child*, all original. *H&J Foulke, Inc.*

See additional photograph on page 158.

EFFanBEE continued

Charlie McCarthy: 1937. Composition head, hands and feet, cloth body; painted hair and eyes; strings at back of head to operate mouth; original clothes; all in very good condition. (For photograph see *8th Blue Book*, page 163.)

MARK:
"EDGAR BERGEN'S CHARLIE McCARTHY, AN EFFanBEE PRODUCT"

17—20in (43—51cm)	**$375**
Mint-in-box with button	**500**

15in (38cm) *Barbara Joan* as the Ice Queen. See color photograph on page 161. *H&J Foulke, Inc.*

Historical Dolls: 1939. All-composition, jointed at neck, shoulders and hips. Three each of 30 dolls portraying the history of American fashion, 1492—1939. "American Children" heads used with elaborate human hair wigs and painted eyes; elaborate original costumes using velvets, satins, silks, brocades, and so forth; all in excellent condition. Came with metal heart bracelet.
Marks: On head: "EFFANBEE AMERICAN CHILDREN"
On body: "EFFANBEE ANNE SHIRLEY"
21in (53cm)   **$1250—1500**
See color photograph on page 80.

Historical Doll Replicas: 1939. All-composition, jointed at neck, shoulders and hips. Series of 30 dolls, popular copies of the original historical models (see above). Human hair wigs, painted eyes; original costumes all in cotton, copies of those on the original models. Came with metal heart bracelet. All in excellent condition. (For photograph see *8th Blue Blue*, page 76.)
Mark: On torso: "EFFanBEE
ANNE SHIRLEY"
14in (36cm)   **$425—450**

Suzette: 1939. All-composition, jointed at neck, shoulders and hips; mohair wig, eyes painted to the side, closed mouth; original clothes; all in very good condition. Came with metal heart bracelet.

Mark: SUZETTE
EFF AN BEE
MADE IN
U.S.A.

11½in (29cm)   **$200—215**

11½in (29cm) **Suzette,** all original. *H&J Foulke, Inc.*

Tommy Tucker: 1939—1949. Composition head with painted hair or mohair wig, flirting eyes, closed mouth, chubby cheeks; composition hands, stuffed body; original clothes; all in very good condition. Also called **Mickey** and **Baby Bright Eyes.** Came with paper heart tag. Sizes: 15—24in (38—61cm).

Mark: On head: "EFFANBEE U.S.A."

16—18in (41—46cm)   **$225—250**
22—24in (56—61cm)   **300—350**

Suzanne: 1940. All-composition jointed at neck, shoulders and hips; mohair wig, sleep eyes, closed mouth; original clothes; all in very good condition. Came with metal heart bracelet. (For photograph see *8th Blue Book,* page 165.)

Mark: SUZANNE
EFFANBEE
MADE IN U.S.A

14in (36cm)   **$225—250**

Little Lady: 1940—1949. All-composition, jointed at neck, shoulders and hips, separated fingers; mohair or human hair wig, sleep eyes, closed mouth; same face as **Anne**

14in (36cm) **Tommy Tucker,** all original. *H&J Foulke, Inc.*

Shirley; original clothes; all in very good condition. (During "war years" some had yarn wigs and/or painted eyes.) Various sizes.

Mark: On back:
"EFFanBEE
U.S.A.

Paper heart:
'I am Little Lady' "

14—15in (36—38cm)   **$210—235**
17—18in (43—46cm)   **260—285**
20—21in (51—53cm)   **325—335**
Brown complexion,
   20—21in (51—53cm)   **450**

EFFanBEE continued

LEFT: 14in (36cm) *Little Lady*, all original. *H&J Foulke, Inc.* RIGHT: 14in (36cm) *Honey*, all original. *H&J Foulke, Inc.*

Portrait Dolls: 1940. All-composition, jointed at neck, shoulders and hips; mohair wigs, sleep eyes; in costumes, such as ballerina, ***Bo-Peep, Gibson Girl***, bride and groom, dancing couple, all original, in excellent condition. (For photograph see *7th Blue Book*, page 152.)
Mark: None
11in (28cm) **$200—225**

Sweetie Pie: 1942. Composition head and limbs, cloth torso; caracul wig, flirty eyes, closed mouth; original clothes; all in very good condition. Available in 16in (41cm), 20in (51cm) and 24in (61cm). (For photograph see *8th Blue Book*, page 167.)
Mark: "EFFANBEE © 1942"
16—18in (41—46cm) **$225—250**
22—24in (56—61cm) **300—350**
All composition,
16in (41cm) **250—265**

Candy Kid: 1946. All-composition toddler, jointed at neck, shoulders and hips; molded hair, sleep eyes; original clothes; all in very good condition. Came with paper heart tag. See color photograph on page 80.
Mark: "EFFanBEE"
12in (31cm) **$275**

Honey: 1949—1955. All-hard plastic, jointed at neck, shoulders and hips; synthetic, mohair or human hair, sleep eyes; original clothes; all in excellent condition.
Mark: EFFANBEE
14in (36cm) **$175—200**
18in (46cm) **225—250**
24in (61cm) **300—325**

Effanbee Club Limited Edition Dolls: 1975—on. All-vinyl jointed doll; original clothes; excellent condition.

1975 *Precious Baby*	$350
1976 *Patsy*	350
1977 *Dewees Cochran*	175
1978 *Crowning Glory*	150
1979 *Skippy*	350
1980 *Susan B. Anthony*	150
1981 *Girl with Watering Can*	150
1982 *Princess Diana*	125
1983 *Sherlock Holmes*	125
1984 *Bubbles*	125
1985 *Red Boy*	125
1986 *China Head*	125

26in (66cm) French bébé marked only "PARIS." For further information see page 178. *Kay & Wayne Jensen Collection.*

16in (41cm) French fashion lady by F. Gaultier. For further information see page 186. *H & J Foulke, Inc.*

BELOW: 15in (38cm) Effanbee composition *Barbara Joan* designed by Dewees Cochran, also called the *Ice Queen*, all original. For further information see page 158. *H & J Foulke, Inc.*

24in (61cm) girl with dolly face incised "Made in Germany," all original. For further information see page 190. *H & J Foulke, Inc.*

7½in (19cm) unmarked German girl, all original. For further information see page 190. *H & J Foulke, Inc.*

LEFT: 21½in (55cm) exceptionally rare Kämmer & Reinhardt bisque character doll dated circa 1909 and marked with an impressed "105 K★R 55." This doll brought a record price when it sold at a Sotheby's auction in February 1989 — **$169,576!** This was the highest known price to date for a doll. *Photo courtesy of Sotheby's.*

ABOVE: 13in (33cm) googly by J. D. Kestner #221 with original label. For further information see page 200. *Kay & Wayne Jensen Collection.*

7½in (19cm) all-bisque Kestner googly, fully jointed including elbows and knees. For further information see page 199. *Kay & Wayne Jensen Collection.*

13½in (34cm) googly by Armand Marseille #253, all original. For further information see page 200. *Private Collection.*

18in (46cm) 172 googly by Hertel, Schwab & Co. For further information see page 201. *Billie Nelson Tyrrell.*

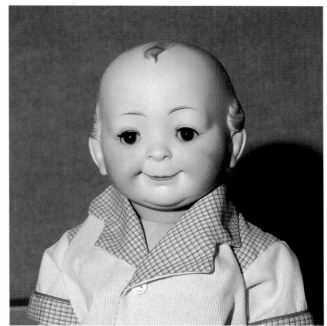

16in (41cm) 173 googly by Hertel, Schwab & Co. For further information see page 201. *Billie Nelson Tyrrell.*

18-1/2in (46cm) French bébé incised "2 H." For further information see page 179. *Private Collection.*

RIGHT: 20in (51cm) Gebrüder Heubach pouty character #7347. For further information see page 230. *Private Collection.*

BELOW RIGHT: 18½in (47cm) Gebrüder Heubach lady #7925. For further information see page 230. *Private Collection.*

BELOW: 5in (13cm) Gebrüder Heubach all-bisque character girl. For further information see page 233. *H & J Foulke, Inc.*

17in (43cm) French fashion lady by Huret, swivel neck, jointed wood body. For further information see page 240. *Private Collection.*

16in (41cm) Ideal composition *Judy Garland*, all original. For further information see page 243. *Rosemary Dent Collection.*

19in (48cm) French bébé by Jullien. For further information see page 249. *Private Collection.*

21in (53cm) French bébé by Jumeau incised "E 10 J." For further information see page 252. *Private Collection.*

19in (48cm) French bébé by Jumeau with incised mark. For further information see page 252. *Kay & Wayne Jensen Collection.*

12in (31cm) K & K toddler, all original with label. For further information see page 255. *H & J Foulke, Inc.*

LEFT: 29in (74cm) smiling character girl #203 by Jumeau. For further information see page 254. *Private Collection.*

Three character dolls by Kämmer & Reinhardt:12-1/2in (32cm) mold #102 boy with molded hair, 13-1/2in (34cm) mold #109 girl, 12in (31cm) mold 107 boy. For further information see page 261. *Private Collection.*

16in (41cm) *Max* and *Moritz* comic characters by Kämmer & Reinhardt, molds #123 and 124. For further information see page 264. *Private Collection.*

7½in (19cm) Kämmer & Reinhardt mold #126 character on five-piece toddler body. For further information see page 260. *Kay & Wayne Jensen Collection.*

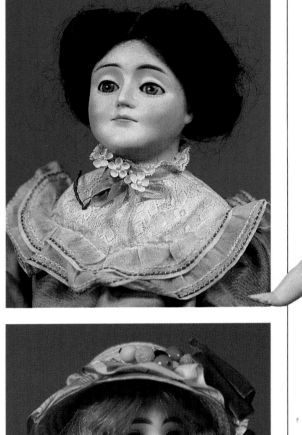

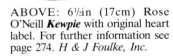

20in (51cm) *Gibson Girl* by J.D. Kestner. For further information see page 273. *Private Collection.*

ABOVE: 6½in (17cm) Rose O'Neill *Kewpie* with original heart label. For further information see page 274. *H & J Foulke, Inc.*

16in (41cm) Kestner child incised "7" with open mouth and square cut teeth. For further information see page 265. *Kiefer Collection.*

ABOVE: 21in (53cm) *Baby Betty* by Arman Marseille. For further information see page 299. *H & J Foulke, Inc.*

17in (43cm) Käthe Kruse Doll I, all-cloth with molded hair. For further information see page 286. *Kiefer Collection.*

20in (51cm) Kley & Hahn mold #526 character girl. For further information see page 280. *Billie Nelson Tyrrell.*

ABOVE: 16½in (42cm) *Fany*, mold #231 by Armand Marseille. For further information see page 301. *Private Collection.*

24in (61cm) toddler by Armand Marseille, mold #341 with wig, cloth torso, composition limbs. For further information see page 304. *Private Collection.*

12in (31cm) character baby by Armand Marseille, mold #560a. For further information see page 302. *H & J Foulke, Inc.*

Falck & Roussel

Maker: Falck & Roussel, Paris, France. Some bisque heads were purchased
   from Francois Gaultier
Date: 1880—1902
Material: Bisque head, composition body
Trademark: Bébé Mignon
Mark:

F.R.
5

Marked F. R. Bébé: Perfect bisque head, paperweight eyes, closed mouth,
   pierced ears, good wig; French-style jointed composition body; appropriate
   clothes; all in good condition.
16—18in (41—46cm)   **$9000—10,000** + +
+Bisque must be excellent quality for this price.
**Not enough price samples to compute a reliable average.

14in (36cm) F. R. Bébé. *Private Collection.*

Maud Tousey Fangel

Maker: Averill Manufacturing Co. and Georgene Novelties, New York, N.Y.,
U.S.A.
Date: 1938
Material: All-cloth
Size: 10in (25cm) and up
Designer: Maude Tousey Fangel
Mark: "M.T.F. ©" at side of face on hair, but often inside the seam

Maud Tousey Fangel Doll: All-cloth with printed face in several variations which came dressed as a baby or child; some bodies are of printed cloth, some plain; soft stuffed, flexible arms and legs; original or appropriate clothes; all in good condition. ***Snooks, Sweets, Peggy-Ann*** and possibly other names.
12—14in (31—36cm)   **$550—600**

14in (36cm) Fangel child with printed cloth body with matching skirt and bonnet ruffle. *H&J Foulke, Inc.*

French Bébé
(Unmarked)

Maker: Numerous French firms
Date: Ca. 1880—1925
Material: Bisque head, jointed composition body
Mark: None, except perhaps numbers, Paris, France or DEP

Unmarked French Bébé: Perfect bisque head, swivel neck, lovely wig, set paperweight eyes, closed mouth, pierced ears; jointed French body; pretty costume; all in good condition.

Early, fine quality (desirable face):
14—16in (36—41cm)   **$3600—4000**
20—22in (51—56cm)   **5000—5500**
Standard quality:
17—19in (43—48cm)   **2400—2600**
22—24in (56—61cm)   **3000—3400**
Open Mouth:
1890s:
16—18in (41—46cm)   **1700—1900**
24—25in (61—64cm)   **2400—2600**

1920s:
16—18in (41—46cm)   **650—750**
22—24in (56—61cm)   **850—900**
DEP:
14—16in (36—41cm)   **1900—2200**
21—24in (53—61cm)   **3000—3200**

See color photograph on page 161.

French Bébé
(Unknown Manufacturers)

H.

Marked H Bébé: Ca. late 1870s. Perfect pressed bisque socket head of fine quality, paperweight eyes, pierced ears, closed mouth, cork pate, good wig; French-style wood and composition jointed body with straight wrists; appropriate clothes; all in excellent condition.

Mark:

$$2 \cdot H$$

19in (48cm)
Approximate size scale:
Size 0 = 16½in (42cm)
    2 = 19in (48cm)
    3 = 21in (56cm)
    4 = 24in (61cm)

$35,000—40,000**

J.M.

Marked J.M. Bébé: Ca. late 1870s. Perfect pressed bisque socket head, paperweight eyes, closed mouth, pierced ears, good wig; French-style composition body; appropriate clothes; all in good condition.

Mark:

$$5$$

$$\mathcal{J} \, \underset{\triangle}{\mathbb{Q}} \, \mathcal{M}$$

26in (66cm)

$18,000—22,000**

**Not enough price samples to compute a reliable average.

19in (48cm) 2 H Bébé. See page 166 for color photograph. *Private Collection.*

26in (66cm) ***J.M. Bébé.*** *Private Collection.*

French Bébés (Unknown Manufacturers) continued

B.L.

Marked B.L. Bébé: Ca. 1880 possibly by Lefebvre or perhaps Jumeau for the Louvre department store. Perfect bisque socket head, closed mouth, paperweight eyes, pierced ears, good wig; French-style jointed composition body; appropriate clothes; all in good condition. (For photograph see *Doll Classics*, page 41 or *5th Blue Book*, page 54.)

Mark:

B. 9 L.

18—21in (46—53cm) **$3800—4000**

21in (53cm) **R.R. Bébé** with Jumeau tick marks on back of her head. *Private Collection.*

R.R.

Marked R.R. Bébé: Ca. 1880s. Some possibly made by Jumeau. Perfect bisque head, closed mouth, paperweight eyes, pierced ears, good wig; French-style jointed composition body; appropriate clothes; all in good condition.

Mark:

R 10 R

21—23in (53—58cm) **$4800—5200****

M.

Marked M. Bébé: Ca. Mid 1890s. Perfect bisque socket head, closed mouth, paperweight eyes, pierced ears, good wig; French-style jointed composition body; appropriate clothes; all in good condition. Some dolls with this mark may be *Bébé Mascottes.*

Mark:

M
4

14—16in (36—41cm) **$2700—3000****
21—23in (53—58cm) **3800—4200****

**Not enough price samples to compute a reliable average.

14in (36cm) Bébé incised "M" over "4." *Private Collection.*

French Fashion-Type

Maker: Various French firms
Date: Ca. 1860—1930
Material: Bisque shoulder head, jointed kid body, some with bisque lower limbs or wood arms; or fully-jointed wood body sometimes covered with kid.

(See also **Bru, Jumeau, Gaultier, Gesland, Huret, Rohmer** and **Barrois**)

French Fashion Lady: Perfect unmarked bisque shoulder head, swivel or stationary neck, kid body, kid arms -- some with wired fingers or old bisque arms; original or old wig, lovely blown glass eyes, closed mouth, earrings; appropriate old clothes; all in good condition. Fine quality bisque.

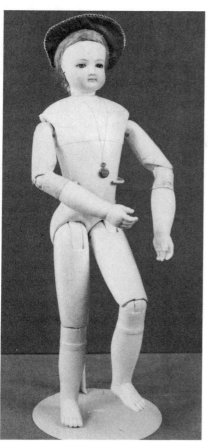

12—13in (31—33cm)	**$1800 up***
15—16in (38—41cm)	**2300 up***
18—19in (46—48cm)	**2800 up***
21in (53cm)	**3200 up***
Fully-jointed wood body,	
16—19in (38—48cm)	**3800 up +**

Molded blonde hair, blue bow, cobalt eyes, swivel neck,
21in (53cm) **3500****

*Allow at least $400 additional for kid-over-wood upper and bisque lower arms.

*Greatly depending upon the appeal of the face.

*Allow extra for original clothing.

+ Allow extra for joints at ankle and waist.

**Not enough price samples to compute a reliable average.

More photographs on page 182.

18in (46cm) kid-over-wood fashion with bisque lower arms and feet. *Yvonne Baird Collection.*

French Fashion-Type (continued)

21in (53cm) fashion with stiff neck and cobalt blue eyes. *Private Collection.*

17in (43cm) fashion with swivel neck and bisque hands. *Private Collection.*

Freundlich

Maker: Freundlich Novelty Corp., New York, N.Y., U.S.A.
Date: 1923—on
Material: All-composition

Baby Sandy: 1939—1942. All-composition with swivel head, jointed shoulders and hips, chubby toddler body; molded hair, smiling face, larger sizes have sleep eyes, smaller ones painted eyes; appropriate clothes; all in good condition. (For photograph see *8th Blue Book*, page 172.)
Mark: On head: "Baby Sandy"
　　　　　On pin: "The Wonder Baby
　　　　　Genuine Baby Sandy Doll"

8in (20cm)	**$125**
12in (31cm)	**150—175**
14—15in (36—38cm)	**250—275**

General Douglas MacArthur: Ca. 1942. All-composition portrait doll, molded hat, painted features, one arm to salute if desired; jointed shoulders and hips; original khaki uniform; all in good condition.
Mark: Cardboard tag: "General MacArthur"
18in (46cm) **$250**

Military Dolls: Ca. 1942. All-composition with molded hats, jointed shoulders and hips, character face, painted features; original clothes. *Soldier, Sailor, WAAC*, and *WAVE*, all in good condition. (For photograph see *7th Blue Book*, page 161.)
Mark: Cardboard tag
15in (38cm) **$135—165**

18in (46cm) *General MacArthur. H&J Foulke, Inc.*

Frozen Charlotte
(Bathing Doll)

Maker: Various German firms
Date: Ca. 1850s—early 1900s
Material: Glazed china; sometimes bisque
Size: 1—18in (3—46cm)
Mark: None, except for "Germany," or numbers or both

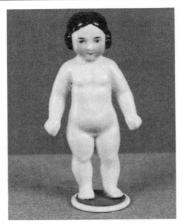

5in (13cm) Frozen Charlotte with pink tint and early hairdo. *Yvonne Baird Collection.*

Frozen Charlotte: All-china doll, black or blonde molded hair parted down the middle, painted features; hands extended, legs separated but not jointed; no clothes; perfect condition. Good quality.

2—3in (5—8cm)	$ 40—50*
4—5in (10—13cm)	90—110*
6—7in (15—18cm)	135—165*
9—10in (23—25cm)	225—250*
14—15in (36—38cm)	350—375*
Pink tint, early hairdo	
5in (13cm)	200—225
Pink tint with bonnet,	
5in (13cm)	325—350
Tinted bisque, blonde hair,	
5in (13cm)	135—160
with lovely boots	200
Parian-type (untinted bisque),	
5in (13cm)	160—185
Alice style with pink boots (bisque),	
5in (13cm)	275
Black china, 5in (13cm)	125
Blonde hair, molded bow,	
5½ (14cm)	150
Wig, lovely boots,	
5in (13cm)	165

*Allow extra for pink tint, fine decoration and modeling, unusual hairdo.

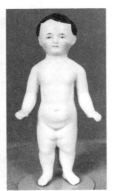

LEFT: 7in (18cm) Frozen Charlotte with beautifully molded hair. *Private Collection.*
RIGHT: 6in (15cm) Frozen "Charlie" with boy hairdo. *H&J Foulke, Inc.*

Fulper

Maker: Heads by Fulper Pottery Co. of Flemington, N.J., U.S.A. for other companies, often Amberg or Horsman
Date: 1918—1921
Material: Bisque heads; composition ball-jointed or jointed kid bodies
Mark: "Fulper—Made in U.S.A."

*Made in
U.S.A
13*

Fulper Child Doll: Perfect bisque head, good wig; kid jointed or composition ball-jointed body; set or sleep eyes, open mouth; suitably dressed; all in good condition. Good quality bisque.

Kid body, 16—19in (41—48cm)	**$350—400***
Composition body, 18—20in (46—51cm)	**475—525***

Fulper Baby or Toddler: Same as above, but with bent-limb or jointed toddler body.

14—16in (36—41cm)	**$450—550***
20—22in (51—56cm)	**650—750***
17in (43cm) very cute toddler, at auction	**800**

*Do not pay as much for a doll with poor bisque.

20½in (52cm) Fulper character boy. *Kiefer Collection.*

Gaultier

Maker: Francois Gauthier (name changed to Gaultier in 1875); St. Maurice, Charenton, Seine, Paris, France (This company made only porcelain parts, not bodies.)
Date: 1860 to 1899 (then joined S.F.B.J.)
Material: Bisque head for kid or composition body; all-bisque

---

Marked F. G. Fashion Lady: 1860 to 1930. Bisque swivel head on bisque shoulder plate, original kid body, kid arms with wired fingers or bisque lower arms and hands; original or good French wig, lovely large stationary eyes, closed mouth, ears pierced; dressed; all in good condition.

Mark: "F.G." on side of shoulder

11½—13in (29—33cm)	**$1300—1600***
16—18in (41—46cm)	**1900—2300***
21—23in (53—58cm)	**2600—2900***
26—27in (66—69cm)	**3200—3500***
Wood body, 16—18in (41—46cm)	**3000—3500***
Late doll in ethnic costume:	
8—9in (20—23cm)	**550—600**

*Allow extra for original clothes.

For color photograph see page 161.

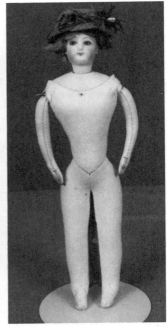

17½in (45cm) F.G. lady on jointed wood body. *Private Collection.*

11½in (29cm) F.G. type lady on stiff kid body. *H&J Foulke, Inc.*

Marked F. G. Bébé: Ca. 1879—1887. Bisque swivel head on shoulder plate and gusseted kid body with bisque lower arms or chunky jointed composition body; good wig, large bulgy paperweight eyes, closed mouth, pierced ears; dressed; all in good condition.

Mark:

F . 7. G

(or other size number) So "called Block letters" mark.

10½—12in (27—31cm)	$3000—3200
16—18in (41—46cm)	3500—3700
21—23in (53—58cm)	4000—4500
26—28in (66—71cm)	5000—5600
33—35in (83—89cm)	7000

11in (28cm) F.G. child with block mark. *Yvonne Baird Collection.*

Marked F. G. Bébé: Ca. 1887—1900 and probably later. Bisque head, composition jointed body; good French wig, beautiful large set eyes, closed mouth, pierced ears; well dressed; all in good condition.

Mark: So-called "Scroll" mark.

5—6in (13—15cm)	$ 600—700
15—17in (38—43cm)	2200—2500
21—23in (53—58cm)	2800—3100
28—29in (71—74cm)	3700—4000
Open mouth:	
8in (20cm)	550—600
15—17in (38—43cm)	1500—1800
20—22in (51—56cm)	1900—2200
27—29in (69—74cm)	2700—3000

21in (53cm) F.G. child with scroll mark. *Private Collection.*

German Bisque
(Unmarked or Unidentified Marks)

Maker: Various German firms
Date: 1860s—on
Material: Bisque head, composition, kid or cloth body
Mark: Some numbered, some "Germany," some both

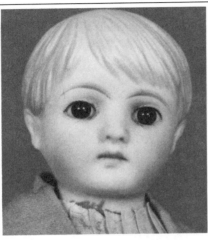

13in (33cm) molded hair boy with glass eyes, all original. *Private Collection.*

16½in (42cm) molded hair lady with glass eyes and decorated bodice. *Private Collection.*

Molded Hair Doll: Ca. 1880. Tinted bisque shoulder head with beautifully molded hair (usually blonde), painted eyes (sometimes glass), closed mouth; original kid or cloth body; bisque lower arms; appropriate clothes; all in good condition.

5—7in (13—18cm)	**$110—135**
11—13in (28—33cm)	**200—250***
15—18in (38—46cm)	**300—350***
23—25in (38—64cm)	**500—600***
With glass eyes	
18—22in (46—56cm)	**600—700***

Unusual hairdo,	
18—22in (46—56cm)	**600 up**
With glass eyes,	**850 up**
With glass eyes and	
decorated bodice	**950 up**

*Allow extra for unusual hairdo and glass eyes.

So-called ***American School Boy:*** Glass eyes. (For photograph see *7th Blue Book*, page 168.)

14—15in (36—38cm)	**$425—475**
20in (51cm)	**650**

German Bisque continued

Hatted or Bonnet Doll: Ca. 1880—1920. Bisque head with painted molded hair and molded fancy bonnet with bows, ribbons, flowers, feathers, and so forth; painted eyes and facial features; original cloth body with bisque arms and legs; good old clothes or nicely dressed; all in good condition.

8—9in (20—23cm)	**$ 135—165**
12—15in (31—38cm)	
"Marqueritas" stone bisque	
(Hertwig & Co.)	**200—250***
18—22in (46—56cm)	
fine quality (A.B.G.)	**750—850***
20in (51cm) blonde hair,	
molded blue hat,	
glass eyes	**3000****
All bisque,	
6—7in (15—18cm)	**150—200***

*Allow extra for unusual style.
**Not enough price samples to compute a reliable range.

9in (23cm) bonnet doll with molded hat. *H&J Foulke, Inc.*

20in (51cm) fashion-type doll. *Private Collection.*

Child Doll with closed mouth: Ca. 1880—1890. Perfect bisque head; kid or cloth body, gusseted at hips and knees with good bisque hands or jointed composition body; good wig; nicely dressed; all in good condition.

Kid or cloth body:

12—13in (31—33cm)	**$ 450—500**
15—17in (38—43cm)	**550—650***
20—22in (51—56cm)	**750—850***
26in (66cm)	**1000—1100***
20in (51cm) German fashion,	
swivel neck	**850—875**

Composition body:

13—15in (33—38cm)	**1250—1450***
19—21in (48—53cm)	**1800—2000***
24—25in (61—64cm)	
	2250—2450*

*Allow extra for fine quality.

19in (48cm) closed mouth child 136, fine quality. *Private Collection.*

German Bisque continued

Child Doll with open mouth "Dolly Face:" 1888 on. Perfect bisque head, ball-jointed composition body or kid body with bisque lower arms; good wig, glass eyes, open mouth; dressed; all in good condition.

13in (33cm) "C" Dolly Face child. *H&J Foulke, Inc.*

Very good quality:

12in (31cm)	**$325—350**
14—16in (36—41cm)	**425—450**
18—20in (46—51cm)	**500—550**
23—24in (48—51cm)	**600—650**
28—30in (71—76cm)	**900—1000**

Standard quality:

12—14in (31—36cm)	**250—275**
16—18in (41—46cm)	**325—375**
22—24in (56—61cm)	**450—500**
28—30in (71—76cm)	**700—800**

See color photograph on page 163.

Tiny child doll: 1890 to World War I. Perfect bisque socket head of good quality, five-piece composition body of good quality with molded and painted shoes and stockings; good wig, set or sleep eyes, open mouth; cute clothes; all in good condition.

Very good quality:

5—6in (13—15cm)	**$200—225**
8—10in (20—25cm)	**250—300**

Fully-jointed body,

7—8in (18—20cm)	**325—375**

Closed mouth:

4½—5½in	**275—300**
8in (20cm)	**450—550**

#39-13, five-piece mediocre body,

glass eyes, 5in (13cm)	**200**
painted eyes	**85**

Standard quality:

5—6in (13—15cm)	**85**
8—10in (20—25cm)	**110—125**

See color photograph on page 163.

23in (48cm) *Pansy IV. H&J Foulke, Inc.*

German Bisque continued

Character Baby: 1910—on. Perfect bisque head, good wig or solid dome with painted hair, sleep eyes, open mouth; composition bent-limb baby body; suitably dressed; all in good condition.

8—9in (20—23cm)	$225—275*
13—15in (33—38cm)	450—500*
18—20in (46—51cm)	550—600*
22—24in (56—61cm)	750—850*
Painted eyes:	
7—8in (18—20cm)	225—275*
12in (31cm)	425—450*

*Allow more for open/closed mouth, closed mouth or unusual face.

21in (53cm) A7 character boy. *Private Collection.*

7½in (19cm) tiny child doll, standard quality. *H&J Foulke, Inc.*

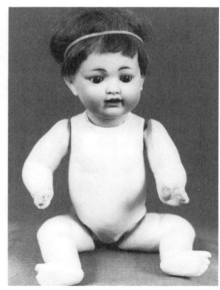

13in (33cm) unmarked character baby. *H&J Foulke, Inc.*

German Bisque continued

Character Child: 1910—on. Bisque head with good wig or solid dome head with painted hair, sleep or painted eyes, open or closed mouth, expressive character face; jointed composition body; dressed; all in good condition.
17—18in (43—46cm)   **$ 2000 up***

#*111, 128* (For photograph see *7th Blue Book*, page 173 and *8th Blue Book*, page 182.)

18—20in (45—51cm)   **16,000****

*Depending upon individual face.

**Not enough price samples to compute a reliable range.

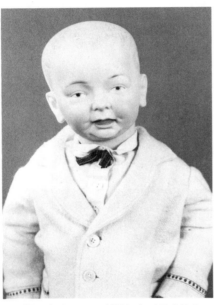

20in (51cm) character child incised "1." *Esther Schwartz Collection.*

Infant, unmarked or unidentified maker: 1924—on. Perfect bisque head with molded and painted hair, glass sleep eyes; cloth body, celluloid or composition hands; dressed; all in good condition.

10—12in (25—31cm) long **$325—375***

15—18in (38—46cm) long **525—625***

*More depending upon appeal and rarity of face.

Gesland

Maker: Heads: François Gaultier, Paris, France
Bodies: E., F. & A. Gesland, Paris, France
Date: Late 1860s—on
Material: Bisque head, stockinette stuffed body on wire frame, bisque or composition lower arms and legs
Mark: Head:

F. G   Body: Sometimes stamped E. Gesland

Fashion lady: Perfect bisque swivel head, good wig, paperweight eyes, closed mouth, pierced ears; stockinette body with bisque hands and legs; dressed; all in good condition.
Beautiful early face:
16—20in (41—51cm) **$3400—3800**
Typical F.G. face:
16—20in (41—51cm) **2800—3200**

Bébé: Perfect bisque swivel head; composition shoulder plate, good wig, paperweight eyes, closed mouth, pierced ears; stockinette body with composition lower arms and legs; dressed; all in good condition. (For photograph see *8th Blue Book*, page 183.)
16—18in (41—46cm) **$3800—4200***
21—24in (53—61cm) **4500—5000***
30—32in (76—81cm) **6000—6500***
*For beautiful early face.

17½in (45cm) Fashion lady with F.G. head. *Private Collection.*

Giebeler-Falk

Maker: Giebeler-Falk Doll Corporation, New York, N.Y., U.S.A.
Date: 1918—1921
Material: Aluminum head, sometimes aluminum hands and feet, wood or composition torso, arms and legs
Size: 16, 18, 20, 22 and 25in (41, 46, 51, 56 and 64cm)
Mark:

U. S. PAT.

Marked Giebeler-Falk Doll: Aluminum head with smiling face, open/closed mouth with painted upper teeth, metal sleeping eyes, chin dimple, mohair wig; jointed wood or composition body, sometimes with metal hands and feet with jointed ankles; appropriate clothing; all in good condition.
16—20in (41—51cm) **$325—425**

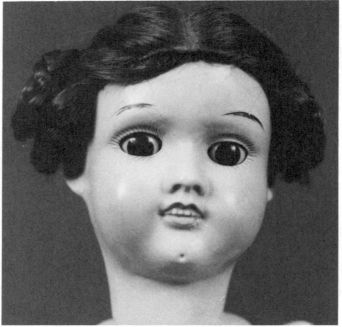

20in (51cm) Giebeler-Falk girl. *H&J Foulke, Inc.*

Gladdie

Maker: Heads made in Ohrdruf area, Germany for George Borgfeldt, New York, N.Y., U.S.A.
Date: 1929
Material: Ceramic or bisque head, cloth torso, composition arms and legs
Size: 16—23in (41—58cm)
Designer: Helen W. Jensen
Mark:
[sic] *Gladdie Copyright By Helen W. Jensen*

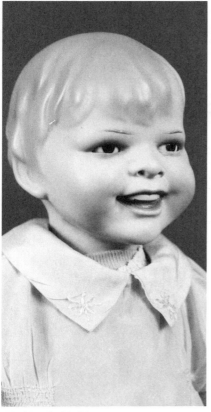

Marked Gladdie: Biscaloid or ceramic head, molded and painted hair, glass eyes, open/closed mouth with molded teeth, laughing face; cloth torso, composition arms and legs; dressed; all in good condition.
16—19in (41—48cm) **$ 850—950**
Bisque head, 13in (33cm) (For photograph see *8th Blue Book*, page 201.)
3200**
**Not enough price samples to compute a reliable range.

20in (51cm) *Gladdie* with ceramic head. *Esther Schwartz Collection.*

Godey's Little Lady Dolls

Maker: Ruth Gibbs, Flemington, N.J., U.S.A.
Date: 1946
Material: China head and limbs, cloth body
Size: Most 7in (18cm); a few 9, 10, 12 or 13in (23, 25, 31 or 33cm)
Designer: Herbert Johnson
Mark: Paper label inside skirt "Godey's Little Lady Dolls;" "R. G." incised on
   back plate.

Ruth Gibbs Doll: China head with painted black, brown, blonde or auburn
   hair and features; pink cloth body with china limbs and painted slippers
   which often matched the hair color; original clothes, usually in an old-
   fashioned style.

7in (18cm)	**$ 60—70**
12 or 13in (31 or 33cm) undressed	**150—160**

13in (33cm) doll with molded necklace. *H & J Foulke, Inc.*

Goebel

Maker: F. & W. Goebel porcelain factory, near Coburg, Thüringia, Germany. Made heads for Max Handwerck and others.

Date: 1879—on

Material: Bisque heads, composition bodies; also all-bisque

Mark: "B" + number; "Germany" sometimes A, C, G, H, K, S, SA & T

Goebel Child Doll: 1895—on. Perfect bisque socket head, good wig, sleep eyes, open mouth; composition jointed body; dressed; all in good condition. Some mold **#120.**

Mark:

120 5/0
Germany

4½—5in (12—13cm)	**$160—175**
14—16in (36-41cm)	**300—350**
21—24in (53—61cm)	**450—500**

Socket head, open/closed mouth with molded teeth, gusseted kid body, bisque hands. (For photograph see *8th Blue Book*, page 203.)

18—20in (46—51cm)	**650—750**

22in (56cm) 120 child. *Wayne & Kay Jensen Collection.*

Pincushion Half Doll: Ca. 1915. Perfect china half figure usually of a lady with molded hair and painted features, sometimes with molded clothing, hats or accessories; lovely modeling and painting. Most desirable have fancy clothing or hair ornamentation and extended arms. (For photograph see *7th Blue Book*, page 188.)

Mark:

2½in (6cm)	**$ 85—95**
4in (10cm)	**150 up***
Half-bisque child, 3½in (9cm)	**95—110**

*Depending upon rarity.

3½in (9cm) half-bisque child of type made by Goebel. *H & J Foulke, Inc.*

Goebel continued

Goebel Character Baby: Ca. 1910. Perfect bisque socket head, good wig, sleep eyes, open mouth with teeth; composition jointed baby body; dressed; all in good condition. (For photograph see *6th Blue Book*, page 171.)

14—16in (36—41cm)	**$ 400—450**
19—21in (48—53cm)	**500—600**
23in (58cm) baby with clockwork eyes, at auction	**1750**

Goebel Character Doll: Ca. 1910. Perfect bisque head with molded hair in various styles, some with hats, character face smiling or somber with painted features; papier-mâché five-piece body; all in excellent condition.
6½in (17cm)   **$250—300**

9in (23cm) character girl of type made by Goebel. *H & J Foulke, Inc.*

Googly-Eyed Dolls

Maker: J. D. Kestner, Armand Marseille, Hertel, Schwab & Co., Heubach, H. Steiner, Goebel and other German and French firms
Date: Ca. 1911—on
Material: Bisque heads and composition or papier-mâché bodies or all-bisque

---

All-Bisque Googly: Jointed at shoulders and hips, molded shoes and socks; mohair wig, glass eyes, impish mouth; undressed; in perfect condition.

4½in (12cm)	**$ 450**
6in (15cm)	**550**
Swivel neck,	
4½in (12cm)	**550**
6in (15cm)	**650**
Jointed elbows and knees (Kestner), swivel neck,	
5in (13cm)	**1800**
7in (18cm)	**2900**
Stiff neck, 5in (13cm)	**1400**
Painted eyes,	
4½in (12cm)	**350**
6in (15cm)	**475**
Baby, 4½in (12cm)	**400—425**
K&R 131, 10in (25cm) Soldier, all original, at auction	**6900**

For color photograph see page 164.

4½in (12cm) 189 all-bisque Kestner googly with glass eyes and swivel neck. *H & J Foulke, Inc.*

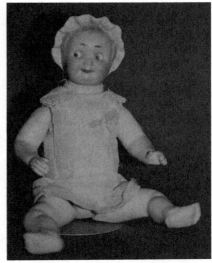

9½in (24cm) R.A. #44 googly with molded bonnet. *Courtesy of Mary Lu Trowbridge.*

Googly-Eyed Dolls continued

Painted eyes, composition body: Perfect bisque swivel head with molded hair, painted eyes to the side, impish mouth; five-piece composition toddler or baby body jointed at shoulders and hips, some with molded and painted shoes and socks; cute clothes; all in good condition.

A.M., E. Heubach, Goebel, R.A.

6—7in (15—18cm)	$350—375*
10in (25cm)	600—650*

Gebrüder Heubach

6—7in (15—18cm)	425—475*

*Allow extra for unusual models.

For photograph see page 199.

Glass eyes, composition body: Perfect bisque head, mohair wig or molded hair, sleep or set large googly eyes, impish mouth closed; original composition body jointed at neck, shoulders and hips, sometimes with molded and painted shoes and socks; cute clothes; all in nice condition.

JDK 221: See color photograph on page 164.

12—13in (31—33cm) Toddler	$3500—4000
17—18in (43—46cm) Toddler	5500

AM #323 and other similar models by H. Steiner, E. Heubach, Goebel and Recknagle:

6½—7in (17—18cm)	550—650
9—10in (23—25cm)	850—950
12—14in (31—36cm)	1500—1600
Baby body, 10—11in (25—28cm)	750—850

AM #253: Watermelon mouth: See color photograph on page 164.

6½—7½in (17—19cm)	650—700
9in (23cm)	950

SFBJ #245:

8in (20cm), five-piece body	1200
11in (28cm) jointed body	2500
15in (38cm)	4200—4600**

K ★ R 131:

8in (20cm), five-piece body	2200—2500**
15—16in (38—41cm)	6500—7500**

AM #240, 241, 200:

11—12in (28—31cm)	2400—2700

G. Heubach Einco:

14—15in (36—38cm)	6000—6500**
Elizabeth: 9in (23cm)	1000—1200

Oscar Hitt:

15in (38cm)	7000—7500**

Hertel, Schwab & Co. #165, 163:

11in (28cm) Toddler	3000
12in (31cm) Baby	3000

**Not enough price samples to compute a reliable range.

Googly-Eyed Dolls continued

Hertel, Schwab & Co. #172, 173: See color photograph on
page 165.

16—18in (44—46cm)	**5800—6500**

Demalcol (Dennis, Malley, & Co. London, England):

9—11in (23—28cm)	**550—650**

Kley & Hahn 180:

16½in (43cm)	**3100**

B.P. 686:

12—14in (31—36cm)	**1700—2200**

P.M. 950:

10½in (27cm) toddler	**2000****

**Not enough price samples to compute a reliable range.

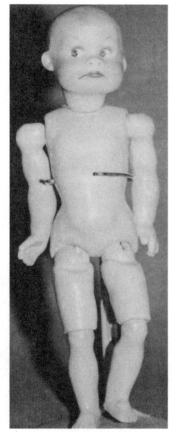

G. Heubach Einco googly. *Courtesy of Lesley Harford.*

8½in (22cm) G. Heubach 9566 googly. *Courtesy of Mary Lu Trowbridge.*

7½in (19cm) A.M. 323 googly. *H & J Foulke, Inc.*

Googly-Eyed Dolls continued

Composition face: 1911—1914. Made by various companies in 9½—14in (24—36cm) sizes; marked with paper label on clothing. Called "Hug Me Kiddies," "Little Bright Eyes," as well as other trade names. Round all-composition or composition mask face, wig, round glass eyes looking to the side, watermelon mouth; felt body; original clothes; all in very good condition.
12—14in (31—36cm)   **$750—850**

14in (36cm) composition head googly. *Esther Schwartz Collection.*

Googly with molded hat: 1915. Perfect bisque head with glass side-glancing eyes, watermelon mouth, molded hat; jointed composition body. Made for Max Handwerck, possibly by Hertel, Schwab & Co. All were soldiers: "U.S." (Uncle Sam hat); "E," (English Bellhop-type hat); "D," (German); "T," (Austrian/Turk - two faces).

Mark: "Dep
Elite"
12—13in (31—33cm)   **$2000—2500**

10½in (27cm) double-faced googly with molded hat, Austrian and Turk. *Esther Schwartz Collection.*

Greiner

Maker: Ludwig Greiner of Philadelphia, Pa., U.S.A.
Date: 1858—1883
Material: Heads of papier-mâché, cloth bodies, homemade in most cases, but later some Lacmann bodies were used.
Size: Various, 13—over 35in (33—over 89cm)
Mark: Paper label on back shoulder:

GREINER'S IMPROVED PATENTHEADS Pat.March 30тн'58	or	GREINER'S PATENT DOLL HEADS No7 Pat. Mar. 30'58. Ext.'72

Greiner: Blonde or black molded hair, painted features; homemade cloth body, leather arms; nice old clothes; entire doll in good condition.

'58 label: (For photograph see page 8.)

| 20—23in (51—58cm) | $ 900—1200 |
| 28—30in (71—76cm) | 1500—1700 |

Much worn:

| 20—23in (51—58cm) | 550—650 |
| 28—30in (71—76cm) | 800—900 |

Glass eyes,

| 20—23in (51—58cm) | 1700—1900** |

'72 label:

| 19—22in (48—56cm) | 475—525 |
| 29—31in (71—79cm) | 750—850 |

**Not enough price samples to compute a reliable range.

24in (61cm) Greiner with '72 label. *Kay & Wayne Jensen Collection.*

28in (71cm) Greiner with '72 label. *H & J Foulke, Inc.*

Hamburger & Co.

Maker: Hamburger & Co., New York, N.Y., U.S.A. doll importer and producer contracted with various German doll factories.

Date: 1889—1909

Material: Bisque head, jointed composition body

Hamburger Viola: 1903. Perfect bisque socket head, original or appropriate wig, sleep or set eyes, open mouth; ball-jointed composition body; dressed; entire doll in good condition. (For photograph see *8th Blue Book*, page 211.)

Mark:

Made in
Germany
Viola
H. 6 Co.

23—25in (58—64cm) **$450—500**

Other Hamburger Trademarks:

Santa 1900. Made by Simon & Halbig. (See page 361.)

Dolly Dimple 1907. Made by Gebrüder Heubach. (See page 230.)

18in (46cm) *Santa*, S&H 1249 made for Hamburger & Co. by Simon & Halbig. *Carole Stoessel Zovanar Collection.*

Heinrich Handwerck

Maker: Heinrich Handwerck, doll factory, Waltershausen, Thüringia, Germany. Heads by Simon & Halbig.
Date: 1855—on
Material: Bisque head, composition ball-jointed body or kid body
Trademarks: Bébé Cosmopolite, Bébé de Réclame, Bébé Superior
Mark: "Germany—Handwerck" sometimes with "S & H" and numbers *69, 79, 89, 99, 109, 119* and others

Hch 6/0 H.
HANDWERCK— *Germany*

Marked Handwerck Child Doll: Ca. 1885—on. Perfect bisque socket head, original or good wig, sleep or set eyes, open mouth, pierced ears; ball-jointed body; dressed; entire doll in good condition.

No mold number:

14—16in (36—41cm)	$ 375—400
19—21in (43—53cm)	450—475
23—25in (58—64cm)	525—625
28—30in (71—76cm)	850—950
33—35in (84—89cm)	1200—1500
42in (107cm)	2500—2700

Shoulder head, kid body

19—21in (48—53cm)	350—375

#69, 79, 89, 99, 109, 119:

14—16in (36—41cm)	425—475
19—21in (43—53cm)	550—600
23—25in (58—64cm)	650—750
28—30in (71—76cm)	1000—1100
33—35in (84—89cm)	1500—1800
42in (107cm)	2900—3200

#79, 89 closed mouth:

12in (31cm)	1250
18—20in (46—51cm)	1700—2000
24in (61cm)	2400

22in (56cm) Handwerck 69 child. *H & J Foulke, Inc.*

20in (51cm) Handwerck 119 child, all original. *H & J Foulke, Inc.*

Max Handwerck

Maker: Max Handwerck, doll factory, Waltershausen, Thüringia, Germany. Some heads by Goebel.

Date: 1900—on

Material: Bisque head, ball-jointed composition or kid body

Trademarks: Bébé Elite, Triumph-Bébé

Mark: also "Bébé Elite"

Max
HANDWERCK
Germany

Max Handwerck
Bebe Elite
B 90/785
6
germany

2 83/60
30.5

MAX HANDWERCK.
Germany

24in (61cm) 283 Max Handwerck child. *H & J Foulke, Inc.*

Marked Max Handwerck Child Doll: Perfect bisque socket head, original or good wig, set or sleep eyes, open mouth, pierced ears; original ball-jointed body; well dressed; all in good condition. Some mold #283.

16—18in (41—46cm)	$ 375—425
19—21in (48—53cm)	450—475
25—26in (64—66cm)	650—750
30—31in (76—79cm)	900—950
38in (97cm)	1900

Marked Bébé Elite Character: Perfect bisque socket head with sleep eyes, open mouth with upper teeth, smiling character face; bent-limb composition baby body; appropriate clothes; all in good condition. (For photograph see *6th Blue Book*, page 171.)

14—16in (36—41cm)	$400—450
19—21in (48—53cm)	500—600
25in (64cm)	750—800

Carl Hartmann

Maker: Carl Hartmann, Neustad, Thüringia; Stockheim, Bavaria, Germany
Date: 1899 trademark
Material: Bisque head, composition body
Size: Various
Mark: Globe Baby
     DEP
     Germany
     C : H

Marked Globe Baby: Perfect bisque head, mohair or human hair wig, sleep eyes, open mouth with upper teeth; good quality five-piece composition body with molded shoes and socks; dressed; all in very good condition.
8in (20cm) **$250—300**

8in (20cm) *Globe Baby*.
H & J Foulke, Inc.

Karl Hartmann

Maker: Karl Hartmann, doll factory, Stockheim/Upper Franconia, Germany
Date: 1911—1926
Material: Bisque head, jointed composition body
Mark:

Marked Karl Hartmann Doll: Perfect bisque head, good wig, glass eyes, open mouth; jointed composition body; suitable clothing; all in good condition.

22—24in (56—61cm)   **$550—650**
28—30in (71—76cm)   **850—950**

30in (76cm) Karl Hartmann child. *H & J Foulke, Inc.*

19in (48cm) French ***Bébé Mascotte***. For further information see page 306. *Private Collection.*

23in (58cm) French bébé incised "B 9 M," by Alexandre Mothereau. For further information see page 313. *Private Collection.*

12in (31cm) Japanese warriors, ca. 1920. For further information see page 318. *Betty Lunz Collection.*

18½in (47cm) early German papier-mâché head, kid body. This type of head known as *kinderkopfe* was used for both males and children. For further information see page 322. *Private Collection.*

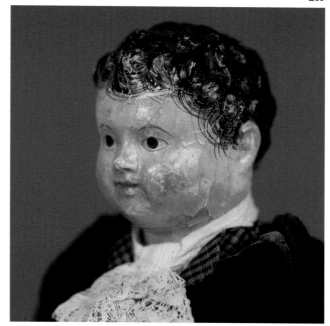

35in (89cm) early German papier-mâché head with glass flirty eyes. For further information see page 322. *Richard Wright Antiques.*

23in (58cm) French bébé incised "P 11 G" by Pintel & Godchaux. For further information see page 332. *Private Collection.*

13in (33cm) *Raggedy Ann & Andy* by Georgene Novelties with awake and asleep faces, all original. For further information see page 336. *Jan Foulke Collection.*

10in (25cm) German Character baby with molded cap by Recknagel, mold #28. For further information see page 340. *H & J Foulke, Inc.*

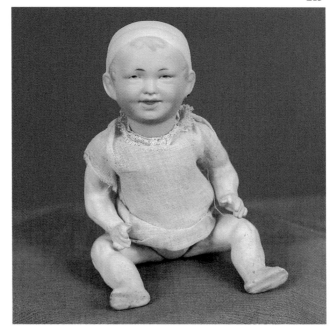

20½in (52cm) character boy by S.F.B.J., mold #233. For further information see page 344. *Private Collection.*

20½in (52cm) character boy by S.F.B.J., mold #237. For further information see page 344. *Private Collection.*

23½in (60cm) French bébé, size 4.5 by Schmitt. For further information see page 349. *Private Collection.*

23in (58cm) character baby by Franz Schmidt, mold #1272. For further information see page 348. *H & J Foulke, Inc.*

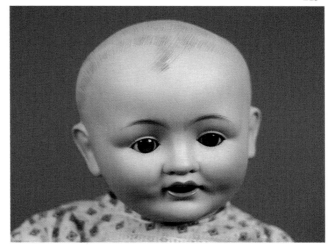

11in (28cm) character child made for Bruno Schmidt by Bähr & Pröschild, mold #537 (so-called **Wendy**). For further information see page 347. *Private Collection.*

216

16in (41cm) Schoenhut boy #205 with carved hair. For further information see page 352. *Yvonne Baird Collection.*

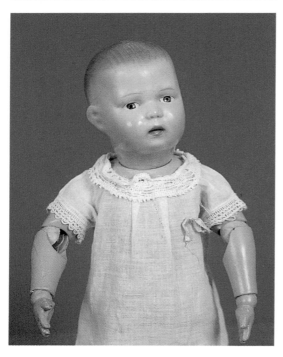

14in (36cm) Schoenhut toddler with baby face and molded hair, #107, original shift. For further information see page 354. *Private Collection.*

16in (41cm) Simon & Halbig child, mold 969, with slightly open mouth and four upper square cut teeth. For further information see page 361. *Ruth Noden Collection.*

16in (41cm) 1911 Schoenhut girl #100 with carved hair. For further information see page 352. *Nancy Smith Collection.*

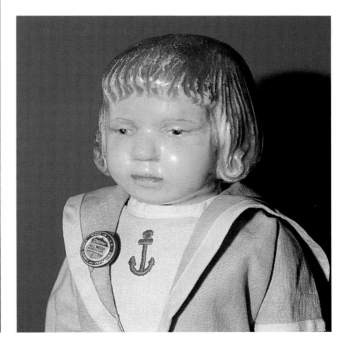

ABOVE: 14in (36cm) Simon & Halbig mold #1468 flapper lady. For further information see page 366. *Gladyse Hills Hilsdorf Collection.*

19in (48cm) character baby mold #1498 Simon & Halbig. For further information see page 366. *Richard Wright Antiques.*

25in (64cm) Simon & Halbig mold #1159 lady, all original. For further information see page 366. *Private Collection.*

22in (56cm) Simon & Halbig character child mold #151. For further information see page 364. *Billie Nelson Tyrrell.*

13in (33cm) French bébé by Jules Steiner, Figure A, size 5, all original. For further information see page 375. *Kay & Wayne Jensen Collection.*

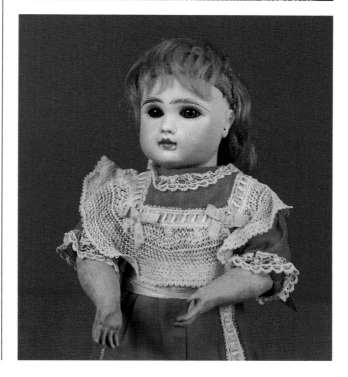

18½in (47cm) doll by Jules Steiner with bisque shoulders, hips, lower arms and lower legs. For further information see page 374. *Kay & Wayne Jensen Collection.*

8in (20cm) *Ginny* by Vogue, 1952 model with "poodle cut." For further information see page 380. *Kay & Wayne Jensen Collection.*

RIGHT: 16in (41cm) lady with wax head and arms with molded gloves, all original. For further information see page 385. *Private Collection.*

24in (61cm) English wooden doll of the Queen Anne period, early 1700s, cloth upper arms, glass eyes. For further information see page 392. *Private Collection.*

21in (53cm) English wooden doll of the Georgian period, ca. 1740, all-wood, all original. For further information see page 392. *Private Collection.*

RIGHT: 17in (43cm) English wooden doll of the William & Mary period, ca. 1690, pegged wood body, cloth upper arms, wood lower arms with fork hands. For further information see page 392. *Private Collection.*

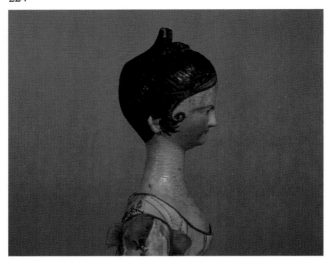

26in (66cm) German wooden doll with yellow tuck comb, fully articulated with ball and socket joints, ca. 1810. For further information see page 393. *Private Collection.*

Hertel, Schwab & Co.

Maker: Stutzhauser Porzellanfabrik, Hertel Schwab & Co., Stutzhaus, near Ohrdruf, Thüringia, Germany

Date: 1910 on

Material: Bisque heads to be used on composition, cloth or leather bodies, all-bisque dolls, pincushion dolls

Mark:

Made in Germany 15 1/2   152 4   Made in Germany 136/10

Marked Character Baby: Perfect bisque head, molded and painted hair or good wig, sleep or painted eyes, open or open/closed mouth with molded tongue; bent limb baby body; dressed; all in good condition.

#130, 142, 150, 151, 152:

11—12in (28—31cm)	**$400—425**
16—18in (41—46cm)	**525—575**
22—24in (56—61cm)	**750—850**
25in (64cm)	**950**
Toddler,	
21in (53cm)	**800**

#125 (so-called "Patsy Baby"):
11—12in (28—31cm)   **600—800**

#126 (so-called "Skippy"):
10in (25cm)   **700—900****

#127 (so-called "Patsy"):
16in (41cm)   **700—900****

**Not enough price samples to compute a reliable range.

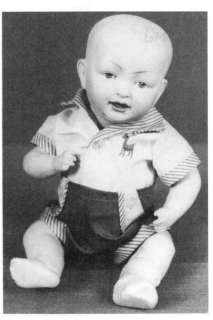

11½in (29cm) 142 character baby. *H & J Foulke, Inc.*

20½in (52cm) 152 character baby. *H & J Foulke, Inc.*

Hertel, Schwab & Co. continued

Child Doll: Ca. 1910. Perfect bisque head, mohair or human hair wig, sleep eyes, open mouth with upper teeth; good quality jointed composition body (some marked K & W); dressed; all in good condition. Mold # *136*. (For photograph see *8th Blue Book*, page 79.)

16—18in (41—46cm)	**$425—475**
22—24in (56—61cm)	**525—625**

149 character child. *Jackie Kaner.*

Marked Character Child: Perfect bisque head, painted or sleeping eyes, closed mouth; jointed composition body; dressed; all in good condition.

#134, 149, 141:
16—18in (41—46cm)	**$4700—5200**

#154 (closed mouth):
16—17in (41—43cm) jointed body	**2100—2300**

#154 (open mouth):
20in (51cm) toddler	**1250—1350**

#169 (closed mouth):
13in (33cm)	**1800—2000**
19—21in (48—53cm) toddler	**3200—3500**

All-Bisque Doll: Jointed shoulders and hips; good wig, glass eyes, closed or open mouth; molded and painted shoes and stockings; undressed; all in good condition. Mold ***#208***.

4—5in (10—13cm)	**$225—250**
7in (18cm)	**350—375**
8in (20cm)	**475—525**
Swivel neck, 6in (15cm)	**400—450**

Hertel, Schwab & Co. continued

Marked Googly: Perfect bisque head, large glass side-glancing sleeping eyes, wig or molded hair, impish closed mouth; composition body; cute clothes; all in good condition.

#163, 165:
  12in (31cm)
    baby   **$3000**
  11in (28cm)
    toddler   **3000**
#172, 173: (See color
  photographs on page 165.)
    15—16in (38—41cm) **5800—6500****

**Not enough price samples to compute a reliable range.

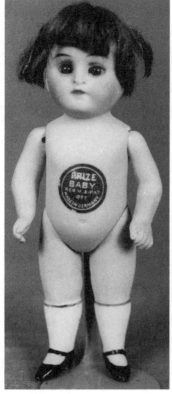

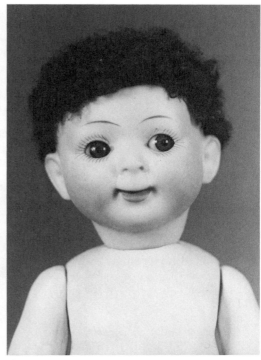

5¾in (15cm) 208 all-bisque girl. *H & J Foulke, Inc.*

9½in (24cm) 165 googly. *Richard Wright Antiques.*

Ernst Heubach

Maker: Ernst Heubach, porcelain factory, Köppelsdorf, Thüringia, Germany
Date: 1887—on
Material: Bisque head; kid, cloth or composition bodies
Mark:

D.E.P. 1902 Heubach · Kopplesdorf.
300·14/0
Germany
— 2/0

Heubach Child Doll: Ca. 1888—on. Perfect bisque head, good wig, sleep eyes, open mouth; kid, cloth or jointed composition body; dressed; all in good condition.

#275, kid or cloth body:
12—13in (31—33cm)	$160—175
16—18in (41—46cm)	225—265
21—23in (53—58cm)	325—375

#250, composition body:
8—9in (20—23cm)	165—185
13—15in (33—38cm)	235—285
18—20in (46—51cm)	350—400
23—24in (58—61cm)	425—475
28in (71cm)	550—575

Painted bisque, **#250**,
7—8in (18—20cm)	95—110

#312 SUR,
28in (71cm)	650

23in (58cm) 275 shoulder head child. *H & J Foulke, Inc.*

Character Baby: 1910—on. Perfect bisque head, good wig, sleep eyes, open mouth (sometimes also wobbly tongue and pierced nostrils); composition bent-limb baby or toddler body; dressed; all in good condition.

#300, 320, 342 and others:
6in (15cm)	$250
8—10in (20—25cm)	250—300
13—15in (33—38cm)	375—425
19—21in (48—53cm)	500—550
24—25in (61—64cm)	750—850

#320, jointed composition body,
17in (43cm)	450
28in (71cm)	750—800

Toddler:
9in (23cm)	
five-piece body:	300—350
13—14in (33—36cm)	475—525
23—25in (58—64cm)	800—900

17in (43cm) 320 character child. *H & J Foulke, Inc.*

Ernst Heubach continued

Character Children: 1910—on. Perfect bisque shoulder head with molded hair in various styles, some with hair bows, painted eyes, open/closed mouth; cloth body with composition lower arms. (For photograph see *8th Blue Book*, page 221.)

#262 and others,
   12in (31cm) **$375—425****

Infant: Ca. 1925. Perfect bisque head, molded and painted hair, sleep eyes, closed mouth; cloth body, composition or celluloid hands, appropriate clothes; all in good condition.

#349, 339, 350: 10—12in (25—31cm)   **$475—575****
#338, 340: 14—16in (36—41cm)   **700—800****

Googly: Perfect bisque character head, molded hair, painted eyes, impish mouth; five-piece composition body; dressed; all in good condition. Mold *#260, 261, 263, 264*.

6—8in (15—20cm)   **$350—450**

**Not enough price samples to compute a reliable range.

10½in (27cm) E. Heubach 349 infant. *Jimmy & Faye Rodolfos Collection.*

8in (20cm) E. Heubach googly. *H & J Foulke, Inc.*

Gebrüder Heubach

Maker: Gebrüder Heubach, porcelain factory, Licht and Sonneberg, Thüringia, Germany

Date: 1820—on; doll heads 1910—on

Material: Bisque head, kid, cloth or jointed composition body or composition bent-limb body, all bisque

Mark:

Heubach Character Child: Ca. 1910. Perfect bisque head, molded hair, glass or intaglio eyes, closed or open/closed mouth, character face; jointed composition or kid body; dressed; all in good condition. (For photographs of Heubach dolls see *Focusing On Dolls*, pages 30-68.)

#5636 laughing child, glass eyes,	
13—15in (33—38cm)	**$1500—1800**
#5689 smiling child (For photograph see *6th Blue Book*,	
page 197), 28—29in (71—74cm)	**3000—4000**
#5730 Santa, JCB, 32—34in (81—87cm)	**3200—3500**
#5777 Dolly Dimple, JCB, 19in (48cm)	**2200—2400**
#6969, 6970, 7246, 7347, 7407, 8017, 8420, pouty child,	
glass eyes, JCB: (See color photograph on page 167.)	
12—13in (31—33cm)	**2000—2300**
18—20in (46—51cm)	**2800—3000**
27in (69cm)	**4500—4700**
#7684 Screamer, 12in (31cm)	**800**
#7622 and other socket head pouties, intaglio eyes,	
17—19in (43—48cm)	**900—1100**
#7679 Whistler socket head, 14in (36cm)	**1000—1100**
#7665, Smiling, 16in (41cm)	**1600**
#7788 Coquette, JCB, 14in (36cm)	**950**
#7852 molded coiled braids shoulder head,	
19in (48cm)	**2400**
#8035, 17in (43cm) at auction	**4100**
#7911, 8191 grinning, JCB, 15in (38cm)	**900—1000**
#7925, 7926 (See color photograph on page 167.)	**2500****
#8192, JCB:	
14—16in (36—41cm)	**600—650**
18—22in (46—56cm)	**900—1000**
#7602 and other socket head pouties, JCB	
14—16in (36—41cm)	**550—700**

**Not enough price samples to compute a reliable range.

Gebrüder Heubach continued

Shoulder heads, pouty or smiling, intaglio eyes,

14—16in (36—41cm)	**425—500**
26in (64cm)	**800—850**
#10532, 20—22in (51—56cm)	**1100—1300**
#10586, 10633, JCB, 18—20in (46—51cm)	**600—700**
#11173 Tiss Me, 8in (20cm)	
(For photograph see *8th Blue Book*, page 224.)	**1400—1600****
Baby Bo Kaye, 6½in (17cm)	**800**
Cat head, composition body, 7in (18cm)	**800****

**Not enough price samples to compute a reliable range.

8in (20cm) square mark, open/closed mouth with molded tongue. *H & J Foulke, Inc.*

6½in (17cm) **Baby Bo Kaye** #1(3 or 5)060, all original. *H & J Foulke, Inc.*

Baby with molded pink hair bow, mold #7764. *Richard Wright Collection.*

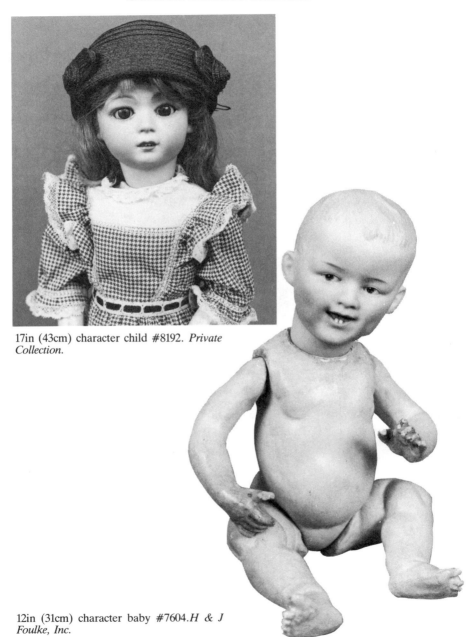

17in (43cm) character child #8192. *Private Collection.*

12in (31cm) character baby #7604.*H & J Foulke, Inc.*

All-Bisque: (For photographs see *Focusing On Dolls*, pages 71—77.)

Position Babies,	
5in (13cm)	**$325—375**
Boy or Girl with bows or hair band:	
7—8in (18—20cm)	**750—850**
9in (23cm)	**950**
Bunny Boy or Girl,	
5½in (14cm)	**275—300**
All-bisque boy or girl,	
4in (10cm)	**250—275**
5—6in (13—15cm)	**400—500**
Chin-Chin character,	
4in (10cm)	**225—250**
Action figures:	
6in (15cm)	**275—325**
4in (10cm)	**150—175**

See color photograph on page 167.

18½in (47cm) shoulder head lady, usually mold #7925 or #7926. See color photograph on page 167. *Private Collection.*

Heubach Babies: Ca. 1910. Perfect bisque head, molded hair, intaglio eyes, open or closed mouth, character face; composition bent-limb body; dressed; all in nice condition.

#6894, 7602, 6898, 7759

and other pouty babies:

6in (15cm)	**$225—250**
10in (25cm)	**375—400**
14in (36cm)	**500—525**
18in (46cm)	**700—750**
#7604 laughing,	
13—14in (33—36cm)	**550—650**
#7764 molded hair bow,	
13in (33cm)	**1500**
#7877, 7977 Baby Stuart,	
10in (25cm)	**1000—1100**

Horsman

Maker: E. I. Horsman Co., New York, N.Y., U.S.A. Also distributed dolls as a *verleger* for other manufacturers and imported French and German dolls.
Date: 1878—on

Billiken: 1909. Composition head with peak of hair at top of head, slanted slits for eyes, watermelon mouth; velvet or plush body; in very good condition.
Mark: Cloth label on body; "Billiken" on right foot
12in (31cm) **$300—350**

Baby Bumps: 1910. Composition head with molded hair and painted features; stuffed cloth body. Good condition with some wear. (For photograph see *8th Blue Book*, page 226.)
Mark: None
12—14in (31—36cm)   **$165—185**
Black   **250**

11in (28cm) *Peterkin*, all original and boxed. *Lesley Hurford Collection.*

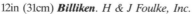

12in (31cm) *Billiken. H & J Foulke, Inc.*

Horsman continued

Can't Break 'Em Characters: Ca. 1910. Heads and hands of "Can't Break 'Em" composition, hard stuffed cloth bodies with swivel joints at shoulders and hips; molded hair, painted eyes, character faces; appropriate clothes; all in good condition. (For photograph see *8th Blue Book*, page 226.)
Mark: "E.I.H.1911"
10—12in (25—31cm) **$125—150**

Peterkin: 1914—1930. All-composition with character face, molded hair, painted eyes to side, watermelon mouth; various boy and girl clothing or simply a large bow; all in good condition.
11in (28cm) **$200—300****

**Not enough price samples to compute a reliable range.

Gene Carr Character: 1916. Composition head with molded and painted hair, eyes painted open or closed, wide smiling mouth with teeth; cloth body with composition hands; original or appropriate clothes; all in good condition. Names such as: *"Snowball"* (Black Boy); *"Mike"* and *"Jane"* (eyes open); *"Blink"* and *"Skinney"* (eyes closed). Designed by Bernard Lipfert from Gene Carr's cartoon characters. (For photograph see *7th Blue Book*, page 210.)
Mark: None
13—14in (33—36cm)   **$250—300**
Black *Snowball*   **550**

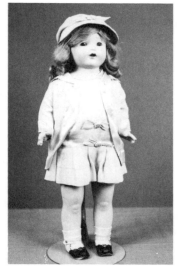

24in (61cm) girl-type "Mama" doll, all original. *H & J Foulke, Inc.*

14in (36cm) "Mama" doll baby, all original. *H & J Foulke, Inc.*

Mama Dolls: Ca. 1920—on. Composition head, cloth body, composition arms and lower legs; mohair wig or molded hair, sleep eyes; original clothes; all in very good condition.

Mark: "E. I. H. Co." or "HORSMAN"

Babies:

12—14in (31—36cm)	**$125—150**
18—20in (46—51cm)	**175—200**

Girls:

14—16in (36—41cm)	**150—175**
22—24in (56—61cm)	**225—275**

See page 235 for photographs.

Jackie Coogan: 1921. Composition head with molded hair, painted eyes, closed mouth; cloth torso with composition hands; appropriate clothes; all in good condition. (For photograph see *8th Blue Book*, page 228.)

Mark: "E. I. H. Co. 19 © 21"

14in (36cm) **$450—500**

Marked Tynie Baby: 1924. Solid dome infant head with sleep eyes, closed mouth, slightly frowning face; cloth body with composition arms; appropriate clothes; all in good condition. Designed by Bernard Lipfert.

Mark: © 1924
E.I. Horsman Inc.
Made in
Germany

Bisque head,

12in (31cm) h.c. **$ 650**

Composition head,

15in (38cm) long **250—275**

All-bisque with swivel neck, glass eyes, wigged or solid dome head,

(For photograph see *8th Blue Book*, page 228.)

9—10in (23—25cm) **1500**

HEbee-SHEbee: 1925. All-composition, jointed at shoulders and hips, painted eyes, molded white chemise and real ribbon or wool ties in molded shoes; all in good condition. Blue shoes indicate a *HEbee*, pink ones a *SHEbee*. (For photograph see *7th Blue Book*, page 212.)

11in (28cm) **$450—500**

Fair condition

(some peeling) **275**

Ella Cinders: 1925. Composition head with molded hair, painted eyes; cloth body with composition arms and lower legs; original clothes; all in fair condition. From the comic strip by Bill Conselman and Charlie Plumb, for the Metropolitan Newspaper Service. (For photograph see *8th Blue Book*, page 229.)

Mark: "1925 © MNS"

18in (46cm) **$500—550**

Baby Dimples: 1928. Composition head with molded and painted hair, tin sleep eyes, open mouth, smiling face; soft cloth body with composition arms and legs; original or appropriate old clothes; all in good condition.

Mark: " ©

E. I. H. CO. INC."

16—18in (41—46cm)	**$185—210**
22—24in (56—61cm)	**250—275**

Child Dolls: Ca. 1930s and 1940s. All-composition with swivel neck, shoulders and hips; mohair wig, sleep eyes; original clothes; all in good condition. (For photograph see *8th Blue Book*, page 229.)

Mark: "HORSMAN"

13—14in (33—36cm)	**$135—165**
16—18in (41—46cm)	**185—210**
Chubby Toddler,	
16—18in (41—46cm)	**185—210**

15in (38cm) composition *Tynie Baby*. H & J Foulke, Inc.

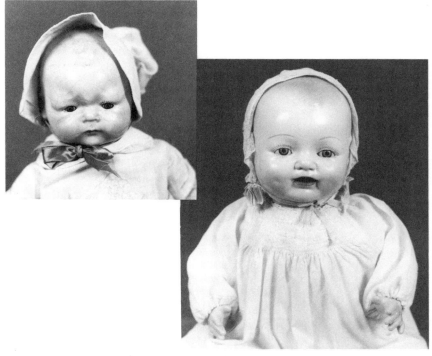

18in (46cm) *Baby Dimples*. H & J Foulke, Inc.

House of Puzzy

Maker: Herman Colin, House of Puzzy, Baltimore, Md., U.S.A.
Date: 1948
Material: All-composition
Size: 15in (38cm)
Mark: Puzzy ©
H. of P. U.S.A.

Marked Puzzy: All-composition jointed at neck, shoulders and hips with character face having molded red hair, very large black eyes and very bulgy cheeks; clothes; all in good condition. (For photograph see *5th Blue Book*, page 248.)
15in (38cm)   **$250—300****

Marked Sizzy: All-composition jointed at neck, shoulders and hips with character face having molded blonde hair with topknot, blue painted eyes, and watermelon mouth; original clothes; all in good condition.
14in (36cm)   **$175—225****

**Not enough price samples to compute a reliable range.

14in (36cm) *Sizzy*, replaced clothes. *Miriam Blankman Collection.*

Mary Hoyer

Maker: The Mary Hoyer Doll Mfg. Co., Reading, Pa., U.S.A.
Date: Ca. 1925—on
Material: First all-composition, later all-hard plastic
Size: 14 and 18in (36 and 46cm)
Mark: Embossed on torso:

"The
Mary Hoyer
Doll"

or in a circle:

"ORIGINAL
Mary Hoyer
Doll"

Marked Mary Hoyer: Material as above; swivel neck; jointed shoulders and hips, original wig, sleep eyes with eyelashes, closed mouth; all in excellent condition. Original tagged factory clothes or garments made at home from Mary Hoyer patterns.

Composition, 14in (36cm)	**$300—350**
Hard plastic, 14in (36cm)	**375—425**

14in (36cm) Mary Hoyer doll, all original.
H & J Foulke, Inc.

Huret

Maker: Maison Huret, Paris, France
Date: 1850—on
Material: China or bisque heads; kid or wood jointed bodies, sometimes with pewter hands and feet
Mark: "Huret" or "Maison Huret" stamped on body

Marked Huret Doll: China or bisque shoulder head, good wig, painted or glass eyes, closed mouth; kid body; beautifully dressed; all in good condition.

16—19in (41—48cm)	**$ 5000 up**
Wood body, 16—19in (41—48cm)	**8000 up**
Gutta-percha body, 16—19in (41—48cm)	**10,000 up**
Child, 18in (46cm), wood jointed body, at auction	**17,500**
Marked Huret shoes	**1000**

17in (43cm) French fashion lady, swivel neck, jointed wood body. See color photograph on page 168. *Private Collection.*

Ideal

Maker: Ideal Novelty and Toy Co., Brooklyn, N.Y., U.S.A.
Date: 1907—on

Uneeda Kid: 1914—1919. Composition head with molded brown hair, blue painted eyes, closed mouth; cloth body with composition arms and legs with molded black boots; original bloomer suit, yellow slicker and rain hat; carrying a box of Uneeda Biscuits; all in good condition, showing some wear.
16in (41cm) **$350—400**

Snoozie: 1933. Composition head, character expression with yawning mouth, sleeping eyes, molded hair, composition arms and legs or rubber arms, cloth body; baby clothes; all in good condition. 13, 16 and 20in (33, 41 and 51cm). (For photograph see *7th Blue Book*, page 216.)
Mark: ©
　　　By B. LIPFERT
16—20in (41—51cm) **$165—185**

Shirley Temple: 1935. For detailed information see pages 357 to 359.

Mama Doll: Ca. 1920—on. Composition head, cloth body, composition arms and lower legs; mohair wig or molded hair, sleep eyes; appropriate old clothes; all in very good condition. (For photograph see *8th Blue Book*, page 233.)
Mark:

14—16in (36—41cm) **$135—165**

16in (41cm) *Uneeda Kid*, all original. *H & J Foulke, Inc.*

Flossie Flirt,
20in (51cm)   **225—250**

Betsy Wetsy: 1937—on. Composition head with molded hair, sleep eyes; soft rubber body jointed at neck, shoulders and hips; drinks, wets; appropriate clothes; all in good condition. This doll went through many changes including hard plastic head on rubber body, later vinyl body, later completely vinyl. Various sizes.
Mark: "IDEAL"
14—16in (36—41cm) rubber body   **$90—110**

Snow White: 1937. All-composition, jointed at neck, shoulders and hips; black mohair wig, lashed sleep eyes, open mouth; original dress with velvet bodice and cape, and rayon skirt with figures of seven dwarfs; in good condition. 11in (28cm), 13in (33cm) and 18in (46cm) sizes. (For photograph see *Doll Classics*, page 190.)
Mark: On body:
"SHIRLEY TEMPLE/18"
On dress: "An Ideal Doll"
11—13in (28—33cm)   **$425—450**
18in (46cm)   **425—475**
Molded black hair, painted blue box, painted eyes,
13—14in (33—36cm)   **150—175**

Betty Jane: 1943. All-composition ***Shirley Temple***-type doll with jointed neck, shoulders and hips; lashed sleeping eyes (sometimes flirty), open mouth with teeth; all original; very good condition. (For photograph see *7th Blue Book*, page 217.)
Mark: IDEAL
18
18in (46cm) **$225—250**

Flirty-eyed Baby: 1938. Composition head, lower arms and legs, cloth body; flirty eyes, closed mouth, molded hair; original clothing; all in good condition. (For photograph see *8th Blue Book*, page 234.)
Mark: "IDEAL DOLL"
16—18in (41—46cm) **$160—185**

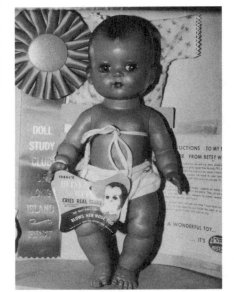

Black ***Betsy Wetsy***, hard plastic head, all original. *Courtesy of Carolyn Tracz.*

Deanna Durbin: 1938. All-composition, jointed at neck, shoulders and hips; original human hair or mohair wig, sleep eyes, smiling mouth with teeth; original clothing; all in good condition. Various sizes.

Mark: Metal button with picture: "DEANNA DURBIN, IDEAL DOLL, U.S.A."

14in (36cm)	$350—400
20—21in (51—53cm)	525—575
24—25in (61—64cm)	650—700

Judy Garland as Dorothy of the Wizard of Oz: 1939. All-composition, jointed at neck, shoulders and hips; dark human hair wig, dark sleep eyes, open mouth with teeth; original dress; all in good condition. See color photograph on page 168.

Mark: On head and body: "IDEAL DOLL"

16in (41cm) **$1000 up**

21in (53cm) ***Deanna Durbin***, all original with pin. *H & J Foulke, Inc.*

Ideal continued

Flexy Dolls: 1938—on. Head, hands and feet of composition; arms and legs of flexible metal cable, torso of wire mesh; in original clothes; all in good condition.

Mark: On head: "Ideal Doll"

12in (31cm)

Baby Snooks (Fanny Brice)	**$225—250**
Mortimer Snerd	**225—250**
Soldier	**150—200**
Children	**150—200**

Composition and wood segmented characters: 1940. Molded composition heads with painted features, wood segmented bodies. Label on front torso gives name of character.

Pinocchio, 10½in (27cm)	**$225—250**
King-Little, 14in (36cm)	**200—225**
Jiminy Cricket, 9in (23cm)	**200—225**

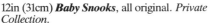

12in (31cm) ***Baby Snooks***, all original. *Private Collection.*

10½in (27cm) ***Pinocchio***. *H & J Foulke, Inc.*

Ideal continued

Toni and P-90 and P-91 Family: 1948—on. Series of girl dolls. Most were completely of hard plastic with jointed neck, shoulders and hips, nylon wig, sleep eyes, closed mouth; original clothes; all in excellent condition. Various sizes, but most are 14in (36cm).

14in (36cm) ***Miss Curity***, all original. *Esther Schwartz Collection.*

Mark: On head: "IDEAL DOLL"
On body: "IDEAL DOLL
P-90
Made in USA"

Toni,
14—15in (36—38cm)	**$150—175**
21in (53cm)	**275—325**

Mary Hartline,
14in (36cm)	**175—200**
22in (56cm)	**275—325**

Betsy McCall, vinyl head,
14in (36cm)	**150—175**

Harriet Hubbard Ayer,
vinyl head,
14in (36cm)	**150—175**

Miss Curity,
14in (36cm)	**175—200**

Sara Ann,
14in (36cm)	**175—200**

Saralee: 1950. Black vinyl head, painted hair, sleep eyes, open/closed mouth; cloth body, vinyl limbs; original clothes; all in excellent condition. Designed by Sarah Lee Creech; modeled by Sheila Burlingame.
17—18in (43—46cm)	**$250**
Undressed	**100**

See photograph on page 246.

14in (36cm) ***Toni***, all original. *H & J Foulke, Inc.*

LEFT: 14in (36cm) ***Harriet Hubbard Ayer***, all original. *H & J Foulke, Inc.*

Ideal continued

Saucy Walker: 1951. All-hard plastic, jointed at neck, shoulders and hips with walking mechanism; synthetic wig, flirty eyes, open mouth with tongue and teeth; original clothes; all in excellent condition. (For photograph see *8th Blue Book*, page 238.)

Mark: "IDEAL DOLL"

16—17in (41—43cm)   **$ 85—110**
20—22in (51—56cm)   **125—150**

Miss Revlon: 1955. Vinyl head with rooted hair, sleep eyes, closed mouth, earrings; hard plastic body with jointed waist and knees, high-heeled feet, vinyl arms with polished nails; original clothes; all in good condition. (For photograph see *6th Blue Book*, page 213.)

Mark: On head and body:
"IDEAL DOLL"

Miss Revlon, 17—19in (43—48cm)   **$125—135**
Little Miss Revlon, 10½in (27cm)   **75—95**

Peter and Patty Playpal: 1960. Vinyl heads with rooted hair, sleep eyes; hard vinyl body, jointed at shoulders and hips; appropriate clothes; all in excellent condition. (For photograph see *7th Blue Book*, page 221.)

Mark: Peter: "IDEAL TOY CORP.
           BE—35—38"
     Patty: "IDEAL DOLL
           G-35"

35—36in (89—91cm):
    Peter   **$300**
    Patty   **250**
18in (46cm)
    Patty   **125**
42in (107cm)
    Daddy's Girl   **800 up**
29in (74cm)
    Miss Ideal   **325**

10½in (27cm) *Little Miss Revlon*, all original. *H & J Foulke, Inc.*

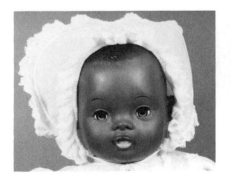

LEFT: 18in (46cm) *Saralee*, all original. *Leone McMullen Collection.*

Italian Hard Plastic

Maker: Bonomi, Ottolini, Ratti, Furga and other Italian firms
Date: Later 1940s and 1950s
Material: Heavy hard plastic, sometimes painted, or plastic coated papier-mâché
Mark: Usually a wrist tag; company name on head
Ottolini - Lion head trademark

Italian Hard Plastic: Heavy, fine quality material jointed at shoulders and hips; human hair wig, sleep eyes, sometimes flirty, often a character face; original clothes; all in excellent condition.

15—17in (38—43cm)   **$ 95—115**
19—21in (48—53cm)   **135—165**

19in (48cm) Bonomi girl, all original., *H & J Foulke, Inc.*

Japanese Bisque Caucasian Dolls

Maker: Various Japanese firms; heads were imported by New York importers, such as Morimura Brothers, Yamato Importing Co. and others.

Date: 1915—on

Material: Bisque head, composition body

Mark: Morimura Brothers
Various other marks with Japan or
Nippon, such as J. W., F. Y., and others

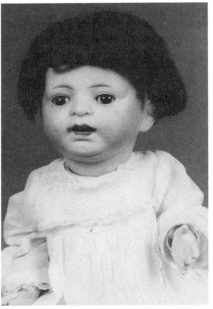

14in (36cm) Morimura Brothers character baby. *H&J Foulke, Inc.*

Character Baby: Perfect bisque socket head with solid dome or wig, glass eyes, open mouth with teeth, dimples; composition bent-limb baby body; dressed; all in good condition.

9—10in (23—25cm)	**$135—165***
14—15in (36—38cm)	**225—275***
20—22in (51—56cm)	**425—475***
Hilda look-alike,	
19in (48cm)	**600—700***

Child Doll: Perfect bisque head, mohair wig, glass sleep eyes, open mouth; jointed composition or kid body; dressed; all in good condition.

14—16in (36—41cm)	**$235—265***
20—22in (51—56cm)	**325—350***

*Do not pay as much for doll with inferior bisque head.

Jullien

Maker: Jullien, Jeune of Paris, France
Date: 1875—1904 when joined with S.F.B.J.
Material: Bisque head, composition and wood body
Mark: "JULLIEN" with size number

JuLLiEN
1

Marked Jullien Bébé: Bisque head, lovely wig, paperweight eyes, closed
    mouth, pierced ears; jointed wood and composition body; pretty old clothes;
    all in good condition.

17—19in (43—48cm)	**$3500—3800**
24—26in (61—66cm)	**4600—4900**
Open mouth, 23—24in (58—61cm)	**2200—2500**

19in (48cm) Jullien. See color photograph on page 169. *Private Collection.*

Jumeau

Maker: Maison Jumeau, Paris, France
Date: 1842—on
Material: Bisque head, kid or composition body
Trademark: Bébé Jumeau (1886)
Bébé Prodige (1886)
Bébé Francais (1896)

25in (64cm) Jumeau fashion lady on kid body.
Yvonne Baird Collection.

Fashion Lady: Late 1860s—on. Usually marked with number only on head, blue stamp on body. Perfect bisque swivel head on shoulder plate, old wig, paperweight eyes, closed mouth, pierced ears; all-kid body or kid with bisque lower arms and legs or cloth Lacmann body with leather arms; appropriate old clothes; all in good condition.
Mark:
JUMEAU
MEDAILLE D'OR
PARIS

12—13in (31—33cm)	$ 2650—3150*
18—20in (46—51cm)	3650—4150*
25—27in (64—69cm)	5500—6500*
Wood body,	
27in (69cm)	15,000**

Later face (sometimes with large eyes):

14—15in (36—38cm)	2500—2800*
20in (51cm)	3500*

Portrait face (so-called):

18—21in (46—53cm)	6000—6800

*Add 25% for original wig and clothing.
**Not enough price samples to compute a reliable range.

Period Clothes:

Fashion Lady Clothing:

Dress	$500—1000
Boots	200
Elaborate wig	300
Nice wig	150

Bébé Clothing:

Jumeau shift	225
Jumeau shoes	200—400
Jumeau dress	500 up

Jumeau continued

Long-Face Triste Bébé: Ca. 1870s. Usually marked with number only on head, blue stamp on body. Perfect bisque socket head with beautiful wig, blown glass eyes, closed mouth, applied pierced ears; jointed composition body with straight wrists; lovely clothes; all in good condition.

22—24in (56—61cm)	**$19,000—22,000**
28—30in (71—76cm)	**24,000 up**

Size 11 = 24in (61cm)
    14 = 29in (74cm)

Portrait Jumeau: Ca. 1870s. Usually marked with size number only on head, blue stamp on body; skin or other good wig; unusually large paperweight eyes, closed mouth, pierced ears; jointed composition body with straight wrists; nicely dressed; all in good condition.

13—14in (33—36cm)	**$ 4800—5300**
16—18in (41—46cm)	**5600—6600**
24—25in (61—64cm)	**8500—9500**
Extreme large almond eyes, 22in (56cm) size 4 at auction	**23,800**

LEFT: 24in (61cm) Long-face Triste Bébé. *Private Collection.*

ABOVE: 15in (38cm) Portrait Bébé. *Private Collection.*

Jumeau continued

E. J. Bébé: Ca. 1880. Head incised as below, blue stamp on body. Perfect bisque socket head with good wig, paperweight eyes, closed mouth, pierced ears; jointed composition body with straight wrists; lovely clothes; all in good condition.

Mark: On head: **DÉPOSÉ E. 7 J.**

10in (25cm) #1	$5000*
14—15in (36—38cm)	5500—6000
20—22in (51—56cm)	6500—7200
26—28in (61—71cm)	10,000—12,000
EJA, 26in (66cm) only	18,500

*Tête-style face 25% less.

Incised Jumeau Depose Bebe: Ca. 1880. Head incised as below, blue stamp on body. Perfect bisque socket head with good wig, paperweight eyes, closed mouth, pierced ears; jointed composition body with straight wrists; lovely clothes; all in good condition. See color photograph on page 171.

Mark: Incised on head:

"JUMEAU
DEPOSE"

16—17in (41—43cm)	$5500—6000
26—27in (66—69cm)	8000—8500

21in (53cm) E 10 J. See color photograph on page 169. *Private Collection.*

Jumeau continued

Tête Jumeau Bébé: 1879—1899, then through S.F.B.J. Red stamp on head as indicated below, blue stamp or "Bebe Jumeau" oval sticker on body. Perfect bisque head, original or good French wig, beautiful stationary eyes, closed mouth, pierced ears; jointed composition body with jointed or straight wrists; original or lovely clothes; all in good condition.

Mark:
DÉPOSÉ
TETE JUMEAU
Bᵀᴱ SGDG
6

10in (25cm) #1	**$3500**
12—13in (31—33cm)	**3000—3200**
15—16in (38—41cm)	**3500—3800**
18—20in (46—51cm)	**4000—4500**
21—23in (53—58cm)	**4800—5200**
25—27in (64—69cm)	**5500—6500**
31—33in (79—84cm)	**7500—8500**
Lady body, 20in (51cm)	**5500—6000**

Open mouth:

14—16in (36—41cm)	**2100—2300**
20—22in (51—56cm)	**2600—2800**
24—25in (61—64cm)	**3200—3500**
27—29in (69—74cm)	**3800—4000**
32—34in (81—86cm)	**4200—4500**

Lever eyes, 22in (56cm) original box, at auction **4750**
Phonograph, boxed with five discs, mint at auction **23,000**

Approximate sizes for E.J.s and Têtes:

1 = 10in (25cm)
2 = 11in (28cm)
3 = 12in (31cm)
4 = 13in (33cm)
5 = 14—15in (36—38cm)
6 = 16in (41cm)
7 = 17in (43cm)
8 = 19in (48cm)
9 = 20in (51cm)
10 = 21—22in (53—56cm)
11 = 24—25in (61—64cm)
12 = 26—27in (66—69cm)
13 = 29—30in (74—76cm)

See additional photograph on page 1.

21½in (55cm) Tête Jumeau. *Private Collection.*

Jumeau continued

#230 Character Child: Ca. 1910. Perfect bisque socket head, open mouth, set or sleep eyes, good wig; jointed composition body: dressed; all in good condition.

16in (41cm)	**$1450**
21—23in (53—58cm)	**1800—2000**

21in (53cm) 1907 Jumeau child. *H&J Foulke, Inc.*

#1907 Jumeau Child: Ca. 1900. Sometimes red-stamped "Tête Jumeau." Perfect bisque head, good quality wig, set or sleep eyes, open mouth, pierced ears; jointed composition body; nicely dressed; all in good condition.

16—18in (41—46cm)	**$2200—2400**
24—25in (61—64cm)	**3000—3200**
33—34in (84—87cm)	**4000—4200**

Jumeau Characters: Ca. 1900. Tête Jumeau mark. Perfect bisque head with glass eyes, character expression; jointed composition body; appropriately dressed; all in good condition.

#203 (See color photograph on page 170.) and others. **$25,000 up**

Princess Elizabeth Jumeau: 1938 through S.F.B.J. Perfect bisque socket head highly colored, good wig, glass flirty eyes, closed mouth; jointed composition body; dressed; all in good condition.

Mark:

19in (48cm) ***Princess Elizabeth*** Jumeau. *Courtesy of Lesley Harford.*

71 UNIS FRANCE 149

306
JUMEAU
1938
PARIS

Body Incised:

JUMEAU
PARIS
Princess

18—19in (46—48cm)	**$1100—1300**
32—33in (81—84cm)	**2400**

K & K

Maker: K & K Toy Co., New York, N.Y., U.S.A.
Date: 1915—on
Material: Bisque or composition head; cloth and composition body
Mark: Size numbers 45, 56 and 60

Germany
K & K
60
Thuringia

K. & K.
39
Made in Germany.

K & K Character Child: Perfect bisque shoulder head, mohair wig, sleep eyes, open mouth with teeth; cloth body with composition arms and legs or cloth or leather legs; appropriate clothes; all in good condition.
18—20in (46—51cm)   **$375—425**
Composition head, 18—20in (46—51cm), all original   **200—225**

12in (31cm) K&K character, all original. See color photograph on page 171. *H&J Foulke, Inc.*

Kamkins

Maker: Louise R. Kampes Studios, Atlantic City, N.J., U.S.A.
Date: 1919—on
Material: Molded mask face, cloth stuffed torso and limbs
Size: About 16—19in (41—48cm)
Mark: Also sometimes stamped with black on foot or back of head: Red paper heart on left side of chest:

KAMKINS
A DOLLY MADE TO LOVE
PATENTED BY L.R. KAMPES
ATLANTIC CITY,   N.J.

KAMKINS
A DOLLY MADE TO LOVE
PATENTED
FROM
L.R. KAMPES
ATLANTIC CITY
N.J.

Marked Kamkins: Molded mask face with painted features, wig; cloth body and limbs; original clothing; all in excellent condition.
18—20in (46—51cm)   **$1100—1200**
Fair to good condition   **650—750**

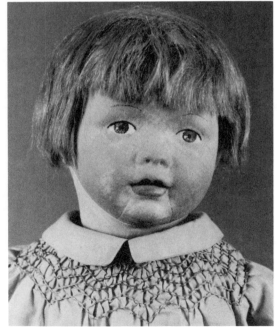

19in (48cm) *Kamkins*, all original. *Private Collection.*

Kämmer & Reinhardt

Maker: Kämmer & Reinhardt of Waltershausen, Thüringia, Germany
Heads often by Simon & Halbig
Date: 1886—on
Material: Bisque socket head, composition body, later papier-mâché, rubber
or celluloid heads, composition bodies
Size: 5½ to 42in (14 to 107cm)
Trademarks: Magestic Doll, Mein Liebling (My Darling), Der Schelm (The
Flirt), Die Kokette (The Coquette)
Mark: In 1895 began using K(star)R, sometimes with "S & H." Mold number
for bisque socket head begins with a 1; for papier-mâché, 9; for cellu-
loid, 7. Size number is height in centimeters. $\mathcal{K}$ ⬡ⒶⓇ R

SIMON & HALBIG
116/A
50

Child Doll: 1886—1895. Perfect
bisque head, original or good wig,
sleep or set eyes, closed mouth,
pierced ears; ball-jointed composition body; dressed; all in good condition.
#192:

6—7in (15—18cm)	$ 475—525*
16—18in (41—46cm)	1800—2200
23—25in (58—64cm)	2500—2800

Open mouth:

7—8in (18—20cm)	425—475*
14—16in (36—41cm)	600—700
20—22in (51—56cm)	850—925
25—27in (64—69cm)	1150—1450

*Allow more for a fully-jointed body.

22in (56cm) 192 child, all original. *H&J Foulke, Inc.*

Kämmer & Reinhardt

Child Doll: 1895—1930s. Perfect bisque head, original or good wig, sleep eyes, open mouth, pierced ears; dressed; ball-jointed composition body; all in good condition. Numbers 15-100 low on neck are centimeter sizes, not mold numbers.

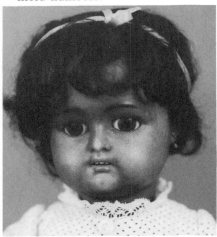

13in (33cm) brown complexion K★R child. *H&J Foulke, Inc.*

#191, 290, 403 or size number only:

12—14in (31—36cm)	**$ 450—500***
16—17in (41—43cm)	**550—600***
19—21in (48—53cm)	**650—750***
23—25in (58—64cm)	**800—900***
29—31in (74—79cm)	**1100—1300***
35—36in (89—91cm)	**1900—2100**
39—42in (99—107cm)	**2800 up**

*Allow $50 additional for flirty eyes.

13in (33cm) brown	**850—950**

Tiny Child Doll: Perfect bisque head, mohair wig, sleep eyes, open mouth; five-piece composition body with molded and painted shoes and socks.

6—7in (15—18cm)	**$350—400**
8—9in (20—23cm)	**425—475**
Walker,	
6—7in (15—18cm)	**400—450**
Closed mouth,	
6in (15cm)	**425—475**
Jointed body,	
8—10in (20—25cm)	**450—500**

6in (15cm) tiny 192 child, all original as Christmas Fairy. *H&J Foulke, Inc.*

Baby #100 (so-called Kaiser Baby): 1909. Perfect bisque solid-dome head, original composition bent-limb body; painted eyes, open/closed mouth; dressed; all in good condition. (For photograph see *8th Blue Book*, page 14.)

10—11in (25—28cm)	**$ 425—475**
14—16in (36—41cm)	**575—675**
20—21in (51—53cm)	**1,000**
Glass eyes (unmarked),	
17—18in (43—46cm)	**2200—2500**

Kämmer & Reinhardt

Character Babies or Toddlers: 1914—on. Perfect bisque head, original or good wig, sleep eyes, open mouth; composition bent-limb or jointed toddler body; nicely dressed; may have voice box or spring tongue; all in good condition. (See *Simon & Halbig Dolls, The Artful Aspect* for photographs of mold numbers not pictured here.)

#126, 22, 26 Baby Body:

10—12in (25—31cm)	$ 375—425
15—18in (38—46cm)	525—625
22—25in (56—64cm)	825—925
30—33in (76—84cm)	1800—2200

#126, 22 Toddler Body:

6—7in (15—18cm)	525—575
9—10in (23—25cm)	550—600
15—17in (38—43cm)	700—800
23—25in (58—64cm)	1200—1500
28—30in (71—76cm)	1800—2200

14in (36cm) K★R 121 toddler. *H&J Foulke, Inc.*

Kämmer & Reinhardt

17in (43cm) K★R 126 baby with flirty and naughty eyes. *H&J Foulke, Inc.*

#126 Child Body:
   24in (61cm)   **800**
#121 Baby Body:
   15—17in (38—43cm) **675—775**
   24—25in (61—64cm) **1100—1300**
#122, 128 Baby Body:
   11—12in (28—31cm) **475—525**
   15in (38cm)   **725—750**
   18—20in (46—51cm) **1100—1200**
   30in (76cm)   **2500—2600**
#121, 122, 128 Toddler Body:
   12—14in (31—36cm) **900—1100**
   25—28in (64—71cm) **1800—2200**
#118A Baby Body: 18—20in
   (46—51cm)   **1600—1800****
#119 Baby Body:
   24in (61cm)   **5000****
#135 Baby Body:
   20in (51cm)   **1600—1800****
Composition Head **#926**:
   17in (43cm) five-piece toddler body
           275—325

   *Allow $50 additional for flirty eyes.
**Not enough price samples to compute a reliable range.

See color photograph on page 173.

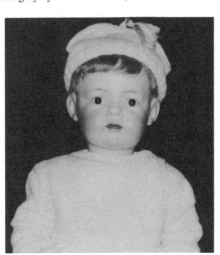

24½in (61cm) K★R 119 baby. *Courtesy of Mary Pat Houston.*

Kämmer & Reinhardt

Character Children: 1909—on. Perfect bisque socket head, good wig, painted or glass eyes, closed mouth; composition ball-jointed body; nicely dressed; all in good condition. (See *Simon & Halbig, The Artful Aspect* for photographs of mold numbers not pictured here.)

#101:

7in (18cm) five-piece body	$ 1000—1100
12in (31cm)	1700—1900
15—17in (38—43cm)	2700—3000
Glass eyes, 16in (41cm)	4500**

#102: See color photograph on page 172.

12in (31cm)	15,000**

#103, 104:

20—22in (51—56cm)	40,000**

#105:

21½in (55cm)	169,576 at auction***

#106:

22in (56cm)	47,000**

#107: See color photograph on page 172.

22in (55cm)	22,000**

#109: See color photograph on page 172.

#112, 112x:

10in (25cm)	3200—3500
18in (46cm)	9000
Glass eyes, 16in (41cm)	8500**

#114:

12in (31cm)	2600—3000
15in (38cm)	3600—4000
18—19in (46—48cm)	4500—5500
24in (61cm)	6500
Glass eyes, 17in (43cm), all original and boxed, at auction	8200

#115, 115A:

Baby, 11—12in (28—31cm)	1800—2000**
Toddler, 15—17in (38—43cm)	3500—3900*
21—22in (53—56cm)	4700—5000*

#116, 116A, open/closed mouth:

Baby, 14—16in (36—41cm)	1800—2200
Toddler, 16—17in (36—41cm)	2600—2900

*Allow additional for molded hair.

**Not enough price samples to compute a reliable range.

***See page 162 for color photograph.

Kämmer & Reinhardt

16in (41cm) K★R 114 character girl. *Yvonne Baird Collection.*

Kämmer & Reinhardt

#116A, open mouth:
Baby, 14—16in (36—41cm)	**1600—1900**
Toddler, 18—21in (46—53cm)	**2300—2600**

#117, 117A, closed mouth:
7½in (19cm) five-piece body	**1800**
12—14in (31—36cm)	**3000—3500**
18—20in (46—51cm)	**4500—5000**
23—25in (59—64cm)	**6000—6500**
28—30in (71—76cm)	**7000—8000**

#117n, sleep eyes:
14—16in (36—41cm)	**850—950**

#117n, flirty eyes:
14—16in (36—41cm)	**1000—1200**
20—22in (51—56cm)	**1600—1800**

18in (46cm) K★R 117n character girl with flirty eyes, all original. *Private Collection.*

17in (43cm) K★R 117 **Mein Liebling.** *Yvonne Baird Collection.*

Kämmer & Reinhardt

#123, 124:
  17in (43cm)   **18,000****
#127:
  Baby, 14—15in (36—38cm)   **1000—1100**
  23—25in (59—64cm)   **1800—2100**
  Toddler or child, 13in (33cm)   **1000—1100**
  Toddler, 27in (69cm)   **2200—2300**
#135 Child, 15in (38cm)   **1000****

**Not enough price samples to compute a reliable range.

16in (41cm) K★R 123 and 124 *Max* and *Moritz*. See color photograph on page 173. *Private Collection.*

K★R 127 character baby. *Courtesy of Lesley Harford.*

Kestner

Maker: J. D. Kestner, Jr., doll factory, Waltershausen, Thüringia, Germany. Kestner & Co., porcelain factory, Ohrdruf.

Date: 1816—on

Material: Bisque heads, kid or composition bodies, bodies on tiny dolls are jointed at the knee, but not the elbow, all bisque

Size: Up to 42in (107cm)

Child doll, early socket head: Ca. 1880. Perfect bisque head, plaster dome, good wig, paperweight or sleep eyes; composition ball-jointed body with straight wrists; well dressed; all in good condition. Marked with size number only.

#169, 128, and unmarked pouty face, closed mouth:

    12—14in (31—36cm)
                    $1650—1850
    17—19in (43—48cm)
                    2200—2400
    23—25in (58—64cm)
                    2750—2950

#XI and very pouty face, closed mouth: +

    14—16in (36—41cm)
                    2350—2650
    19—21in (48—53cm)
                    2800—3000
    24—25in (61—64cm)
                    3200—3500

A.T.-type: Closed mouth,

    13in (33cm)   **3500—4000** * * +
    20in (51cm)   **4500—4800** * *

Open mouth, 19in (48cm)
                    2200 * * +

Bru-type, molded teeth, jointed ankles: (For photograph see *8th Blue Book*, page 258.)

    20in (51cm)   **3000** * * +

Open mouth, square cut teeth: (See color photograph on page 174.

    10—11in (25—28cm) **450—500**
    14—16in (36—41cm) **650—750**

26in (66cm) 128 Kestner, closed mouth. *Kay & Wayne Jensen Collection.*

22in (56cm) A.T.-type Kestner. *Esther Schwartz Collection.*

+ Allow less for a kid body.

* * Not enough price samples to compute a reliable range.

Kestner continued

Child doll, early shoulder head: Ca. 1880s. Perfect bisque head, plaster dome, good wig, set or sleep eyes; sometimes head is slightly turned; kid body with bisque lower arms; marked with size letters or numbers. (No mold numbers.)

Closed mouth:

14—16in (36—41cm)	$ 600—650*
20—22in (51—56cm)	750—850*
26in (66cm)	1100*

Open/closed mouth:

16—18in (41—46cm)	650—750

Open mouth:

14—16in (36—41cm)	425—450
20—22in (51—56cm)	525—600
25in (64cm)	675—725

*Allow extra for a very pouty face or swivel neck.

Large early shoulder head child with closed mouth. *Courtesy of Judy Newell.*

Kestner continued

Child doll, bisque shoulder head, open mouth: Ca. 1892. Kid body, some with rivet joints. Plaster dome, good wig, sleep eyes, open mouth; dressed, all in good condition. (See *Kestner, King of Dollmakers* for photographs of mold numbers not pictured here.)

HEAD MARK: 154. 8 dep.
D made in Germany

BODY MARK: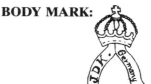

#154, 147, 148, 149, 166, 195:

12—13in (31—33cm)	$300—350*
16—17in (41—43cm)	400—450*
20—22in (51—56cm)	500—550*
26—28in (66—71cm)	750—850*

*Allow additional for a rivet jointed body.

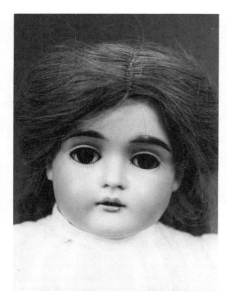

22in (56cm) 166 Kestner shoulder head child. *H&J Foulke, Inc.*

16in (41cm) 154 Kestner shoulder head child. *H&J Foulke, Inc.*

268

Kestner continued

Child doll, open mouth: Bisque socket head on ball-jointed body; plaster dome, good wig, sleep eyes, open mouth; dressed; all in good condition. (See *Kestner, King of Dollmakers* for photographs of mold numbers not pictured here.)

HEAD MARK: made in D Germany. 8. 162.

BODY MARK: Excelsior DRP N. 70686 Germany

Mold numbers 129, 142, 144, 146, 152, 156, 160, 164, 167, 168, 171, 174, 196, 214:

10in (25cm)	$ 550
12—14in (31—36cm)	500—600
18—21in (46—53cm)	625—725
24—26in (61—66cm)	825—925
30in (76cm)	1100—1200
36in (91cm)	1600—1800
42in (107cm)	3200—3500

#155:

7—8in (18—20cm)	500—550

#171: Daisy, blonde mohair wig,

18in (46cm)	700—750

16½in 167 Kestner child. *Wayne & Kay Jensen Collection.*

25in (64cm) 146 Kestner girl. *H&J Foulke, Inc.*

Kestner continued

Character Child: 1909—on. Perfect bisque head character face, plaster pate, wig, painted or glass eyes, closed, open or open/closed mouth; good jointed composition body; dressed; all in good condition. (See *Kestner, King of Dollmakers* for photographs of mold numbers not pictured here.)

#143 (Pre 1897):

7—8in (18—20cm)	**$ 500—600**
12—14in (31—36cm)	
	700—800
18—20in (46—51cm)	
	1050—1250

#178-190,

Painted Eyes:

12in (31cm)	**1800—2000**
15in (38cm)	**2800—3000**
18in (46cm)	**3800—4300**

Glass Eyes:

12in (31cm)	**2800—3200**
15in (38cm)	**3800—4300**
18in (46cm)	**4800—5300**

Boxed set,

15in (38cm)	**7500**

#206,

19in (48cm) at auction	
	12,700**
12in (31cm)	**4000****

#208,

Painted Eyes,

23—24in (58—61cm)	
	12,000**

#239 Toddler,

20in (51cm)	**3800****

#241:

18—22in (46—56cm)	
	4000—4500**

#249:

20—22in (51—56cm)	**1400—1800**

#260:

8in (20cm) Toddler	**550—600**
12—14in (31—36cm)	**700—800**
18—20in (46—51cm)	**800—1000**

#220 Toddler:

18in (46cm)	**6500****
27in (69cm)	**9500****

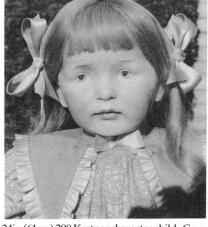

24in (61cm) 208 Kestner character child. *Courtesy of Sylvia Whatley.*

20in (51cm) JDK 249 character child. *Wayne & Kay Jensen Collection.*

**Not enough price samples to compute a reliable range.

Kestner continued

*16in (41cm) 183 Kestner character child.
Esther Schwartz Collection.*

11½in (29cm) 206 Kestner character child.
Esther Schwartz Collection.

11in (28cm) 143 Kestner character child,
all original. *H&J Foulke, Inc.*

Kestner continued

Character Baby: 1910—on. Perfect bisque head, molded and/or painted hair or good wig, sleep or set eyes, open or open/closed mouth; bent-limb body; well dressed; nice condition. (See *Kestner, King of Dollmakers* for photographs of mold numbers not pictured here.)

Mark:

made in
F. Germany. 10
211
J. D. K.

#211, 226, 262, 263, JDK solid dome:

11—13in (28—33cm)	$ **425—475**
16—18in (41—46cm)	**650—750**
20—22in (51—56cm)	**850—950**
25in (64cm)	**1300—1500**
16in (41cm) toddler	**850—950**

#234, 235, 238 shoulder heads:

16—18in (41—46cm)	**650—750**

Hilda, #237, 245, solid dome:

11—13in (28—33cm)	**2200—2500**
16—17in (41—43cm)	**3200—3800**
20—22in (51—56cm)	**4500—4800**
24in (61cm)	**5500—6500**

#247:

12—13in (31—33cm)	**1000—1100**
14—16in (36—41cm)	**1600—1800**

#257:

9—10in (23—25cm)	**425—450**
17—20in (43—51cm)	**800—900**
Toddler 20in (51cm)	**1000—1100**

20½in (52cm) JDK 257 character baby. *H&J Foulke, Inc.*

Solid dome, fat-cheeked: (For photograph see *8th Blue Book*, page 263.):

11—12in (28—31cm)	**600—650**
19—21in (48—51cm)	**1100—1300**

All-bisque:

9—10in (23—25cm)	**650—750**

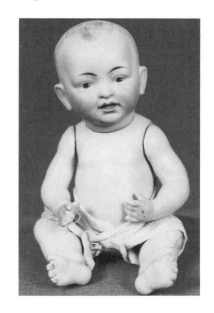

11½in (29cm) JDK character baby with painted eyes. *H&J Foulke, Inc.*

Kestner continued

18in (46cm) JDK 226 character baby. *H&J Foulke, Inc.*

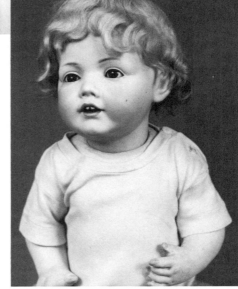

24in (61cm) JDK 237 **Hilda** character baby. *H&J Foulke, Inc.*

Kestner continued

All-Bisque Child: Perfect all-bisque child jointed at shoulders and hips; mohair wig, sleeping eyes, open mouth with upper teeth; blue or pink painted stockings, black strap shoes. Naked or with appropriate clothes. Very good quality.

#150:

4—5in (10—13cm)	**$225—250***
6in (15cm)	**300—325***
7in (18cm)	**350—375***
8in (20cm)	**475—525***
9in (23cm)	**600—700**
11in (28cm)	**850—950**

*Allow $25-50 extra for yellow boots (Kestners).

Gibson Girl: Ca. 1910. Perfect bisque shoulder head with good wig, glass eyes, closed mouth, up-lifted chin; kid body with bisque lower arms (cloth body with bisque lower limbs on small dolls); beautifully dressed; all in good condition; sometimes marked "Gibson Girl" on body. See color photograph on page 174.

#172:

10in (25cm)	**$1100**
15in (38cm)	**1700—2100**
20—21in (51—53cm)	**3300—4100**

Lady Doll: Perfect bisque socket head, plaster dome, wig with lady hairdo, sleep eyes, open mouth with upper teeth; jointed composition body with molded breasts, nipped-in waist, slender arms and legs; appropriate lady clothes; all in good condition. (For photograph see *7th Blue Book*, page 248.)

Mark: *made in*
D germany. 8.
162.

#162:

16—18in (41—46cm)	**$1200—1400**

8½in (22cm) Kestner 150 all-bisque child. *H&J Foulke, Inc.*

Kewpie

Maker: Various
Date: 1913—on
Size: 2in (5cm) up
Designer: Rose O'Neill, U.S.A. U.S. Agent: George Borgfeldt & Co., New York, N.Y., U.S.A.
Mark: Red and gold paper heart or shield on chest and round label on back

---

All-Bisque: Made by J. D. Kestner and other German firms. Often have imperfections in making. Sometimes signed on foot "O'Neill". Standing, legs together, arms jointed, blue wings, painted features, eyes to side.

2½in (5—6cm)	$ 85—95
4—5in (10—13cm)	100—125
6in (15cm)	150—165
7in (18cm)	200—250
8—9in (20—23cm)	350—400
10in (25cm)	650
12—13in (31—33cm)	1200—1500
Jointed hips, 4in (10cm)	400—450
Shoulder head, 3in (8cm)	425
Black Hottentot, 5in (13cm)	450
Button hole, 2in (5cm)	150—165
Pincushion, 2—3in (5—8cm)	225—250
Painted shoes and socks, 5in (13cm)	325—350

See color photograph on page 174.

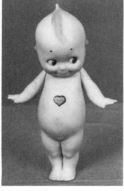

10½in (27cm) all-bisque ***Kewpie*** with heart label. *H&J Foulke, Inc.*

4½in (12cm) all-bisque ***Kewpie*** with jointed hips. *H&J Foulke, Inc.*

Kewpie continued

Action Kewpies (sometimes stamped: ©):

Thinker, 4in (10cm)	$ 250—275
Kewpie with cat, 3½in (9cm)	400—450
Kewpie holding pen, 3in (8cm)	350—400
Reclining or sitting 3-4in (8—10cm)	375—400
Gardener, Sweeper, Farmer, 4in (10cm)	450—475
Kewpie 2in (5cm) with rabbit, rose, turkey, pumpkin, shamrock, etc.	250—300
Doodledog:	
3in (9cm)	1100—1300
1½in (4cm)	600—650
Huggers, 3½in (9cm)	175—200
Guitar player, 3½in (9cm)	300—325
Traveler, 3½in (9cm)	275—300
Governor, 3½in (9cm)	350—375
Kewpie and *Doodledog* on beach, 3½in (9cm)	2800
Kewpie sitting on inkwell, 3½in (9cm)	600
Kewpie Traveler with *Doodledog,* 3½in (9cm)	850
Kewpie Soldiers 5—6in (13—15cm)	650—750
Kewpie with basket	450—475
Kewpie with drum	2400
Kewpie at tea table	1700
Kewpie driving chariot	2800
Kewpie Mountain with 17 figures	17,000

Kewpie holding basket. *Richard Wright Antiques.*

Kewpie lying on back. *Sandy Coons Collection.*

Kewpie continued

Bisque head on chubby jointed composition toddler body, glass eyes: Made
by J. D. Kestner.
Mark:
           "Ges. gesch.
        O'Neill J.D.K."

10in (25cm) five-piece body	$3300—3800**
12—14in (31—36cm)	4300—5300**

Bisque head on cloth body (For photograph see *8th Blue Book*, page 270.):
  Mold *#1377* made by Alt, Beck & Gottschalck

12in (31cm) Glass eyes	$2600—2800**
Painted eyes	1600—2000**

**Not enough price samples to compute a reliable range.

12in (31cm) JDK *Kewpie*, composition body. *Esther Schwartz Collection.*

Kewpie continued

Celluloid: Made by Karl Standfuss, Deuben near Dresden, Saxony, Germany. Straight standing, arms jointed, blue wings; very good condition.

2½in (6cm)	**$ 35**
5in (13cm)	**75**
8in (20cm)	**125—150**
Black, 2½in (6cm)	**65—75**

All-Composition: Made by Cameo Doll Co., Rex Doll Co., and Mutual Doll Co., all of New York, N.Y., U.S.A. All-composition, jointed at shoulders, some at hips; good condition.

8in (20cm)	**$125**
11—13in (28—33cm)	**165—185**
Black, 12—13in (31—33cm)	**250—275**
Talcum container, 7in (18cm)	**150—175**

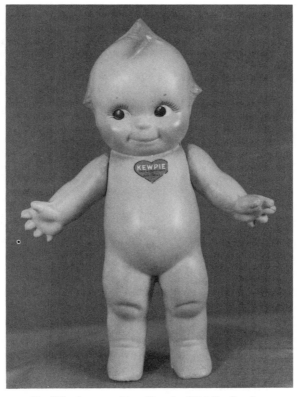

11in (28cm) composition ***Kewpie.*** *H&J Foulke, Inc.*

Kewpie continued

All-Cloth: Made by Richard G. Kreuger, Inc., New York, N.Y., U.S.A. Patent number 1785800. Mask face with fat-shaped cloth body, including tiny wings and peak on head. Cloth label sewn in side seam.

10—12in (25—31cm)	**$135—165**
18in (46cm) with tagged dress and bonnet	**325—350**

Hard Plastic: Ca. 1950s.

Standing Kewpie, one piece with jointed arms, 8in (20cm)	**$ 85**
Fully jointed with sleep eyes; all original clothes, 13in (33cm)	**325—375****

**Not enough price samples to compute a reliable range.

Vinyl: Ca. 1960s.

Kewpie Baby with hinged body 16in (41cm)	**$165—185**

13in (33cm) hard plastic **Kewpie** baby with sleep eyes, all original. *Courtesy of Carolyn Guzzio.*

12in (31cm) **Cuddle Kewpie** with label. *H&J Foulke, Inc.*

Kley & Hahn

Maker: Kley & Hahn, doll factory, Ohrdruf, Thüringia, Germany. Heads by Hertel, Schwab & Co. (100 series), Bähr & Pröschild (500 series) and J. D. Kestner (250, 680 and Walkure).
Date: 1902—on
Material: Bisque head, composition body
Trademarks: Walküre, Meine Einzige, Special, Dollar Princess
Mark:

> ＞K&H＜
> Germany   *K H*
> *Walküre*

Child Doll: Perfect bisque head, wig, glass eyes, open mouth; jointed composition child body; fully dressed; all in good condition.
#250 or *Walküre:*

16—18in (41—46cm)	**$425—475**
22—24in (56—61cm)	**525—625**
29—30in (74—76cm)	**850—950**

Character Child: Perfect bisque head, wig, glass or painted eyes, closed mouth; jointed composition child or toddler body; fully dressed; all in good condition.
#520, 526, 536, 546, 549:

15—16in (36—38cm)	**$3000—3200**
19—21in (48—53cm)	**4000—4500**

#154, 166, closed mouth, jointed body:

16—17in (41—43cm)	**2100—2300**
15in (38cm) baby	**1200**

#154, 166, open mouth:

20in (51cm) toddler	**1300—1500**
20in (51cm) baby	**1000—1200**

20in (51cm) 250 Walküre. *H&J Foulke, Inc.*

K&H 546 character girl. *Jackie Kaner.*

Kley & Hahn continued

#169, closed mouth:	
13in (33cm) toddler	**1800—2000**
19—21in (48—53cm) toddler	**3200—3500**
20in (51cm) baby	**2200**
#169, open mouth: 23in (58cm)	**1500****

See color photograph on page 175.

Character Baby: Perfect bisque head with molded hair or good wig, sleep or painted eyes, open or closed mouth; bent-limb baby body; nicely dressed; all in good condition.

#138, 158, 160, 167, 176, 525, 531:	
11—13in (28—33cm)	**$ 450—500***
18—20in (46—51cm)	**650—750***
24in (61cm)	**1000***
28in (71cm)	**1200—1500**
26—27in (66—69cm) toddler	**1800—2000**

*Allow $100—150 extra for a toddler or jointed body.

Two-Face Baby, 13in (33cm)	**2200****

**Not enough price samples to compute a reliable range.

28in (71cm) K&H 167 character baby. *H&J Foulke, Inc.*

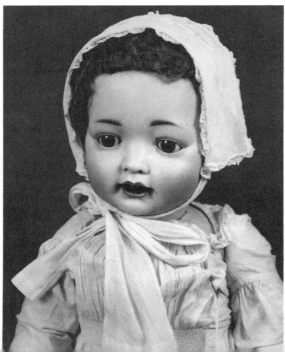

Kling

Maker: Kling & Co., porcelain factory, Ohrdruf, Thüringia, Germany
Date: 1836—on (1870—on for dolls)
Material: Bisque or china shoulder head, cloth body, bisque lower limbs; bisque socket head, composition body, all-bisque
Mark:  and numbers, such as *167, 176, 189, 190, 203, 372, 377*

China shoulder head: Ca. 1880. Black- or blonde-haired china head with bangs, sometimes with a pink tint; cloth body with china limbs or kid body; dressed; all in good condition.
#188, 189, 200 and others:

13—15in (33—38cm)	**$225—275**
18—20in (46—51cm)	**325—375**
24—25in (61—64cm)	**450—500**

Bisque shoulder head: Ca. 1880. Molded hair or mohair wig, painted eyes, closed mouth; cloth body with bisque lower limbs; dressed; in all good condition. Mold numbers such as *140* and *186.*

12—14in (31—36cm)	**$275—350**
18—20in (46—51cm)	**450—500**
23—25in (58—64cm)	**550—600**

Molded hair, glass eyes, molds *153* and *154*, 19—20in (48—51cm)   **800—900****
**Not enough price samples to compute a reliable range.

5in (13cm) 189 Kling china head with pink tint. *H&J Foulke, Inc.*

3¼in (8cm) 186 Kling bisque shoulder head. *H&J Foulke, Inc.*

Kling continued

Bisque head: Ca. 1890. Mohair or human hair wig, glass sleep eyes, open mouth; kid or cloth body with bisque lower arms or jointed composition body; dressed; all in good condition.

#373 or **377** shoulder head:

13—15in (33—38cm)	**$350—375**
19—22in (48—56cm)	**450—500**

#370 or **372** socket head:

14—16in (36—41cm)	**375—425**
22—24in (56—61cm)	**525—625**

#123 shoulder head, cloth body, 9—10in (23—25cm)   **200—225**

All-bisque Child: Jointed shoulders and hips; wig, glass eyes, closed mouth; molded footwear (usually two-strap boots with heels.)

Mark: Kling bell
and/or
"36-10n"

4in (10cm)   **$225**

8in (20cm) Kling bisque shoulder head with glass eyes, all original. *H&J Foulke, Inc.*

4¼in (11cm) Kling all-bisque 36.10. *H&J Foulke, Inc.*

Knickerbocker

Maker: Knickerbocker Doll & Toy Co., New York, N.Y., U.S.A.
Date: 1937
Material: All-composition
Mark: (Embossed on dwarfs)
"WALT DISNEY
KNICKERBOCKER TOY CO."

Composition Seven Dwarfs: All-composition jointed at shoulders, stiff hips, molded shoes, individual character faces, painted features; mohair wigs or beards; jointed shoulders, molded and painted shoes; original velvet costumes and caps with identifying names: "Sneezy," "Dopey," "Grumpy," "Doc," "Happy," "Sleepy" and "Bashful." Very good condition.

9in (23cm)	**$150—175 each**
Mint-in-box, at auction	**275 each**

Composition Snow White: All-composition jointed at neck, shoulders and hips; black mohair wig with hair ribbon, brown lashed sleep eyes, open mouth; original clothing; all in good condition.

20in (51cm)	**$ 400—450**
With molded black hair and blue ribbon, 13in (33cm)	**250—275**
Complete Set of ***Snow White and Seven Dwarfs*** with tags, excellent	**2200**
Cloth Seven Dwarfs; 14in (36cm) excellent	**225 each**

9in (23cm) all-composition ***Grumpy, Sleepy*** and ***Dopey***, all original. *H&J Foulke, Inc.*

König & Wernicke

Maker: König & Wernicke, doll factory, Waltershausen, Thüringia, Germany.
Heads by Hertel, Schwab & Co. and Bahr & Pröschild
Date: 1912—on
Material: Bisque heads, composition bodies or all-composition
Trademarks: Meine Stolz, My Playmate
Mark: K ε W
1070   Body Mark:

K & W Character: Bisque head with good wig, sleep eyes, open mouth;
composition baby or toddler body; appropriate clothes; all in good condition.

#98, 99, 100, 1070:

14—16in (36—41cm)	$ 475—525*
19—21in (48—53cm)	650—750*
24—25in (61—64cm)	850—950*
28in (71cm) toddler	**1100**

*Allow $50 extra for flirty eyes.
*Allow $100—150 extra for toddler body.

18in (46cm) incised K&W toddler. *Yvonne Baird Collection.*

Richard G. Krueger, Inc.

Maker: Richard G. Krueger, Inc., New York, N.Y., U.S.A.
Date: 1917—on
Material: All-cloth, mask face
Mark: Cloth tag or label

All-Cloth Doll: Ca. 1930. Mask face
with painted features, rosy cheeks,
painted eyes with large black pupil
and two highlights each eye, curly
thick painted upper lashes, curly
mohair wig on cloth cap; oil cloth
body with hinged shoulders and
hips. Simple dotted swiss dress with
attached undie, pink taffeta coat
and hat with lace trim. All in excellent condition.
Label:

> Krueger, N.Y.
> Reg. U.S. Pat Off.
> Made in U.S.A.

16in (41cm)	**$100—115**
20in (51cm)	**135—165**

Pinocchio: Ca. 1940. Mask character face with black yarn hair, attached ears, round nose, large oval
eyes, curved mouth; cloth torso,
wood jointed arms and legs; original clothes, all in good condition.
15in (38cm)   **$250**

15in (38cm) *Pinocchio. H&J Foulke, Inc.*

Käthe Kruse

Maker: Käthe Kruse, Bad Kösen, Germany
Date: 1910—on
Material: Molded muslin head (hand-painted), jointed cloth body, later of hard plastic material.
Mark: On cloth: "Käthe Kruse" on sole of foot, sometimes also "Germany" and a number
Hard plastic on back: Turtle mark and "Käthe Kruse"

Käthe Kruse
81971

*Made in
Germany*

Cloth Käthe Kruse: Molded muslin head, hand-painted; jointed at shoulders and hips:
Doll I (1910), painted hair, wide hips, 16—17in (41—43cm):

Mint, all original	**$3000—3200**
Good condition, suitably dressed	**1800—2000**
With jointed knees (1911)	**3600 up**

Doll IH (after 1929), wigged, 16—17in (41—43cm): (For photograph see *Doll Classics*, page 174.)

Mint, all original	**1800—2000**
Good condition, suitably dressed	**1100—1300**

Doll II "Schlenkerchen" Smiling Baby (1922—on). (For photograph see *5th Blue Book*, page 235.)

13in (33cm)	**1200****

Doll V & VI Babies ***"Traumerchen"*** (closed eyes) and ***"Du Mein"*** open eyes, some heads of Magnesit, 1925—on

19½—23½in (50—60cm)	**3000—3700**

Doll VII (1927—on) & ***Doll X*** (1935—on):

14in (36cm)	**1200**
with ***Du Mein*** head (1928—1930)	**1500**

Doll VIII (1929—on) "German Child" 20½in (52cm) wigged, turning head:

Mint, all original	**1800—2000**
Good condition, suitably dressed	**1100—1300**

Doll IX "Little German Child" (1929—on) wigged, turning head:

14in (36cm)	**1200**

Bambino (Ca. 1925) 8—9in (20—23cm)   **500****
See color photograph on page 175.

**Not enough price samples to compute a reliable range.

U.S. Zone Germany: Dolls IX or ***X*** with cloth or Magnesit heads, very thick paint finish: all original, very good condition. (1945—1951)

14in (36cm)	**$650—700**

Käthe Kruse continued

16in (41cm) Doll I, all original. *Private Collection.*

20½in (52cm) Doll VIII, all original. *Joanna Ott Collection.*

20in (51cm) Du Mein, Doll V. *Private Collection.*

14in (36cm) Doll VII with Du Mein head, rarely found. *Esther Schwartz Collection.*

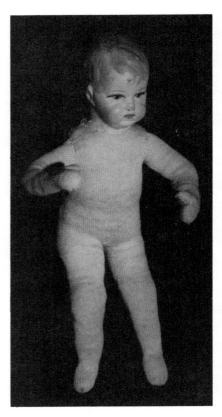

8in (20cm) *Bambino*, plaster-type head, stockinette body. *Lesley Harford Collection.*

Hard Plastic Head: Ca. 1950s—on. Hard plastic head with lovely wig, painted eyes; pink muslin body; original clothes; all in excellent condition.
U.S. Zone Germany
    14in (36cm)   **$500—550**
Ca. 1952—1975:
    14in (36cm)   **425—475**
    18—20in (46—51cm)   **575**
1975—on:
    14in (36cm)   **350—400**
    18—20in (46—51cm)   **450—500**
    20in (51cm) ***Du Mein***   **550**

Hanna Kruse Dolls:
    10in (25cm) ***Däumlinchen*** with foam rubber stuffing (1957—on)   **175—225**
    13in (32cm) ***Rumpumpel Baby*** (1959—on)   **350**

Käthe Kruse continued

All-Hard Plastic (Celluloid) Käthe Kruse: Wig or molded hair and sleep or painted eyes; jointed neck, shoulders and hips; original clothes; all in excellent condition. Turtle mark. (1955—1961).
16in (41cm)   **$350—375**

13in (32cm) ***Rumpumpel Baby***, all original. *H&J Foulke, Inc.*

14in (36cm) Doll IX boy and Doll X girl, all original. (Doll X has same face as Doll VII, but has a turning head.) *H&J Foulke, Inc.*

16in (41cm) Hard plastic (celluloid) with turtle mark. *H&J Foulke, Inc.*

Gebrüder Kuhnlenz

Maker: Gebrüder Kuhnlenz, porcelain factory, Kronach, Bavaria
Date: 1884—on
Material: Bisque head, composition or kid body
Size: Various
Mark: " G.K. "

Gbr 165 K
9
Germany 44-31

Gbrk

and/or numbers, such as:
41-28   56-18   44-15

The first two digits are mold number; second two are size number.

G. K. doll with closed mouth: Ca. 1885—on. Perfect bisque socket head, inset glass eyes, closed mouth, round cheeks; jointed composition body; dressed; all in good condition.

#32, 31:

10in (25cm)	**$ 650—700***
16—18in (41—46cm)	**1000—1200***
22—24in (56—61cm)	**1500—1700***

#34, Bru-type, French JCB, Gosset label:

16—18in (41—46cm)	**2500****

#38 shoulder head, kid body:

14—16in (36—41cm)	**550—600**
22—23in (56—58cm)	**800—900**

*Allow more for a very pretty doll.
**Not enough price samples to compute a reliable range.

G. K. child doll: Ca. 1890—on. Perfect bisque socket head with distinctive face, almost a character look, long cheeks, sleep eyes, open mouth, molded teeth; jointed composition body, sometimes French; dressed; all in good condition.

#41, 44, 56:

18—20in (46—51cm)	**$ 750—800**
24—26in (61—66cm)	**1000—1100**

#165:

18in (46cm)	**425—450**
22—24in (56—61cm)	**475—525**
34in (86cm)	**1150—1250**

#61 shoulder head:

19—22in (48—56cm)	**450—500**

20in (51cm) Kuhnlenz 61-28 shoulder head.
Kay & Wayne Jensen Collection.

Gebrüder Kuhnlenz continued

G. K. Tiny Dolls: Perfect bisque socket head, wig, stationary glass eyes, open mouth with molded teeth; five-piece composition body with molded shoes and socks; all in good condition. Usually mold *#44*.

7—8in (18—20cm) crude body **$175**
better body **225**

All-bisque with swivel neck, pegged shoulders and hips, white painted stockings, light blue boots, black straps.
7½in (19cm) **$700**

7in (18cm) Kuhnlenz 44-17 child. *H&J Foulke, Inc.*

7½in (19cm) Kuhnlenz 44-17 all-bisque. *H&J Foulke, Inc.*

Lanternier

Maker: A Lanternier & Cie. porcelain factory of Limoges, France
Date: 1915—1924
Material: Bisque head, papier-mâché body
Mark:

FABRICATION
FRANÇAISE

AL ε Cⁱᵉ
LIMOGES
A   1

Marked Lanternier Child: Ca. 1915. Perfect bisque head, good or original wig, large stationary eyes, open mouth, pierced ears; papier-mâché jointed body; pretty clothes; all in good condition.

23in (58cm) *Cherie. Kay & Wayne Jensen Collection.*

Cherie, Favorite or *La Georgienne*
16—18in (41—46cm) $ 650—750*
22—24in (56—61cm)   **850—950***
28in (71cm)   **1300—1500***
*Allow extra for lovely face and bisque.

Lanternier Lady: Ca. 1915. Perfect bisque head with adult look, good wig, stationary glass eyes, open/closed mouth with molded teeth; composition lady body; dressed; all in good condition. (For photograph see *7th Blue Book*, page 271.)
Lorraine
16—18in (41—46cm)   **$850—1250***
*Depending upon costume and quality.

Marked Toto: Ca. 1915. Perfect bisque smiling character face, good wig, glass eyes, open/closed mouth with molded teeth, pierced ears; jointed French composition body; dressed; all in good condition. (For photograph see *8th Blue Book*, page 295.)
17—19in (43—48cm)   **$900—1000**

Lenci

Maker: Enrico & Elenadi Scavini, Turin, Italy
Date: 1920—on
Material: Pressed felt head with painted features, jointed felt bodies
Size: 5—45in (13—114cm)
Mark: "LENCI" on cloth and various
paper tags; sometimes stamped
on bottom of foot

Lenci di E. SCAVINI
TURIN (Italy)
Made in ITALY
N. 159G
Pat. Sept. 8, 1921, Pat. N. 142433
Bré SGDG.X 87395. Brevetta 501.198

Lenci: All-felt (sometimes cloth torso) with swivel head, jointed shoulders
and hips; painted features, eyes usually side-glancing; original clothes, often
of felt or organdy; in excellent condition.

Miniatures and Mascottes:

8—9in (20—23cm) Regionals	**$ 250—275**
Children or unusual costumes	**350—400**

Children #300, 109, 149, 159, 111:

13in (33cm)	**800 up**
16—18in (41—46cm)	**950 up**
20—22in (51—56cm)	**1250 up**

20½in (52cm) Lenci with unusual face. *H&J Foulke, Inc.*

17in (43cm) early Lenci, all original and boxed. *Esther Schwartz Collection.*

Lenci continued

"Lucia" face, 14in (36cm)	**$ 600 up**
Ladies and long-limbed novelty dolls, 24—28in (61—71cm)	**1600 up**
Glass eyes, 20in (51cm)	**2800—3000**
Celluloid-type, 6in (15cm)	**40—50**
"Surprised Eye" (round painted eyes) fancy clothes, 20in (51cm)	**2000—2500**
#1500, scowling face, 17—19in (43—48cm)	**1600—1800**
Baby, 14—18in (36—46cm)	**1800 up**
Teenager, long legs, 17in (43cm)	**900 up**
Orientals, 18in (46cm)	**3500—4000**
Sports Series, 17in (43cm)	**2000**
Golfer, 23in (58cm)	**2900**
Benedetta, 18in (46cm)	**2000 up**
1927 Catalog	**1650**
1931 Catalog	**800**

Collector's Note: Mint examples of rare dolls will bring higher prices. To bring the prices quoted, Lenci dolls must be clean and have good color. Faded and dirty dolls bring only about one-third to one-half these prices.

9in (23cm) Lenci Mascotte, all original. *H&J Foulke, Inc.*

13in (33cm) Lenci #111, all original. *H&J Foulke, Inc.*

Lenci-Type

Maker: Various Italian, French and English firms such as Marguerin, Alma and others
Date: 1920—1940
Material: Felt and cloth
Size: 6in (15cm) up
Mark: Various paper labels, if any

Felt or Cloth Doll: Mohair wig, painted features; original clothes or costume.
Child dolls, 16—18in (41—46cm) up to **$750** depending upon quality
Foreign costume,

7½—8½in (19—22cm)	**$35—45**
12in (31cm)	**80—90**

16in (41cm) Lenci-type child with glass eyes, all original. *H&J Foulke, Inc.*

Limbach

Maker: Limbach Porzellanfabrik, Limbach, Thüringia,
Germany (porcelain factory)
Date: Factory started in 1772
Material: Bisque head, composition body; all bisque
Mark:

MADE IN GERMANY

All-Bisque Child: Ca. 1900. Child all of bisque (sometimes pink bisque) with
wire jointed shoulders and hips; molded hair (often with a blue molded bow)
or bald head with mohair wig, painted eyes, closed mouth, white stockings,
blue garters, brown slippers or strap shoes.

Mark:

P.23

GERMANY

4—5in (10—13cm)	$ 75—85
Glass eyes,	
5in (13cm)	**150—165**
Character, jointed arms only,	
4—5in (10—13cm)	**75—85**

All-Bisque Baby: Ca. 1910. Baby
with painted hair and facial features; wire jointed shoulders and
hips, bent arms and legs; bare feet.
(For photograph see *8th Blue
Book*, page 299.)
Mark: Clover and number with P.

4—5in (10—13cm)	$ 75—95
11—12in (28—31cm)	**500**

4in (10cm) all-bisque character of the type
made by Limbach. *H&J Foulke, Inc.*

Limbach continued

Limbach Child Doll: 1893—1899; 1919—on. Perfect bisque head, good wig, glass eyes, open mouth with teeth; composition jointed body; dressed; all in good condition.

Wally, Rita, or ***Norma*** after 1919.

17—19in (43—48cm)   **$450—500****

23—24in (58—61cm)   **600—650****

Incised with clover (1893—1899):

  14—17in (36—43cm)   **900—1200****

**Not enough price samples to compute a reliable range.

14½in (37cm) Limbach child with incised clover. *Private Collection.*

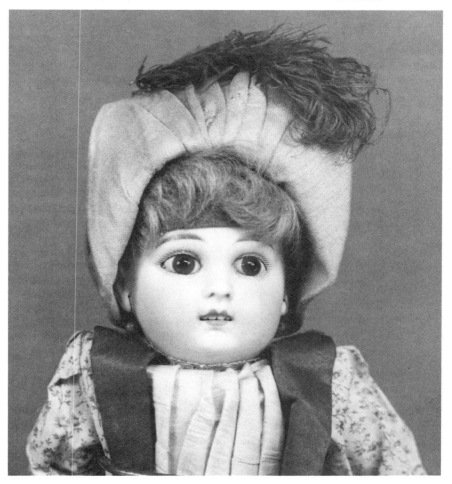

Albert Marque

Maker: Unknown, possibly artist produced
Date: 1916
Material: Bisque head, jointed composition body with bisque lower arms
Size: 22in (56cm) one size only
Designer: Albert Marque, French sculptor
Mark: a Marque

A. Marque Doll: Bisque head with wistful character face, mohair wig, paper-weight eyes, closed mouth; jointed composition body of special design with bisque lower arms and hands, fixed wrists; appropriate clothes (some original ones from Paris designer Margaines-Lacroix).

22in (56cm)   **$43,000**
With two faint hairline cracks, two fingers broken, at auction   **22,000**

22in (56cm) A. Marque child. *Courtesy of Richard W. Withington, Inc.*

Armand Marseille

(A.M.)

Maker: Armand Marseille of Köppelsdorf, Thüringia, Germany (porcelain and doll factory)

Date: 1885—on

Material: Bisque socket and shoulder head, composition, cloth or kid body

Marks:

A.M.-DEP
Nº. 3600.
3.
Made in Germany.

A0½M
Florodora
Armand Marseille
Made in Germany

1894
A M 5/0 DEP
Germany

18" Made in Germany
A. (Baby 2½ Betty) M.
D. R. G. M.

Child Doll: 1890—on. Perfect bisque head, nice wig, set or sleep eyes, open mouth; composition ball-jointed body or jointed kid body with bisque lower arms; pretty clothes; all in good condition.

#390, (larger sizes marked only "A. [size] M."), **Florodora** (composition body):

9—10in (23—25cm)	$ 225—250
12—14in (31—36cm)	215—265
16—18in (41—46cm)	300—325
20in (51cm)	375
23—24in (58—61cm)	450—500
28—29in (71—74cm)	600—650
30—32in (76—81cm)	700—850
35—36in (89—91cm)	1100—1300
40—42in (102—107cm)	1800—2100
Five-piece composition body, 6—7in (15—18cm)	150—175
9—10in (23—25cm)	200—225
Closed mouth, 5—5½in (12—14cm)	225

#1894 (composition body):

14—16in (36—41cm)	375—450
21—23in (53—58cm)	600—700

#370, 3200, 1894 Florodora and other shoulder heads:

11—12in (28—31cm)	150—175
14—16in (36—41cm)	200—250
22—24in (56—61cm)	350—400

Queen Louise, Rosebud: See photograph on page 13.

12in (31cm)	300—325
23—25in (58—64cm)	450—550

Baby Betty: See color photograph on page 175.

14—16in (36—41cm) composition body	450—500

#2000, 3600:

16in (41cm)	550—600

Name shoulder head child: 1898 to World War I. Perfect bisque shoulder head marked with doll's name, jointed kid or cloth body, bisque lower arms; good wig, glass eyes, open mouth; well dressed; all in good condition. Names include ***Rosebud, Lilly, Alma, Mabel, Darling, Beauty*** and ***Princess.***

Mark:

Alma
5

12—14in (31—36cm)	**$175—200**
20—22in (51—56cm)	**300—350**
25in (64cm)	**400—450**

18in (46cm) A.M. 3600 child. *H&J Foulke, Inc.*

20in (51cm) ***Florodora*** shoulder head, all original. *H&J Foulke, Inc.*

Character Children: 1910—on. Perfect bisque head, molded hair or wig, glass or painted eyes, open or closed mouth; composition body; dressed; all in good condition.

#230 Fany (molded hair):

  15—16in (38—41cm) **$4500—5000**
  19in (48cm) **7500—8500**

#231 Fany (wigged): See color photograph on page 176.

  15—16in (38—41cm) **3500—4000**

#400 (child body):

  24in (61cm) **3650****

#500, 600:

  15in (38cm) **450—550**

#550 (glass eyes):

  18—20in (46—51cm) **3200—3500**

A.M. (intaglio eyes):

  16—17in (41—43cm) **4500 up**

#620 shoulder head, 16in (41cm) at auction **1200****

**Not enough price samples to compute a reliable range.

12½in (32cm) A.M. 550 character girl. *Private Collection.*

Character Baby: 1910—on. Perfect bisque head, good wig, sleep eyes, open mouth some with teeth; composition bent-limb body; suitably dressed; all in nice condition.

Marks:

Armand Marseille
Germany
990
A 9/0 M

Germany
326
A 11 M

11in (28cm) A.M. 251/248 open mouth toddler.
Wayne & Kay Jensen Collection.

Mold #990, 985, 971, 996, 1330, 326 (solid dome), 980, 991, 327, 329 and others:

13—15in (33—38cm)	$ 375—425
18—20in (46—51cm)	500—550
22in (56cm)	650
24—25in (61—64cm)	750—850

#233:

13—15in (33—38cm)	450—500
20in (51cm)	650—700

#251/248 (open/closed mouth):

12—15in (31—38cm)	1250—1500

#251/248 (open mouth):

12—15in (31—38cm)	650—850

#410 (2 rows teeth):

15—16in (38—41cm)	900—1000

#518:

16—18in (41—46cm)	525—575

#560A: See color photograph on page 176.

15—17in (38—43cm)	525—575

#580, 590 (open/closed mouth):

14—15in (31—38cm)	1000—1100
18—20in (46—51cm)	1400—1600

#590 (open mouth):

16—18in (41—46cm)	850—950

#700, closed mouth, glass eyes, wig

10½in (27cm) baby, at auction	1350
14in (36cm) child	2500**

Kiddiejoy (shoulder head, mamma body):

19in (48cm)	825—850

Melitta, 19in (48cm) toddler

	600—650

**Not enough price samples to compute a reliable range.

20in (51cm) A.M. 990 character baby. *H&J Foulke, Inc.*

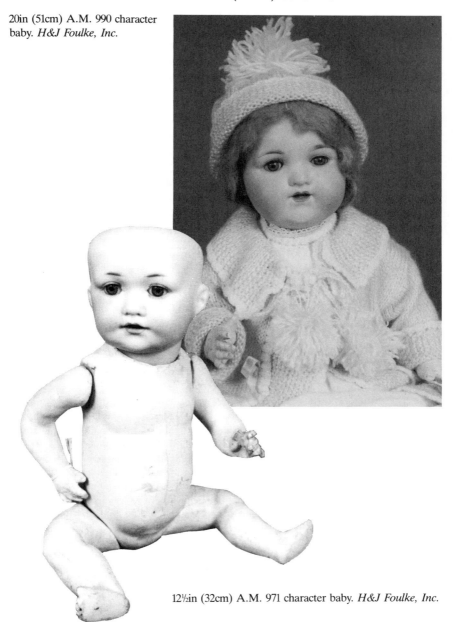

12½in (32cm) A.M. 971 character baby. *H&J Foulke, Inc.*

Armand Marseille (A.M.) continued

13in (33cm) head circumference A.M. 351 baby, composition body. *H&J Foulke, Inc.*

Infant: 1924—on. Solid-dome bisque head with molded and/or painted hair, sleep eyes; composition body or hard-stuffed jointed cloth body or soft-stuffed cloth body; dressed; all in good condition.

Mark:

A. M.
Germany.
351. 14K

#351, 341 Kiddiejoy and Our Pet:
Head circumference:

10in (25cm)	**$275**
12—13in (31—33cm)	**350—425**
15in (38cm)	**600—650**
6in (15cm) compo body	**225**
24in (61cm) wigged toddler (see color photograph on page 176.)	**850**

#352:

17—20in (43—51cm) long	**550—650**

#347:
Head circumference:

12—13in (31—33cm)	**450—500**

10in (25cm) painted bisque ***Just Me***, all original. *H&J Foulke, Inc.*

12in (31cm) A.M. 401 lady, all original. *Mike White Collection.*

Armand Marseille (A.M.) continued

Marked Just Me Character: Ca. 1925. Perfect bisque socket head, curly wig, glass eyes to side, closed mouth; composition body; dressed; all in good condition. (For photograph see *7th Blue Book*, page 285.) Some of these dolls, particularly the painted bisque ones, were used by Vogue Doll Company in the 1930s and will be found with original Vogue labeled clothes.

Mark:

Just ME
Registered
Germany
A 310/5/0 M

9in (23cm)	**$1000—1100**
11in (28cm)	**1200—1400**
Painted bisque: 7—8in (18—20cm)	**600—700**

Lady: 1910—1930. Bisque head with mature face, mohair wig, sleep eyes, open or closed mouth; composition lady body with molded bust, long slender arms and legs; appropriate clothes; all in good condition. (For photograph see *6th Blue Book*, page 271.)

#401 and ***400*** (slim body):

12—13in (31—33cm):	
Open mouth	**$ 800—900**
Closed mouth	**1500—1900**
#300 (H.A.):	
9in (23cm)	**850—900****

**Not enough price samples to compute a reliable range.

Marked Baby Phyllis: Baby Phyllis Doll Co., Brooklyn, N.Y., U.S.A. Heads by Armand Marseille. Perfect solid dome bisque head with painted hair, sleep eyes, closed mouth; cloth body with composition hands; appropriate clothes; all in good condition. (For photograph see *5th Blue Book*, page 57.)

Mark:

BABY PHYLLIS
Made in Germany
24014

Head circumference: 12—13in (31—33cm)	**$400—450**

Marked Baby Gloria: Perfect solid dome head with molded and painted hair, sleep eyes, smiling face with open mouth and two upper teeth, dimples; cloth mama doll body with composition limbs; appropriately dressed; all in good condition. (For photograph see *5th Blue Book*, page 56.)

Mark:

Baby Gloria
Germany

15—16in (38—41cm) long	**$650—700**

Mascotte

Maker: May Freres Cie, 1890—1897; Jules Nicholas Steiner, 1898—on. Paris, France
Date: 1890—1902
Material: Bisque head, composition and wood jointed body
Mark:

"BÉBÉ MASCOTTE
PARIS"

Bébé Mascotte: Bisque socket head, good wig, closed mouth, paperweight eyes, pierced ears; jointed composition and wood body; appropriate clothes; all in good condition.

17—19in (43—48cm)	**$4000—4500**
24—26in (61—66cm)	**5500—6000**

19in (48cm) ***Bébé Mascotte.*** See color photograph on page 209. *Private Collection.*

Mattel — Barbie®

Maker: Mattel, Inc., Hawthorne, Calif., U.S.A.
Date: 1959 to present
Material: Hard plastic and vinyl
Size: 11½—12in (29—31cm)
Mark: 1959—1962: Barbie TM/Pats. Pend./© MCMLVIII/by/Mattel, Inc.
      1963—1968: Midge TM/© 1962/Barbie®/© 1958/by/Mattel, Inc.
      1964—1966: © 1958/Mattel, Inc./U.S. Patented/U.S. Pat. Pend.
      1966—1969: © 1966/Mattel, Inc./U.S. Patented/U.S. Pat. Pend./Made
      in Japan

First Barbie®: 1959. Vinyl; very light complexion, white irises, pointed eyebrows, ponytail, black and white striped bathing suit, holes in feet to fit stand, gold hoop earrings; mint condition.

11½in (29cm) boxed	**$2500**
Doll only, no box or accessories	
Mint	**1500**
Very good	**1200**
Stand	**100—150**
Shoes	**20**

Second Barbie: 1959—1960. Vinyl; very light complexion, same as above, but no holes in feet, some wore pearl earrings; mint condition. Made 3 months only.

11½in (29cm) boxed	**$2200**
Doll only, no box or accessories, very good	**1500**

Third Barbie: 1960. Vinyl; very light complexion, same as above, but with blue irises and curved eyebrows; no holes in feet; mint condition.

11½in (29cm) boxed	**$500**
Doll only	**300—350**

Fourth Barbie: 1960. Vinyl; same as #3 but of flesh-toned vinyl; mint condition.

11½in (29cm) boxed	**$350**
Doll only	**150**

Fifth Barbie: 1961. Vinyl; same as #4; ponytail hairdo of firm Saran; mint condition.

11½in (29cm) boxed	**$175 up**
Doll only	**95**

Other Dolls:

Black Francie: 1967, mint-in-package $500
Ken #1, mint-in-box 125
Ken, bendable knees, mint-in-box 150
Side-Part Barbie, bendable knees, mint-in-box 900—1000
Hair Happenin's Barbie, 1971, mint-in-box 375
Hair Happenin's Francie, 1970, mint-in-box 125
Truly Scrumptious, 1969, mint-in-box 375
   mint, no box 175
Supersize Barbie, bride, mint-in-box 85
   swimsuit, mint-in-box 55
Twiggy, 1967, mint-in-box 125
Midge, bendable knee, mint-in-box 225
Bubble Cut Barbie, 1963—on, mint-in-box 95—125
   Gift Sets 350—500 up
Allen, bendable knee, mint-in-box 200

Most other dolls are in the $15—35 price range except for a few harder to find models.

Outfits:*

Roman Holiday, mint-in-package $400
Gay Parisienne, mint-in-package 400
Easter Parade, mint-in-package 400
Brown mink coat, mint-in-package 800 up
   Not in package 500 up
Barbie Baby Sits, mint-in-package 100
Dogs & Duds, mint-in-package 100
   Dog only 35
Enchanted Evening 150

*Especially desirable are the 1600 series outfits and Jacqueline Kennedy- style clothes.

#2 Barbie, in bridal outfit, also original booklet, shoes, glasses and bathing suit. *Margie Ann Yocom Collection.*

Mattel — Barbie continued

American Girl Barbie, center part, bendable legs, mint-in-box	**$300**
Early (1967—1970):	
Tutti, mint-in-box	**75**
Chris, mint-in-box	**95**
Todd, mint-in-box	**95**
Black ***Julia***, mint-in-box:	
one-piece suit	**75**
two-piece suit	**95**
Fashion Queen Barbie	**125—150**
Swirl Ponytail Barbie	**200—225**

Barbie® is a registered trademark of Mattel, Inc.

#3 Barbie, all original with appropriate carrying case. *Margie Ann Yocom Collection.*

Twiggy, all original. *Margie Ann Yocom Collection.*

Mengersgereuth

Maker: Porzellanfabrik Mengersgereuth, porcelain factory, Mengersgereuth, Sonneberg, Thüringia, Germany

Date: 1908—on

Material: Bisque head, composition or kid body

Mark:

PM
914.
Germany
1

Marked Child: Perfect bisque head, wig, sleep eyes, open mouth; kid body with bisque hands or composition body; appropriate clothing; all in good condition.

Shoulder head with triangle mark, 24—26in (61—66cm)   **$550—650****

Trebor, composition body, 16—18in (41—46cm)   **450—500****

**Not enough price samples to compute a reliable range.

Marked Character Baby: Ca. 1910—on. Perfect bisque socket head, good wig, sleep eyes, open mouth; five-piece composition bent-limb baby body; dressed; all in good condition. Molds *914, 23, Grete* or *Herzi.*

12—14in (31—36cm)   **$350—400**

18—20in (46—51cm)   **500—550**

15in (38cm) P.M. 914 character baby. *H&J Foulke, Inc.*

Metal Heads

Maker: Buschow & Beck, Germany (Minerva); Karl Standfuss, Germany (Juno); Alfred Heller, Germany (Diana)
Date: Ca. 1888—on
Material: Metal shoulder head, kid or cloth body
Mark:

Marked Metal Head: Metal shoulder head on cloth or kid body, bisque or composition hands; dressed; very good condition, not repainted.

With molded hair, painted eyes, 12—14in (31—36cm)	**$110—135**
With molded hair, glass eyes, 12—14in (31—36cm)	**150—175**
18—20in (46—51cm)	**200—225**
With wig and glass eyes, 14—16in (36—41cm)	**225—250**
20—22in (51—56cm)	**275—325**

18in (46cm) metal head with Minerva mark.
H&J Foulke, Inc.

18in (46cm) unmarked metal head boy with molded hair. *H&J Foulke, Inc.*

Monica

Maker: Monica Doll Studios, Hollywood, Calif., U.S.A.
Date: 1941—1951
Material: All-composition
Size: 15in (38cm), 17in (43cm), 20in (51cm), 22in (56cm), 24in (61cm); later 11in (28cm)
Mark: None

Monica: Composition swivel head, human hair rooted in scalp, painted eyes with eye shadow, closed mouth; composition body with adult-type legs and arms, fingers with painted nails; dressed; in good condition (nearly all have crazing on faces).

$350—450

18in (46cm) *Monica. H&J Foulke, Inc.*

Mothereau

Maker: Alexandre Mothereau, Paris, France
Date: 1880—1895
Material: Bisque head, wood and composition body
Trademark: Bébé Mothereau
Mark: B.M.

Bébé Mothereau: Perfect bisque head, beautiful blown glass eyes, closed
mouth, good wig, pierced ears; wood and composition jointed body; beautifully dressed; all in good condition.
26—28in (66—71cm)   **$25,000 up**

23in (58cm) B 9 M. See color photograph on page 210. *Private Collection.*

Pierre Muller

Maker: Pierre Muller, Levallois, Seine, France
Date: 1924
Material: Bisque head, jointed composition body
Trademark: Olympia
Mark:

OLYMPIA
PARIS

Olympia Bébé: Perfect bisque head, glass sleeping eyes, appropriate wig, open mouth with six teeth; jointed composition body; appropriately dressed; all in good condition.

35in (89cm)   **$2000—2500****

**Not enough price samples to compute a reliable range.

35in (89cm) ***Olympia Bébé.*** *Courtesy of Dr. & Mrs. R. L. Terhune.*

Munich Art Dolls

Maker: Marion Kaulitz
Date: 1908—1912
Material: All-composition, fully-jointed bodies
Size: Various
Designer: Paul Vogelsanger, and others
Mark: Sometimes signed on doll's neck

Munich Art Dolls: Molded composition character heads with hand-painted features; fully-jointed composition bodies; dressed; all in good condition.

13in (33cm)   **$1800—2000****
18—19in (46—48cm)   **2700—3000****

**Not enough price samples to compute a reliable range.

13in (33cm) Munich Art Doll. *Esther Schwartz Collection.*

Nancy Ann

Maker: Nancy Ann Storybook Dolls Co., South San Francisco, Calif., U.S.A.
Date: Mid 1930s
Material: Painted bisque, later plastic
Mark: Painted Bisque: **Mark:** Hard Plastic:

"Story	"STORYBOOK
Book	DOLLS
Doll	U.S.A.
U.S.A."	TRADEMARK
	REG."

Also a wrist tag identifying particular model

Marked Storybook Doll: Painted bisque, mohair wig, painted eyes; one-piece body, head and legs, jointed arms; original clothes; excellent condition.

Painted Bisque	**$ 45 up**
Jointed legs,	**65 up**
Swivel neck,	**65 up**
Hard Plastic	**40 up**
Bent-limb baby:	
Painted bisque	**90—100**
Hard plastic	**70—80**
Nancy Ann Style Show, hard plastic, 17in (43cm)	**400 up**
Muffie, hard plastic, 8in (20cm)	**125 up**

Nancy Ann Storybook doll, all original. *H&J Foulke, Inc.*

Ohlhaver

Maker: Gebrüder Ohlhaver, doll factory, Sonneberg, Thüringia, Germany. Heads made by Gebrüder Heubach, Ernst Heubach and Porzellanfabrik Mengersgereuth.

Date: 1912—on

Material: Bisque socket head, ball-jointed composition body

Trademarks: Revalo

Mark:

Revalo
Germany
3

Revalo Character Baby or Toddler: Perfect bisque socket head, good wig, sleep eyes, hair eyelashes, painted lower eyelashes, open mouth; ball-jointed toddler or baby bent-limb body; dressed; all in good condition. (For photograph see *7th Blue Book*, page 296.)

#22:

14—16in (36—41cm)	$475—550*
20—22in (51—56cm)	700—800*

*Allow $150 extra for toddler body.

Revalo Character Doll: Bisque head with molded hair, painted eyes, open/closed mouth; composition body; dressed; all in good condition. (For photograph see *8th Blue Book*, page 320.)

Coquette,

10—12in (25—31cm)	$600—650

Revalo Child Doll: Bisque socket head, good wig, sleep eyes, hair eyelashes, painted lower eyelashes, open mouth; ball-jointed composition body; dressed; all in good condition. Mold ***#150*** or ***#10727***.

16—18in (41—46cm)	$500—550
22in (56cm)	650
25—27in (64—69cm)	750—850

22in (56cm) Revalo head #10727 made by Gebrüder Heubach. *Kay & Wayne Jensen Collection.*

Oriental Dolls

Japanese Traditional Children: 1850—on. Papier-mâché swivel head on shoulder plate, hips, lower legs and feet (early ones have jointed wrists and ankles); cloth midsection, cloth (floating) upper arms and legs; hair wig, dark glass eyes, pierced ears and nostrils; original or appropriate clothes; all in good condition.

12—14in (31—36cm)	**$250—300**
18—20in (46—51cm)	**400—500**
Boy, 18—20in (46—51cm)	**450—550**
Ca. 1920s, 13—15in (33—38cm)	**125—150**
17—18in (43—46cm)	**175—200**
Ca. 1940s, 12—14in (31—36cm)	**85—95**
Traditional Lady, 1920s,	
10—12in (25—31cm)	**150**
17in (43cm) boxed lady with wigs	**450**
1940s, 12—14in (31—36cm)	**85—95**
Traditional Warrior, 1880s, 16—18in (41—46cm)	**500 up**
1920s: 11—12in (28—31cm)	**225 up**
Royal Personnages, 1920s & 1930s,	
4—6in (10—15cm)	**100—125**
12in (31cm)	**225 up**
Bisque Head Child, papier-mâché, wood and cloth body:	
14in (36cm)	**250****
Baby with bent limbs, Ca. 1920s: 8—10in (20—25cm)	**65—85**

**Not enough price samples to compute a reliable range.
See color photograph on page 210.

24in (61cm) sexed Japanese boy. *Lesley Hurford Collection.*

14in (36cm) bisque head, papier-mâché, wood and cloth body. *H&J Foulke, Inc.*

Oriental Dolls continued

Oriental Bisque Dolls: Ca. 1900—on. Made by German firms such as Simon & Halbig, Armand Marseille, J. D. Kestner and others. Bisque head tinted yellow; matching ball-jointed or baby body. (See previous *Blue Book* for photographs of mold numbers not shown here.)

S&H 1329 girl,	
13—14in (33—36cm)	**$1700—2100**
18—19in (46—48cm)	**2400—2600**
A.M. 353 baby, 11—13in (28—33cm)	**800—1000**
J.D.K. 243 baby, 13—15in (33—38cm)	**4250—4750**
18in (46cm)	**6500**
S&H 1099, 1129, and 1199 girl, 14—18in (36—46cm)	**2400—2700**
#220, 16—17in (41—43cm)	**3000—3400**
A.M. girl, 8—9in (20—23cm)	**600—700**
#164, 16—17in (41—43cm)	**2200—2400**
JDK molded hair baby, 17in (43cm) at auction	**8700****
All-bisque S&H, 5½ (14cm)	**550**
7in (18cm)	**750—850**
All-bisque S&H 921 baby: 4in (10cm)	**500—550**
10in (25cm)	**1600**
BSW #500, 14—15in (36—38cm)	**1800—2100**
Unmarked 4½in (12cm) painted eyes	**150—175**
8—9in (20—23cm)	**600—700**

**Not enough price samples to compute a reliable range.

9in (23cm) unmarked German bisque Oriental girl, all original. *H&J Foulke, Inc.*

16in (41cm) JDK 243 baby. *Private Collection.*

Oriental Dolls continued

Baby Butterfly: 1911—1913. Made by E. I. Horsman. Composition head and hands, cloth body; painted black hair, painted features.

13in (33cm)   **$225****

**Not enough price samples to compute a reliable average.

Ming Ming Baby: Quan-Quan Co., Los Angeles and San Francisco, Calif., U.S.A. Ca. 1930. All-composition baby, jointed at shoulders and hips; painted facial features; sometimes with black yarn hair, original costume of colorful taffeta with braid trim; feet painted black or white for shoes. (For photograph see *8th Blue Book*, page 323.)

10—12in (25—31cm)   **$110—135**

17in (43cm) S&H 1199 Oriental, all original. *Regina Steele Collection.*

13in (33cm) Horsman **Baby Butterfly.** *Private Collection.*

Papier-mâché
(So-Called French-Type)

Maker: Heads by German firms such as Johann Müller of Sonneberg and Andreas Voit of Hildburghausen, were sold to French and other doll makers
Date: 1816—1860
Material: Papier-mâché shoulder head, pink kid body
Mark: None

French-type Papier-mâché: Shoulder head with painted black pate, brush marks around face, nailed on human hair wig (often missing), set-in glass eyes, closed or open mouth with bamboo teeth, pierced nose; pink kid body with stiff arms and legs; appropriate old clothes; all in good condition, showing some wear.

18—20in (46—51cm)	**$1400—1700**
24—26in (61—66cm)	**2000—2300**
Painted eyes,	
12—14in (31—36cm)	**750—850**

14in (36cm) French-type papier-mâché lady.
Private Collection.

Papier-mâché
(German)

Maker: Various German firms of Sonneberg such as Johann Müller, Müller & Strasburger, F. M. Schilling, Heinrich Stier, A. Wislizenus, and Cuno & Otto Dressel

Date: 1816—on

Material: Papier-mâché shoulder head, cloth body, sometimes leather arms or kid body with wood limbs

---

Papier-mâché Shoulder Head: Ca. 1820s to 1850s. Unretouched shoulder head, molded hair, painted eyes; cloth or kid body; original or appropriate old clothing; entire doll in fair condition.

22—24in (56—61cm)	**$ 900—1200**
Glass eyes: 19in (48cm) short hair	**1400—1700**
Flirty eyes: 23in (58cm) long hair	**2500—2700**

See color photographs on page 211.

18½ (47cm) papier-mâché with glass eyes and pierced nose. *Private Collection.*

Molded Hair Papier-mâché: (so-called Milliners' models.) 1820s—1860s. Unretouched shoulder head, various molded hairdos, eyes blue, black or brown, painted features; original kid body, wooden arms and legs; original or very old handmade clothing; entire doll in fair condition.

Long curls:	
9in (23cm)	**$ 500**
13in (33cm)	**650**
Covered wagon hairdo:	
11in (28cm)	**450**
15in (38cm)	**675**
7in (18cm)	**275—325**
Side curls with braided bun,	
9—10in (23—25cm)	**600—700**
13—15in (31—38cm)	**1000—1200**
Center part with molded bun,	
12in (28cm)	**950**
Side curls with high beehive, (apollo knot)	
17in (43cm)	**1600—1800**
10in (25cm)	**850**

Papier-Mâché (German) continued

Sonneberg-type Papier-mâché: Ca. 1880—1910. Shoulder head with molded and painted black or blonde hair, painted eyes, closed mouth; cloth body sometimes with leather arms; old or appropriate clothes; all in good condition, showing some wear.

Mark: Usually unmarked. Some marked:

```
M & S
Superior
2015
```

14—16in (36—41cm)	**$250—275**
19—21in (48—53cm)	**350—400**
24—25in (61—64cm)	**475—525**
Glass eyes, 23in (58cm)	**750****

See additional photograph on page 324.

Patent Washable-type: 1880s to 1914. See page 136.

**Not enough price samples to compute a reliable range.

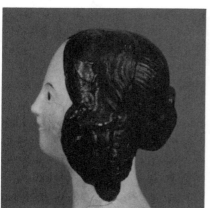

17½ (45cm) papier-mâché lady with molded fancy hairdo. *Private Collection.*

15in (38cm) Sonneberg-type papier-mâché with glass eyes. *H&J Foulke, Inc.*

Papier-Mâché (German) continued

Papier-mâché: Ca. 1920—on. Papier-mâché head and hands or arms, hard
  stuffed cloth body or full composition body; good hair wig, painted eyes,
  original child clothes; all in good condition of excellent quality.

4in (10cm)	**$45—50**
8—9in (20—23cm)	**65—75**
12in (31cm)	**90—100**

Gura: Ca. 1950.
  13in (33cm)   **40—50**

6in (15cm) 1920s papier-mâché girl, all original. *H&J Foulke, Inc.*

17in (43cm) Sonneberg-type papier-mâché
with molded hair ribbon. *H&J Foulke, Inc.*

Parian-Type
(Untinted Bisque)

Maker: Various German firms
Date: Ca. 1860s through 1870s
Material: Untinted bisque shoulder head, cloth or kid body, leather, wood, china or combination extremities
Mark: Usually none, sometimes numbers

Unmarked Parian: Pale or untinted shoulder head, sometimes with molded blouse, beautifully molded hairdo, (may have ribbons, beads, comb or other decoration), painted eyes, closed mouth; cloth body; lovely clothes; entire doll in fine condition.

16—18in (41—46cm)	**$ 425—475**
22—24in (56—61cm)	**625—675**
Very fancy hairdo and/or elaborately decorated blouse	**700 up**
Very fancy with glass eyes	**1250 up**
Common, plain style, 8—10in (20—25cm)	**125—165**
16in (41cm)	**300**
24in (61cm)	**475**
Man, molded collar and tie, 17in (43cm)	**700**
Boy, 19in (48cm) short black hair	**1800**
"Augusta Victoria," 17in (43cm)	**900**
Swivel neck, blonde curls, ribbon, glass eyes, 12—15in (31—38cm)	**1300—1400**
Alice hairdo, 21in (53cm)	**750—800**
"Countess Dagmar," 19in (48cm)	**750**
Molded blonde hair, blue ribbon, glass eyes, fashion face, swivel neck, 21in (53cm)	**2500**
Blonde hair, blue glass eyes, 13in (33cm)	**425**

RIGHT: 13in (33cm) unmarked Parian-type lady with glass eyes, pierced ears and molded blue ribbon. *H&J Foulke, Inc.*

FAR RIGHT: 8in (20cm) unmarked Parian. *H&J Foulke, Inc.*

P. D.

Maker: Probably Petit & Dumontier, Paris, France. Some heads made by
   François Gaultier.
Date: 1878 — 1890
Material: Bisque head, composition body
Size: Various
Mark: P.2.D

P. D. Bébé: Perfect bisque head with paperweight eyes, closed mouth, pierced
ears, good wig; jointed composition body (some have metal hands); appropriate clothes; all in good condition.
21—24in (53—61cm)   **$17,000 up**

18½in (47cm) P. 2. D. *Private Collection.*

Dora Petzold

Maker: Dora Petzold, Berlin, Germany
Date: 1920—on
Material: Composition or cloth head, cloth body
Mark:

"DORA PETZOLD
Registered
Trade Mark
Doll
Germany"

Dora Petzold Doll: Molded composition or cloth head with closed mouth, hair wig, pensive character face, painted features; cloth body sometimes with especially long arms and legs; dressed; all in good condition. Many unmarked.

20—28in (51—71cm)   **$850—950**

19in (48cm) signed Dora Petzold girl. *Esther Schwartz Collection.*

Philadelphia Baby

Maker: J. B. Sheppard & Co., Philadelphia, Pa., U.S.A.
Date: Ca. 1900
Material: All-cloth
Size: 18—22in (46—56cm)
Mark: None

Philadelphia Baby. H&J Foulke, Inc.

Philadelphia Baby: All-cloth with treated shoulder-type head, lower arms and legs; painted hair, well-molded facial features, ears; stocking body; good condition.
18—22in (46—56cm) **$1600—1800**
Fair condition, showing wear
1100
All original, mint condition
2600

Piano Baby

Maker: Gebrüder Heubach, Kestner and other German makers
Date: 1880—on
Material: All-bisque
Size: Usually under 12in (31cm), some larger
Mark: Many unsigned; some with maker's particular mark

Piano Baby: All-bisque immobile with molded clothes and painted features; made in various sitting and lying positions. Heubach quality.

4½in (12cm)	**$ 150—175**
7—8in (18—20cm)	**275—375**
11—12in (28—31cm)	**600—700**
Black, 3—4in (8—10cm)	**125—150**

Sitting Heubach child with bathing trunks and cap, 11½in (29cm) at auction
1125

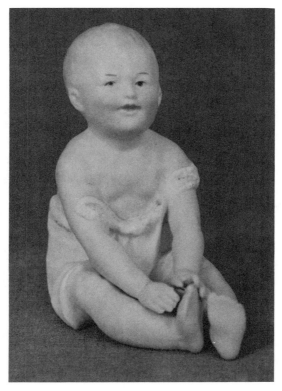

4½in (12cm) piano baby by Heubach. *H&J Foulke, Inc.*

330

Pincushion Dolls*

Maker: Various German firms, such as William Goebel, Dressel, Kister & Co., J. D. Kestner, Simon & Halbig, Limbach, Hertwig & Co., Gebrüder Heubach

Date: 1900—on

Material: China, sometimes bisque

Size: Up to about 9in (23cm)

Mark: "Germany" and numbers; a few with Goebel (see page 197), D&K or Karl Schneider marks.

Pincushions: China half figures with molded hair and painted features; usually with molded clothes, hats, lovely modeling and painting.

Arms close	**$ 30—40**
Arms extending but hands coming back to figure	**45 up**
Hands extended	**75 up**
Bisque child, glass eyes, 2in (5cm)	**175**
Painted eyes, 3in (8cm)	**125**
Flapper with molded dress and cloche, 4in (10cm)	**65 up**
French-style ladies	**400**

*Also called half dolls.

6in (15cm) lady with Karl Schneider mark. *H&J Foulke, Inc.*

5in (13cm) flapper lady. *H&J Foulke, Inc.*

Pincushion Dolls* continued

4in (10cm) lady with molded jacket and hat. *H&J Foulke, Inc.*

2½in (6cm) seated bathing beauty. *H&J Foulke, Inc.*

4½in (12cm) French lady with molded cap. *H&J Foulke, Inc.*

Pintel & Godchaux

Maker: Pintel & Godchaux, Montreuil, France
Date: 1890—1899
Material: Bisque head, jointed composition body
Trademark: Bébé Charmant
Mark:

	B	A
	P 9 G	P 7 G

Marked P.G. Doll: Perfect bisque head, paperweight eyes, closed mouth, good wig; jointed composition and wood body; appropriate clothing; all in good condition.

20—24in (51—61cm)   **$2500—3000**
Open mouth, 23in (58cm)   **1800—2000**

23in (58cm) P 11 G. See color photograph on page 212. *Private Collection.*

Poir

Maker: Eugenie Poir, Paris, France; and New York, N.Y., U.S.A., also Gre-
Poir (French Doll Makers)
Date: 1920s
Material: All-cloth, felt face and limbs or all-felt
Mark: None on doll; paper label on clothes as below

Poir Child: All-fabric movable arms and legs; mohair wig; painted facial
features; original clothes.
17—21in (43—53cm):
    Mint condition   **$600—700**
    Good condition   **400—500**

19in (48cm) Poir-type doll, all original.
H&J Foulke, Inc.

Pre-Greiner
(So-called)

Maker: Unknown and various
Date: Ca. 1850
Material: Papier-mâché shoulder head, stuffed cloth body, mostly homemade,
wood, leather or cloth extremities
Mark: None

Unmarked Pre-Greiner: Papier-mâché shoulder head; molded and painted
black hair, pupil-less black glass eyes; cloth (sometimes kid) stuffed body,
leather extremities; dressed in good old or original clothes; all in good
condition.

18—22in (46—56cm)	**$ 900—1200**
28—32in (71—81cm)	**1600—1900**
Fair condition, much wear, 20—24in (51—61cm)	**700—800**
Flirty eye, 30in (76cm)	**3000**

18in (46cm) Pre-Greiner with glass eyes. *H&J Foulke, Inc.*

Rabery & Delphieu

Maker: Rabery & Delphieu of Paris, France
Date: 1856 (founded)—1899—then with S. F. B. J.
Material: Bisque head, composition body
Mark: "R. D." (from 1890)
Mark: On back of head:
Body mark:
(Please note last two lines illegible)

Marked R. D. Bébé: Ca. 1880s. Bisque head, lovely wig, paperweight eyes, closed mouth; jointed composition body; beautifully dressed; entire doll in good condition.

13—15in (33—38cm)	**$2400—2600***
19—21in (48—53cm)	**3000—3200***
24in (61cm)	**3500—3600***
12in (31cm) Great face	**3300**
Open mouth:	
19—22in (48—56cm)	**2000—2300***

*Must have very good bisque and pretty face.

15in (38cm) R 5/0 D. *Private Collection.*

Raggedy Ann and Andy

Maker: Various
Date: 1915 to present
Material: All-cloth
Size: 4½—39in (12—99cm)
Creator: Johnny B. Gruelle

Early Raggedy Ann or Andy: All-cloth with movable arms and legs; brown yarn hair, button eyes, painted features; legs or striped fabric for hose and black for shoes; original clothes; all in fair condition. (See *Doll Classics*, page 173.)

Mark: "PATENTED SEPT. 7, 1915"
(black stamp on front torso)

16in (41cm)	**$750**
Mint condition	**950**

Molly-'es Raggedy Ann or Andy: 1935—1938, manufactured by Molly-'es Doll Outfitters. Same as above, but with red hair and printed features; original clothes; all in good condition. (For photograph see *8th Blue Book*, page 195.)

Mark:
"Raggedy Ann and Raggedy Andy Dolls
Manufactured by Molly'es Doll Outfitters"
(printed writing in black on front torso)

16in (41cm) **$350—400****

LEFT: Knickerbocker ***Beloved Belindy***, all original with tag. *Esther Schwartz Collection.*
RIGHT: ***Beloved Belindy*** box. *Esther Schwartz Collection.*

Georgene Raggedy Ann or Andy: 1938-1963, manufactured by Georgene Novelties. Same as above, but with red hair and printed features; original clothes; all in good condition. See color photograph on page 212.

Mark: Cloth label sewn in side seam of body.

15—18in (38—46cm)	**$ 95—115***
Fair condition	**150 pair***
With two faces, 12in (31cm)	**400**
Beloved Belindy	**750****

*Allow more for black outlined nose.

**Not enough price samples to compute a reliable range.

Knickerbocker Toy Co. Raggedy Ann or Andy: 1963 to 1982. Excellent
   condition.

12in (31cm)	**$ 20—25**
24in (61cm)	**85—95**
36in (91cm)	**125—150**
Beloved Belindy	**300 up**

Raleigh

Maker: Jessie McCutcheon Raleigh, Chicago, Ill., U.S.A.
Date: 1916—1920
Material: All-composition or composition heads and cloth bodies
Designer: Jessie McCutcheon Raleigh
Mark: None

Raleigh Doll: Composition head, molded hair or wig, sleep or painted eyes;
   composition or cloth body; appropriate clothes; all in good condition. Child
   and baby styles.
   11—13in (28—33cm)   **$375—425**

11in (28cm) Raleigh doll, probably ***Goldilocks***, appears original. *H&J Foulke, Inc.*

Ravca

Maker: Bernard Ravca, Paris, France. After 1939, New York, N.Y., U.S.A.
Date: 1924—on
Material: Cloth with stockinette faces
Size: Various
Mark: Paper label: "Original Ravca Fabrication Francaise"

Ravca Doll: Stockinette face individually needle sculpted; cloth body and
limbs; original clothes; all in excellent condition.
10in (25cm)   **$ 85—95**
17in (43cm)   **210—235**

17in (43cm) Ravca French peasant man. *H&J Foulke, Inc.*

Raynal

Maker: Edouard Raynal, Paris, France
Date: 1922—on
Material: Felt and cloth, sometimes celluloid hands
Trademark: Poupees Raynal
Size: 17—18in (43—46cm)
Mark: "Raynal" on necklace or shoe soles

Raynal Doll: Molded felt mask face with mohair wig, beautifully painted
eyes, closed lips, rosy cheeks; stuffed cloth body (may have celluloid hands);
original clothes often of felt; all in good condition.
17—18in (43—46cm)   **$550—650**

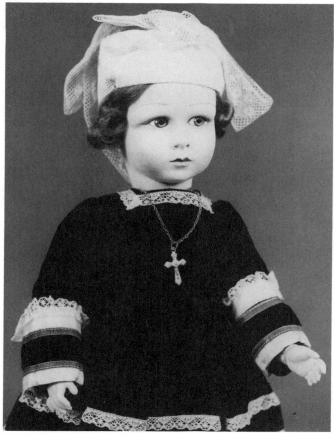

17in (43cm) Raynal girl, all original. *H&J Foulke, Inc.*

Recknagel

Maker: Th. Recknagel, porcelain factory, Alexandrienthal, Thüringia, Germany
Date: 1886—on
Material: Bisque head, composition or wood-jointed body
Size: Usually small
Mark:

1907
R/A DEP
I 9/0

9in (23cm) R.A. girl. *H&J Foulke, Inc.*

R. A. Child: Ca. 1890s-World War I. Perfect marked bisque head, jointed composition or wooden body; good wig, set or sleep eyes, open mouth; some dolls with molded painted shoes and socks; all in good condition.
1907, 1909, 1914, 1924:
8—9in (20—23cm)   **$150—175**
16—18in (41—46cm)   **300—325***
*Fine quality bisque only.

R. A. Character Baby: 1909-World War I. Perfect bisque socket head; cloth baby body or composition bent-limb baby body; painted or glass eyes; nicely dressed; all in good condition. *#127* and others.
Infants, 8—9in (20—23cm) long
                                      $225—275
Character babies, *#23* and others,
7—8in (18—20cm)   **275—325**
Bonnet babies, *#22 & 28:*
10in (25cm)   **450—475**

R.A. Character #31 Max: molded hair; painted features.
8in (20cm)   **$500—600**

10in (25cm) #28 character baby. See color photograph on page 213. *H&J Foulke, Inc.*

Rohmer Fashion

Maker: Madame Marie Rohmer, Paris, France
Date: 1857—1880
Material: China or bisque shoulder head, jointed kid body
Mark:

Rohmer Fashion: China or bisque swivel or shoulder head, jointed kid body, bisque or china arms, kid or china legs; lovely wig, set glass eyes, closed mouth, some ears pierced; fine costuming; entire doll in good condition.
16—18in (41—46cm) **$4500—5500***
*Allow extra for original clothes.

15in (38cm) Rohmer-type china fashion lady. *Private Collection.*

Rollinson Doll

Maker: Utley Doll Co., Holyoke, Mass., U.S.A.
Date: 1916—on
Material: All-cloth
Size: 14—28in (36—71cm)
Designer: Gertrude F. Rollinson
Mark: Stamp in shape of a diamond with a doll in center, around border
"Rollinson Doll Holyoke, Mass."

Marked Rollinson doll: All molded cloth with painted head and limbs; painted hair or human hair wig, painted features (sometimes teeth also); dressed; all in good condition. (See *8th Blue Book*, page 346 and *7th Blue Book*, page 327 for other Rollinson faces.)

Chase-type Baby with molded hair, 18—22in (46—51cm)	$ 850—900**
Toddler with wig, 16in (41cm)	950—1000**
Child with wig, 26in (66cm)	2500**

**Not enough price samples to compute a reliable range.

16in (41cm) Rollinson. *H&J Foulke, Inc.*

S.F.B.J.

Maker: Société Francaise de Fabrication de Bébés & Jouets, Paris, France
Date: 1899—
Material: Bisque head, composition body

Child Doll: 1899—on. Perfect bisque head, good French wig, set or sleep eyes, open mouth, pierced ears; jointed composition body; nicely dressed; all in good condition.

Jumeau-type (no mold number):

14—16in (36—41cm)	$ 900—1100
21—23in (53—58cm)	1500—1700
25—27in (64—69cm)	2000—2200

#301:

12—14in (31—36cm)	600—700
20—23in (51—58cm)	900—1000
28—30in (71—76cm)	1500—1700
Lady Body, 22in (56cm)	1100—1300

#60:

12—14in (31—36cm)	500—550
19—21in (48—53cm)	700—750
28in (71cm)	1100

Bleuette #301, (For photograph see *8th Blue Book*, page 347.)

10in (25cm)	500—600
Walking, Kissing and Flirting:	
22in (56cm)	1600—1700

Mark:

DÉPOSÉ
S.F.B.J.

S.F.B.J
301
PARIS

12in (31cm) S.F.B.J. 60 child. *H&J Foulke, Inc.*

S.F.B.J. continued

Character Dolls: 1910—on. Perfect bisque head, wig, molded, sometimes flocked hair on mold numbers ***237, 266, 227*** and ***235,*** sleep eyes, composition body; nicely dressed; all in good condition. (See previous *Blue Books* for illustrations of mold numbers not shown here.)

Mark:

S.F.B.J
230
PARIS

S.F.B.J
236
PARIS

#226, 235: 15—17in (38—43cm)	**$1650—1850**
#227, 237: See color photograph on page 214.	
9in (23cm)	**1200**
17—19in (43—48cm)	**2300—2500**
#230, (sometimes Jumeau):	
14—16in (36—41cm)	**1400—1500**
20—23in (51—58cm)	**1800—2000**
#233: Screamer, 20in (51cm)	**2400****
#234: Baby, 15in (38cm)	**2600****
#236: Baby, 17—18in (43—46cm)	**1200—1400**
10—12in (25—31cm)	**750—850**
Toddler, 14—15in (36—38cm)	**1500—1600**
27—28in (69—71cm)	**2300—2500**

**Not enough price samples to compute a reliable range.

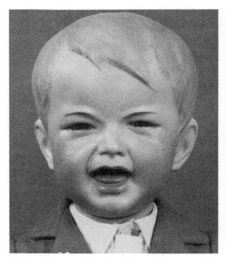

20½in (52cm) S.F.B.J. 233. See page 213 for color photograph. *Private Collection.*

13in (33cm) S.F.B.J. 242 nursing baby. *Private Collection.*

S.F.B.J. continued

#238, 229: Child, 15—16in (38—41cm)   2600—2800
#239: Five-piece crude body not original clothes, 13in (33cm)   4000—4500
#242: Nursing Baby 13in (33cm)   2600**
#245: (See page 200).
#247: Toddler, 16—18in (41—46cm)   2300—2600
  27in (69cm)   3200—3500
#251: Baby, 19in (48cm)   2000—2100
  Toddler, 14—15in (36—38cm)   1500—1600
  27—28in (69—71cm)   2500—2800
#252: Toddler, 12in (31cm)   4500—5000
  18—20in (48—53cm)   7000—7500

**Not enough price samples to compute a reliable range.

13½in (34cm) S.F.B.J. 247 toddler. *Private Collection.*

19in (48cm) S.F.B.J. 252 toddler. *Private Collection.*

Sasha

Maker: Trendon Toys, Ltd., Reddish, Stockport, England.
Date: 1865—1986
Material: All-vinyl
Designer: Sasha Morgenthaler

Sasha: All-vinyl of exceptionally high quality, long synthetic hair, painted features, wistful, appealing expression; original clothing, tiny circular wrist tag; excellent condition.

16in (41cm)	$ 125—150
In cylinder package	225—325
Gregor (boy)	150—175
Cora (black girl)	225—250
Caleb (black boy)	225—250
Black Baby	160—185
White Baby	125—135
Sexed Baby, pre 1979	200—225
Limited Edition Dolls:	
1982 *Pintucks Dress*	250—300
1983 *Kiltie*	250—300
1985 *Prince Gregor*	250—300
Gotz model 1965—69, mint and boxed, at auction	1000

1982 Limited Edition Sasha in "Pintucks" dress. *H&J Foulke, Inc.*

Black baby #4509, sexed girl, all original. *H&J Foulke, Inc.*

Bruno Schmidt

Maker: Bruno Schmidt, doll factory, Waltershausen, Thüringia, Germany.
Heads by Bähr & Pröschild, Ohrdruf, Thüringia, Germany.
Date: 1898—on
Material: Bisque head, composition body
Mark:

2096-4

Marked B. S. W. Child Doll: Ca.
1898—on. Bisque head, good wig,
sleep eyes, open mouth; jointed
composition child body; dressed;
all in good condition. (For photograph see *8th Blue Book*, page 351.)
20—23in (51—58cm)   **$500—575**
28—30in (71—76cm)   **850—950**

**Marked B. S. W. Character
Dolls:** Bisque socket head, glass
eyes; jointed composition body;
dressed; all in good condition.
#2048, 2094, 2096 (so-called
Tommy Tucker), molded hair, open
mouth, (For photograph see *7th
Blue Book*, page 334.)
19—21in (48—53cm)   **$1300—1500**
27—28in (69—71cm)   **2000—2200**
#2048 (closed mouth):
16—18in (41—46cm)   **2100—2400**
#2072:
17—19in (43—48cm)   **2900—3300**
(For photograph see *7th Blue Book*,
page 335.)
#2033 (so-called ***Wendy***) (***537***),
16in (41cm) at auction   **9900**
#2025 (***529***) closed mouth, wigged:
22in (56cm)   **4500—5000****
#2097, character baby open mouth,
wig: 18in (46cm) baby   **650—750**
#425 all-bisque baby:
6½ (17cm)   **250—275**
**Not enough price samples to com-
pute a reliable range.

18in (46cm) B. S. W. 2097 character baby.
H&J Foulke, Inc.

11in (28cm) B. S. W. 537 so-called ***Wendy***. See
color photograph on page 215. *Private Collection.*

Franz Schmidt

Maker: Franz Schmidt & Co., doll factory, Georgenthal near Waltershausen, Thüringia, Germany. Heads by Simon & Halbig, Grafenhain, Thüringia, Germany.

Date: 1890—on

Material: Bisque socket head, jointed bent-limb or toddler body of composition

---

Marked F.S. & Co. Character Baby: Ca. 1910. Perfect bisque character head, good wig, sleep eyes, open mouth, may have open nostrils; jointed bent-limb body; suitably dressed; all in good condition.

#1272, 1295, 1296, 1297, 1310:
Baby,

12—14in (31—36cm)	**$ 475—525**
20—21in (51—53cm)	**700—750**

Toddler,

7in (18cm)	**550—600**
12—15in (31—38cm)	**550—650**
19—21in (48—53cm)	**850—950**

#1286, molded hair with blue ribbon, glass eyes, open smiling mouth,
16in (41cm) toddler   **4000**

Mark:

1295
F. S. & Co.
Made in
Germany
30

Marked S & C Child Doll: Ca. 1890—on. Perfect bisque socket head, good wig, sleep eyes, open mouth; jointed composition child body; dressed; all in good condition. Some are Mold *#293.*

6in (15cm)	**$275—300**
16—18in (41—46cm)	**425—475**
22—24in (56—61cm)	**525—625**
29—30in (74—76cm)	**850—950**

Mark:

S & C
SIMON & HALBIG
28

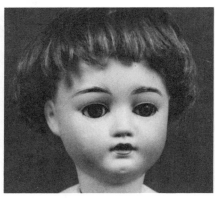

23in (58cm) F.S. & Co. 1272 character baby. See color photograph on page 215. *H&J Foulke, Inc.*

18in (46cm) S&C flapper, pierced nose, flapper body, rubber hands. For full view see page 17. *H&J Foulke, Inc.*

Schmitt

Maker: Schmitt & Fils, Paris, France
Date: 1854—1891
Material: Bisque socket head, composition jointed body
Size: Various
Mark: On both head and body:

Marked Schmitt Bébé: Ca. 1879. Perfect bisque socket head with skin or good wig, large paperweight eyes, closed mouth, pierced ears; Schmitt-jointed composition body; appropriate clothes; all in good condition.

Long face (as shown):
  16—18in (41—46cm)
         $10,000—12,000
  23—25in (58—64cm)
         16,000—18,000
Short face (For photograph see cover
Doll Classics):
  18—20in (46—51cm)
         14,000—15,000
Oval face:
  10—11in (25—28cm)
         8000
  22—24in (56—61cm)
         12,000—14,000
Cup and saucer neck:
  12in (31cm)   **12,000**
  16in (41cm)   **15,000—16,000**
Allow one-third less for dolls which do not have strongly molded faces.

23½in (60cm) Schmitt bébé. See color photograph on page 214. *Private Collection.*

Schoenau & Hoffmeister

Maker: Schoenau & Hoffmeister, Porzellanfabrik Burggrub, Burggrub, Bavaria, Germany. Arthur Schoenau also owned a doll factory.

Date: 1884—on dolls; 1901—on porcelain

Material: Bisque head, composition body

Trademarks: Hanna, Burggrub Baby, Bébé Carmencita, Viola, Kunstlerkopf, Das Lachende Baby.

Mark:

A S

S ⭐PB H
4600
Germany

Child Doll: 1901—on. Perfect bisque head; original or good wig, sleep eyes, open mouth; ball-jointed body; original or good clothes; all in nice condition. ***#1909, 5500, 5800, 5700.*** (For photograph see *7th Blue Book*, page 338.)

14—16in (36—41cm)	$ 275—325
21—23in (53—58cm)	450—550
28—30in (71—76cm)	700—800
33in (84cm)	950—1000
39in (99cm)	1800
#4600: 20in (51cm)	500—550

Character Baby: 1910—on. Perfect bisque socket head, good wig, sleep eyes, open mouth; composition bent-limb baby body; all in good condition. ***#169, 769,*** "Burggrub Baby" or "Porzellanfabrik Burggrub." (For photograph see *8th Blue Book*, page 355.)

13—15in (33—38cm)	$375—425
18—20in (46—51cm)	500—550
23—24in (58—61cm)	700—800

Hanna:

Baby, 14—16in (36—41cm)	$600—650
20—22in (51—56cm)	850—950
Toddler, 14—16in (36—41cm)	750—850

Das Lachende Baby, 1930. (For photograph see *8th Blue Book*, page 355.)

23—24in (58—61cm)	$2000**

Princess Elizabeth, 1932.
Chubby five-piece body.

17in (43cm)	$1900—2100
20—23in (51—58cm)	2400—2700

**Not enough price samples to compute a reliable range.

Schoenau & Hoffmeister continued

Pouty Baby: Ca. 1925. Perfect bisque solid dome head with painted hair, tiny sleep eyes, closed pouty mouth; cloth body with composition arms and legs; dressed; all in good condition. (For photograph see *8th Blue Book*, page 355.)

11—12in (28—31cm) $700—800**

**Not enough price samples to compute a reliable range.

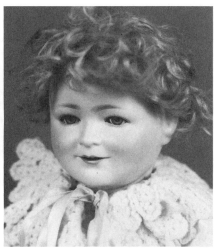

19in (48cm) *Princess Elizabeth*. Private Collection.

20in (51cm) S PB H 4600 child. *H&J Foulke, Inc.*

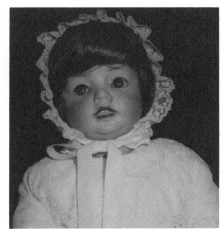

18in (46cm) *Hanna*. Lesley Hurford Collection.

Schoenhut

Maker: Albert Schoenhut & Co., Philadephia, Pa., U.S.A.
Date: 1872—on
Material: Wood, spring-jointed, holes in bottom of feet to fit metal stand
Size: Various models 11—21in (28—53cm)
Designer: Early: Adolph Graziana and Mr. Leslie
Later: Harry E. Schoenhut
Mark: Paper label: Incised:

SCHOENHUT DOLL
PAT. JAN. 17,'11, U.S.A.
& FOREIGN COUNTRIES

Character: 1911—1930. Wooden head and spring-jointed wooden body, marked head and/or body; original or appropriate wig, brown or blue intaglio eyes, open/closed mouth with painted teeth or closed mouth; original or suitable clothing; nothing repainted. Pouty or smiling.
14—21in (36—53cm)
Excellent condition	**$1300—1800***
Good, some wear	**900—1100**

*Depending upon rarity of face.

Character with carved hair: Ca. 1911—1930. Wooden head with carved hair, comb marks, possibly a ribbon or bow, intaglio eyes, mouth usually closed; spring-jointed wooden body; original or suitable clothes.
14—21in (36—53cm):
Excellent condition	**$2000—2300**
Good, some wear	**1600—2000**
Early style	**2500—3000**

See color photographs on pages 216 and 217.

Schoenhut continued

16in (41cm) #300 pouty girl. *Yvonne Baird Collection.*

16in (41cm) #309 pouty girl. *Private Collection.*

16in (41cm) #310 pouty girl. *Esther Schwartz Collection.*

Schoenhut continued

Baby Face: Ca. 1913—1930. Wooden head and fully-jointed toddler or bent-limb baby body, marked head and/or body; painted hair or mohair wig, painted eyes, open or closed mouth; suitably dressed; nothing repainted; all in good condition.

Mark:

Baby,

12in (31cm)	$500—550
15—16in (38—41cm)	650—750

Toddler,

14in (36cm)	800—850
11in (28cm)	800—900
16—17in (41—43cm)	800—850

See color photograph on page 216.

Dolly Face: Ca. 1915—1930. Wooden head and spring-jointed wooden body; original or appropriate mohair wig, decal eyes, open/closed mouth with painted teeth; original or suitable clothes.

14—21in (36—53cm)

Excellent condition,	$750—850
Good condition, some wear,	450—650

16in (41cm) dolly face girl with sleep eyes. *Private Collection.*

Schoenhut continued

Walker: Ca. 1919—1930. All-wood with "baby face," mohair wig, painted eyes; curved arms, straight legs with "walker" joint at hip; original or appropriate clothes; all in good condition. No holes in bottom of feet.

13in (33cm)   **$800—850**

Sleep Eyes: Ca. 1920—1930. Used with "baby face" or "dolly face" heads. Mouths on this type were open with teeth or barely open with carved teeth. (For photograph see *8th Blue Book*, page 259.)

14—21in (36—53cm)
Excellent condition   **$1200—1400**
Good condition   **750—850**

All-Composition: Ca. 1924. Jointed at neck, shoulders and hips, right arm bent, molded blonde curly hair, painted eyes, tiny closed mouth; original or appropriate clothing; in fair condition. (See photograph in *8th Blue Book*, page 359.)

Paper label on back:

13in (33cm)   **$400****

**Not enough price samples to compute a reliable range.

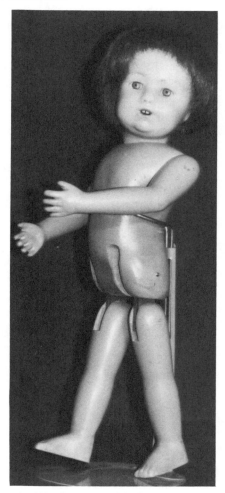

13in (33cm) walker with sleep eyes, open mouth and two metal teeth. *Courtesy of Paula Ryscik.*

Schuetzmeister & Quendt

Maker: Schuetzmeister & Quendt, porcelain factory, Boilstadt, Thüringia, Germany, made heads for Welsch, Kämmer & Reinhardt, Wolf & Co.
Date: 1889
Material: Bisque head, composition body
Distributor: John Bing Co., New York, N.Y., U.S.A.

S & Q Child Doll: Ca. 1900. Perfect bisque head with mohair wig, sleep eyes, open mouth with teeth; jointed composition body; nicely dressed.
Mark:

S & Q
101
Dep.
6.

#101 Jeanette:

16—18in (41—46cm)	$325—375
24—25in (61—64cm)	500—550

S & Q Character Baby: Ca. 1910. Perfect bisque head with mohair wig, sleep eyes, open mouth with tongue and teeth, slightly smiling; composition baby body; nicely dressed; all in good condition.
Mark:

301
S&Q
Germany

#201, 301:

13—15in (33—38cm)	$375—425
18—20in (46—51cm)	500—550
23—24in (58—61cm)	700—800

16in (41cm) S&Q 101. *H&J Foulke, Inc.*

Shirley Temple

Maker: Ideal Novelty Toy Corp., New York, N.Y., U.S.A.
Date: 1934 to present
Size: 7½—36in (19—91cm)
Designer: Bernard Lipfert
Mark: See individual doll listings below. (Ideal used marked Shirley Temple bodies for other dolls).

All-Composition Child: 1934 through late 1930s. Marked head and body, jointed composition body; all original including wig and clothes; entire doll in very good condition. Came in sizes 11—27in (28—69cm)

Mark: On body:

SHIRLEY TEMPLE
13
13

On head: **SHIRLEY TEMPLE**

On cloth label:

Genuine SHIRLEY TEMPLE DOLL REGISTERED U.S. PAT OFF IDEAL NOVELTY & TOY CO	MADE IN USA

11in (28cm)	**$625—675***
13in (33cm)	**550—600***
15—16in (38—41cm)	**500—600***
18in (46cm)	**600—650***
20—22in (51—56cm)	**650—700***
25in (64cm)	**775—825***
27in (69cm)	**950—1050***
Button	**75—85**
Dress, tagged	**100 up**
Trunk	**100—125**

*Allow more for mint-in-box doll or one with unusual outfit.

27in (69cm) flirty-eyed composition *Shirley Temple*, all original and boxed. *H&J Foulke, Inc.*

Shirley Temple continued

18in (46cm) composition **Shirley Temple**, all original. *Private Collection.*

Baby: 1934 through late 1930s. Composition swivel head with molded hair or blonde mohair wig, sleep eyes, open smiling mouth, dimples; cloth body, composition arms and legs; appropriate clothes; all in good condition. Came in six sizes, 16—25in (41—64cm). (For photograph see *7th Blue Book*, page 346.)

Mark: "Shirley Temple" on head
16—18in (41—46cm)   **$850—950**

All-composition Shirley with molded hair: Late 1930s. Made in Japan. (For photograph see *8th Blue Book*, page 362.)
7½in (19cm)   **$225—250**

Hawaiian Shirley: Brown composition with black yarn hair, painted eyes; original grass skirt and ornaments; all in good condition.
13in (33cm)   **$600****
18in (46cm)   **750****
**Not enough price samples to compute a reliable range.

17in (43cm) vinyl **Shirley Temple**, 1957, all original. *H&J Foulke, Inc.*

Shirley Temple continued

Vinyl and Plastic: 1957. Vinyl and plastic, rooted hair, sleep eyes; jointed at shoulders and hips; original clothes; all in excellent condition. Came in sizes 12in (31cm), 15in (38cm), 17in (43cm), 19in (48cm) and 36in (91cm).

Mark: "Ideal Doll ST—12"
              (number denotes size)

12in (31cm)	**$ 165**
15in (38cm)	**225—250**
17in (43cm)	**300—350**
19in (48cm)	**375—400**
36in (91cm)	**1400**
Script name pin	**20**
Name purse	**15**

Vinyl and Plastic: 1973. Vinyl and plastic, rooted hair, painted eyes, smiling mouth; jointed shoulders and hips; original clothes; all in mint condition. (For photograph see *4th Blue Book*, page 302.)

16in (41cm) size only	**$ 90—95**
Boxed	**125**
Boxed dress	**30—35**

15in (38cm) vinyl **Shirley Temple**, 1957, all original. *H&J Foulke, Inc.*

Simon & Halbig

Maker: Simon & Halbig, porcelain factory, Gräfenhain, Thüringia, Germany; purchased by Kämmer & Reinhardt in 1920
Date: 1869—on
Material: Bisque head, kid (sometimes cloth) or composition body
Mark: S 13 H   1079-2
          949   DEP
                S H
                Germany

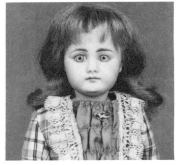

16½in (42cm) S&H 949, closed mouth, swivel neck, shoulder plate, kid body. *Private Collection.*

15½in (39cm) S&H 939, closed mouth. *Yvonne Baird Collection.*

**Not enough price samples to compute a reliable range.

Child doll with closed mouth: Ca. 1879. Perfect bisque socket head on ball-jointed wood and composition body; good wig, glass set or sleep eyes, closed mouth, pierced ears; dressed; all in good condition. See *Simon & Halbig Dolls - The Artful Aspect* for photographs of mold numbers not shown here.

#719, 749, 939:
15—17in (38—43cm)
$2200—2500
22—24in (56—61cm)
3200—3500
27—29in (69—74cm)
4000

#949:
17—20in (43—51cm)
2000—2500

#905, 908:
16—18in (41—46cm)
2500—2700

#929:
16in (41cm) **2400****

#720, 740, 940, 950 (kid body):
9—10in (23—25cm)
500—550
18—20in (46—51cm)
1500—1800

#949 (kid body)
20—22in (51—56cm)
1800—2200

S.H. shoulder head (kid body);
15—17in (38—43cm)
1500—1800**

Young lady, swivel neck, twill-covered body, 9in (23cm) **2500****

Simon & Halbig continued

All-Bisque Child: 1880—on. All-bisque child with swivel neck, pegged shoulders and hips; appropriate mohair wig, glass eyes, open or closed mouth; molded stockings and shoes.

#886 & 890:
Over-the-knee black or blue stockings. (For photograph see page 46.)

5½—6in (14—15cm)	**$ 550—600***
7—7½in (18—19cm)	**700—750***

Early model with five-strap bootines, closed mouth:

7—8in (18—20cm)	**1100—1250***
#939, open mouth, 9in (23cm)	**1650***

*Allow extra for original clothes.

Child doll with open mouth and composition body: Ca. 1889 to 1930s. Perfect bisque head, good wig, sleep eyes, open mouth, pierced ears; original ball-jointed composition body; very pretty clothes; all in nice condition. See *Simon & Halbig Dolls - The Artful Aspect* for photographs of mold numbers not shown here.

#719, 739, 939, 949, 979:

12—14in (31—36cm)	**$1050—1250**
19—22in (48—56cm)	**1900—2200**
29—30in (74—76cm)	**2700—3000**

#1039, 1078, 1079:

10in (25cm)	**500—550**
12—14in (31—36cm)	**450—500**
17—19in (43—48cm)	**525—575**
22—24in (56—61cm)	**625—725**
28—30in (71—76cm)	**1000—1200**
34—35in (86—89cm)	**1800—2100**
42in (107cm)	**3200—3500**
46in (117cm)	**4700**

#1009:

19—21in (48—53cm)	**750—850**

#1248, 1249, Santa:

13—15in (33—38cm)	**650—700**
21—24in (53—61cm)	**1000—1200**
26—28in (66—71cm)	**1400—1600**

#1039 key-wind walking body:

13—14in (33—36cm)	**1500—1600**

#1039 walking, kissing:

20—22in (51—56cm)	**900—1000**

7½in (19cm) all-bisque Simon & Halbig with open mouth, two upper teeth, and one lower tooth, yellow painted hose, black boots with straps. *Private Collection.*

See photographs on pages 9 and 217.

Simon & Halbig continued

15in (38cm) S&H 989 child, 2 square upper teeth. *Private Collection.*

#540, 550, 570 Baby Blanche:
22—24in (56—61cm)   **550—600**

21in (53cm) S&H 1079 child, all original. *H&J Foulke, Inc.*

22in (56cm) S&H 550 child. *H&J Foulke, Inc.*

Simon & Halbig continued

22in (56cm) S&H 570 child. *H&J Foulke, Inc.*

20in (51cm) S&H 1078 child. *H&J Foulke, Inc.*

S&H 1149 child. *Courtesy of Jean Hess.*

Simon & Halbig continued

Child doll with open mouth and kid body: Ca. 1889 to 1930s. Perfect bisque swivel head on shoulder plate or shoulder head with stationary neck, sleep eyes, open mouth, pierced ears; kid body, bisque arms, cloth lower legs; well costumed; all in good condition.

#1010, 1040, 1080:

14—16in (36—41cm)	**$425—475**
21—23in (53—58cm)	**600—650**
#1009 fashion-type body: 17—19in (43—48cm)	**650—750**

#1250, 1260:

14—16in (36—41cm)	**450—500**
22—24in (56—61cm)	**725—775**
29in (74cm)	**950**

Tiny Child doll: Ca. 1889 to 1930s. Usually mold number ***1079*** or ***1078***. Perfect bisque head, nice wig, sleep eyes, open mouth; composition body with molded shoes and socks: appropriate clothes; all in good condition.

7—8in (18—20cm)	**$375**
10in (25cm) walker, five-piece body	**600**
Fully-jointed: 8—10in (20—25cm)	**500—550**

So-called Little Women type: Ca. 1900. Mold number ***1160***. Shoulder head with fancy mohair wig, glass set eyes, closed mouth; cloth body with bisque limbs, molded boots; dressed; all in good condition.

5½—7in (14—18cm)	**$325—375**
10—11in (25—28cm)	**425—475**
Head only: 1½—2½in (4—6cm)	**60—80**
2½—3in (6—8cm)	**130**

Character Child: Ca. 1909. Perfect bisque socket head with wig or molded hair, painted or glass eyes, open or closed mouth, character face, jointed composition body; dressed; all in good condition. (See *Simon & Halbig Dolls - The Artful Aspect* for photographs of mold numbers not shown here.)

#120: 20—23in (51—58cm)	**$ 2300—2600**
#150: 20in (51cm)	**12,000****
#151: See color photograph on page 219. 13in (33cm)	**3900**
18—19in (46—48cm)	**6500**
#153: 16in (41cm)	**8500****
#1279: 15—17in (38—43cm)	**1500—1800**
22—25in (56—64cm)	**2700—3200**
34in (86cm) at auction	**9500**
#1299: 19—21in (48—53cm)	**950—1050**
#1339: 18in (46cm)	**950****
28—32in (71—81cm)	**1700—2000****

Simon & Halbig continued

#1388: 23in (58cm)   **12,000****
#1398: 23in (58cm)   **12,000****
IV, #1448: 18in (46cm)   **12,000****
**Not enough price samples to compute a reliable range.

6in (15cm) S&H 1160 lady. *H&J Foulke, Inc.*

14½in (37cm) S&H 150 character child. *Jackie Kaner.*

13in (33cm) S&H 1279 character child. *Yvonne Baird Collection.*

Simon & Halbig continued

Character Baby: Ca. 1909 to 1930s. Perfect bisque head, molded hair or wig, sleep or painted eyes, open or open/closed mouth; composition bent-limb baby or toddler body; nicely dressed; all in good condition. (See *Simon & Halbig Dolls - The Artful Aspect* for photographs of mold numbers not shown here.)

#1294:

Baby, 17—19in (43—48cm)	$ 650—700
23—25in (58—64cm)	1000—1200
Toddler, 20in (51cm)	1000—1100

#1428:

Baby, 12—13in (31—33cm)	900—1000
Toddler 18in (46cm)	1750—1850
25in (64cm)	2500

#1488:

Toddler, 14—15in (36—38cm)	2800—3000
22—24in (56—61cm)	3500—3700

#1489, Erika:

Baby, 21—22in (53—56cm)	3200—3600

#1498: See color photograph on page 218.

Toddler, 17in (43cm)	3000—3200

Lady doll: Ca. 1910. Perfect bisque socket head, good wig, sleep eyes, pierced ears; lady body, molded bust, slim arms and legs; dressed; all in good condition.

#1159:

12in (31cm)	$ 750—850
16—18in (41—46cm)	1350—1600
22in (56cm)	2300
26—27in (66—69cm)	2600—2700

#1468, 1469: See color photograph on page 218.

13—15in (33—38cm)	2500—4200*

#1303:

15—16in (38—41cm)	7000 up**

#152:

18in (46cm)	10,000 up**

#1308 Man:

13in (33cm)	5250

**Not enough price samples to compute a reliable range.

*Wide range usually indicates imminent rise to higher price.

Simon & Halbig continued

25in (64cm) S&H 1159 lady, all original. See color photograph on page 366. *Private Collection*.

Snow Babies

Maker: Various German firms including Hertwig & Co. and Bähr & Pröschild after 1910.
Date: Ca. 1890 until World War II
Material: All-bisque
Size: 1—3in (3—8cm) usually
Mark: Sometimes "Germany"

Snow Babies: All-bisque with snowsuits and caps of pebbly-textured bisque; painted features; various standing, lying or sitting positions.

1½in (4cm)	**$ 35**
2½in (6cm)	**75—85**
1½in (4cm) snow bear	**35**
1½in (4cm) snowman	**75**
3in (8cm) baby riding snow bear	**165—185**
2½in (6cm) tumbling snow baby	**110—125**
2in (5cm) musical snow baby	**75**
2in (5cm) baby on sled	**75**
3in (8cm) baby on sled	**135—150**
2in (5cm) reindeer pulling snow baby	**165—185**
2in (5cm) early fine quality babies with high hoods	**100—110**
3 small babies on sled	**135—145**
Santa on snow bear	**300—325**
3in (8cm) jointed snow baby	**250—275**
10in (25cm) snow baby shoulder head doll, cloth body, bisque limbs	**400—425**
Santa in car	**350**

Snow Babies on sled. *H&J Foulke, Inc.*

Family of snow bears. *H&J Foulke, Inc.*

Sonneberg Täufling
(So-called Motschmann Baby)

Maker: Various Sonneberg factories such as Heinrich Stier; many handled by exporter Louis Lindner & Söhn, Sonneberg, Thüringia, Germany
Date: 1851—1880s
Material: Papier-mâché, wood and cloth
Size: 8in (20cm) to about 28in (71cm)
Mark: None

Sonneberg Täufling: Papier-mâché or wax-over-composition head with painted hair or wig, glass eyes, closed mouth or open mouth with bamboo teeth; composition lower torso; composition arms and legs jointed at ankles and wrists, cloth covered midsection with voice box, upper arms and legs cloth covered, called floating joints; dressed in shirt and bonnet.

Very good condition:

12—14in (31—36cm)	$ 500—550
18—20in (46—51cm)	750—900
24in (61cm)	1150

Fair condition, with wear:

12—14in (31—36cm)	400—450
18—20in (46—51cm)	650—750
24in (61cm)	850

14in (36cm) Sonneberg Täufling. *H&J Foulke, Inc.*

NOTE: For many years it was thought that these dolls were made by Ch. Motschmann, since some were found stamped with his name; hence, they were called ***Motschmann Babies*** by collectors. However, research has shown that they were made by various factories and that Motschmann was the holder of the patent for the voice boxes, not the manufacturer of the dolls.

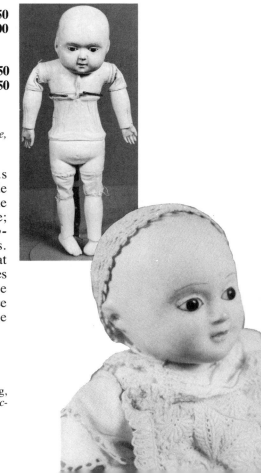

Wax-over-composition Sonneberg Täufling, all original. *Dr. Carole Stoessel Zvonar Collection.*

Steiff

Maker: Fraulein Margarete Steiff, Würtemberg, Germany
Date: 1894—on
Material: Felt, plush or velvet
Size: Various
Mark: Metal button in ear

Steiff "Witch" character. *Kay & Wayne Jensen Collection.*

Steiff Doll: Felt, plush or velvet, jointed; seam down middle of face, button eyes, painted features; original clothes; most are character dolls, many have large shoes to enable them to stand; all in good condition; some wear acceptable.

Children (Character Dolls):
    11—12in (28—31cm) **$ 900**
    16—17in (41—43cm)   **1300—1500**

Caricature or Comic Dolls:
                          1200—3500*
    18in (46cm) Soldiers **3000 up**
    18in (46cm) Dutch   **3000**
    20in (51cm) Sailor, jointed knee
                            3500

*Depending upon rarity, condition and accessories.

Steiff "Mama Katzenjammer." *Kay & Wayne Jensen Collection.*

E.U. Steiner

Maker: Edmund Ulrich Steiner, doll factory, Sonneberg, Thüringia, Germany
Date: 1864—on
Material: Bisque heads, kid, cloth or composition body
Trademark: Magestic
Mark:

MAJESTIC
Reg^d
Germany

E.U. Steiner Child Doll: Ca. 1902. Perfect bisque head, original or appropriate wig, sleep or set glass eyes, open mouth; ball-jointed composition body or kid body; appropriately dressed; entire doll in good condition.

Kid body:

14—16in (36—41cm)	$225—250
22—24in (56—61cm)	350—400

Composition body:

15—17in (38—43cm)	300—350
23—25in (58—64cm)	425—475

25in (64cm) E.U. Steiner child. *H&J Foulke, Inc.*

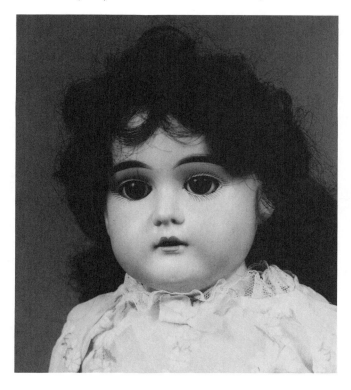

Herm Steiner

Maker: Hermann Steiner of Sonneberg, Thüringia, Germany
Date: 1921—on
Material: Bisque head, cloth or composition body
Size: Various, usually small
Mark:

15
}S(
Germany
2 4 0

Herm Steiner
}S(
Germany

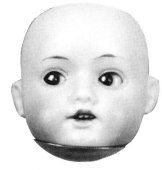

Hermann Steiner #128 child with patented eye having movable pupil, the "Lifelike Steiner Eye." *H&J Foulke, Inc.*

Hermann Steiner infant, cloth body. *H&J Foulke, Inc.*

Herm Steiner Child: Perfect bisque head, wig, sleep eyes, open mouth; jointed composition body; dressed; in good condition.
7—8in (18—20cm) **$150—175**
14—16in (36—41cm) **275—300**
#128 with special eye movement
14in (36cm) **325****

Herm Steiner Infant: Perfect bisque head, molded hair, sleep eyes, closed mouth; cloth or composition bent-limb body; dressed; in good condition.
Head circumference:
7—8in (18—20in) **$225**

Herm Steiner Character Baby: Perfect bisque socket head, good wig, sleep eyes, open mouth with teeth; composition jointed baby body; dressed; all in good condition.
9—11in (23—28cm) **$225—275**
**Not enough price samples to compute a reliable range.

Jules Steiner

Maker: Jules Nicolas Steiner and Successors, Paris, France
Date: 1855—1908
Material: Bisque head, jointed papier-mâché body

Marked C or A Series Steiner Bébé: 1880s. Perfect socket head, cardboard
pate, appropriate wig, sleep eyes with wire mechanism, bulgy paperweight
eyes with tinting on upper eyelids, closed mouth, round face, pierced ears
with tinted tips; jointed composition body with straight wrists and stubby
fingers (sometimes with bisque hands); dressed; all in good condition.
Sometimes with wire-operated sleep eyes. Sizes 4/0 (8in) to 8 (38in). For
Series "A" face see *7th Blue Book*, page 360.
Mark: (incised)

$$S^{IE} \; A \; O$$

(red script)

J Steiner. Bte S.g. Bg. J Bourgoin S½

(incised)

$$S^{IE} \; C \; 4$$

(red stamp)

J. STEINER B.S.G.D.G.

8in (20cm)	**$ 3000**
10in (25cm)	**3200**
15—16in (38—41cm)	**4200—4700**
21—24in (53—61cm)	**6000—7000**
33in (84cm) at auction	**13,000**
Open mouth, lever eyes:	
17in (43cm)	**3800**

23in (58cm) Series C Steiner Bébé. *Private Collection.*

Jules Steiner continued

Round face with open mouth: Ca. 1870s. Perfect very pale bisque socket head, appropriate wig, bulgy paperweight eyes, open mouth with pointed teeth, round face, pierced ears; jointed composition body; dressed; all in good condition.

Mark: None, but sometimes body has a label

Two rows of teeth, (For photograph see *8th Blue Book*, page 378.)

    18—20in (46—51cm)   **$3000****

Kicking, crying bébé, mechanical key-wind body with composition arms and lower legs, 18in (46cm)   **2100—2300**

Motschmann-type body with bisque shoulders, hips and lower arms and legs.

    (For photograph see *7th Blue Book*, page 361 and color photograph on page 220.)

    18—21in (46—53cm)   **4500****

**Not enough price samples to compute a reliable range.

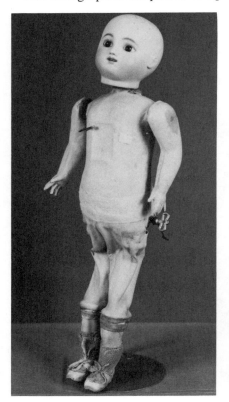

22in (56cm) mechanical kicking-crying Steiner. *Private Collection.*

13in (33cm) Figure C ⅗ Steiner Bébé. *Private Collection.*

Figure A Bébé: Ca. 1887—on. Perfect bisque socket head, cardboard pate, appropriate wig, paperweight eyes, closed mouth, pierced ears; jointed composition body; dressed; all in good condition. See color photograph on page 219.

Mark: (incised)

J. STEINER
Bᵀᴱ S.G.D.G.
PARIS
Fᴵ ᴬᶠ A 15

Body and/or head may be stamped:
"Le Petit Parisien
BEBE STEINER
MEDAILLE d'OR
PARIS 1889"
or paper label of doll carrying flag

8in (20cm)	**$2300—2500***
15—16in (38—41cm)	**4000—4500***
22—25in (56—64cm)	**6000—7000***
10in (25cm) with trunk and wardrobe	**3850**

*Allow slightly more for Figure C.

Bébé Le Parisien: 1892—on. Perfect bisque socket head, cardboard pate, appropriate wig, paperweight eyes, closed or open mouth, pierced ears; jointed composition body; dressed; all in good condition.

Mark: head (incised):

A-19
PARIS

(red stamp):
"LE PARISIEN"
body (purple stamp):
"BEBE 'LE PARISIEN'
MEDAILLE D'OR
PARIS"

Closed mouth:

13—15in (33—38cm)	**$3000—3200**
18—20in (46—51cm)	**4500—5200**
23—25in (58—64cm)	**6000—6500**

Open mouth:

20—22in (51—56cm)	**2500—2700**

22in (56cm) Figure A-15 Steiner Bébé. *Private Collection.*

13in (33cm) A-5 Le Parisien Bébé. *Betty Harms Collection.*

Swaine & Co.

Maker: Swaine & Co., porcelain factory, Hüttensteinach, Sonneberg, Thüringia, Germany
Date: Ca. 1910—on for doll heads
Material: Bisque socket head, composition baby body
Mark: Stamped in green:

Incised Lori: Perfect bisque solid dome head, painted hair, sleep eyes, closed mouth; composition baby body with bent limbs; dressed; all in good condition. (For photograph see *7th Blue Book*, page 363.)
22—24in (56—61cm)   **$2800—3000**

#232: (open-mouth ***Lori***):
(For photograph see *5th Blue Book*, page 299.)
20in (51cm)   **1500—1700**
DIP: (wig, glass eyes, closed mouth):
9—10in (23—25cm)   **600—700**
15in (38cm)   **1150**
DV: (molded hair, glass eyes open/closed mouth):
12—14in (31—36cm)   **1300—1500**
DI: (For photograph see *8th Blue Book*, page 380.) (molded hair, intaglio eyes, open/closed mouth):
12—13in (31—33cm)   **800—850**
B.P., B.O.: (For photograph see *6th Blue Book*, page 322.) (smiling character):
16—18in (41—46cm)
3500—3800**
F.P.:
9in (23cm)   **1600**

**Not enough price samples to compute a reliable range.

15in (38cm) B.P. character. *Private Collection.*

16½in (42cm) DIP toddler. *Private Collection.*

Terri Lee

Maker: TERRI LEE Sales Corp., V. Gradwohl, Pres., U.S.A.
Date: 1946-Lincoln, Neb.,; then Apple Valley, Calif., from 1952-Ca. 1962
Material: First dolls, rubbery plastic composition; later, hard plastic
Size: 16in (41cm) and 10in (25cm)
Mark: embossed across shoulders
First dolls:

> "TERRI LEE
> PAT. PENDING"

raised letters
Later dolls: "TERRI LEE"

Terri Lee Child Doll: Original wig, painted eyes; jointed at neck, shoulders and hips; all original clothing and accessories; very good condition.

16in (41cm): (See additional photograph on page 11.)

Early model	**$225—275**
Hard plastic	**175—225**

Jerri Lee,

16in (41cm)	**225**

Tiny Terri Lee, inset eyes, (For photograph see *8th Blue Book*, page 381.)

10in (25cm)	**125—135**

Tiny Jerri Lee, inset eyes,

10in (25cm)	**185**
Connie Lynn	**350**
Mint-in-box	**400**

Linda Baby (For photograph see *8th Blue Book*, page 381.)   **150—175**

Ginger Girl Scout

8in (20cm)	**95**

10in (25cm) ***Tiny Jerri Lee***, all original. *H&J Foulke, Inc.*

8in (20cm) ***Ginger Girl Scout*** marketed by Terri Lee. *Courtesy of Carolyn Guzzio.*

LEFT: 16in (41cm) ***Terri Lee*** (Patent Pending), redressed. *H&J Foulke, Inc.*

Unis

Maker: Société Française de Fabrication de Bébés et Jouets.
(S. F. B. J.) of Paris and Montruil-sous-Bois, France
Date: 1922—on
Material: Bisque head, composition body
Size: 5in (13cm) up
Mark:

71 UNIS FRANCE 149
301

Unis Child Doll: Perfect bisque head, wood and composition jointed body; good wig, sleep eyes, open mouth; pretty clothes; all in nice condition.

#301 or 60 (fully-jointed body):

8—10in (20—25cm)	**$ 375—425**
15—17in (38—43cm)	**525—575**
23—25in (58—64cm)	**800—900**
28in (71cm) original box	**1200**

Five-piece body:

5in (13cm) painted eyes	**125—150**
6½in (17cm)	**175—200**
11—13in (28—33cm)	**275—325**
Black or brown bisque, 11—13in (28—33cm)	**350—375**

Princess: See page 254.

#251 character toddler:

14—15in (36—38cm)	**1300—1400**

Composition head 301 or 60:

11—13in (28—33cm)	**150—175**

18½in (47cm) Unis 301 child. *Kiefer Collection.*

6½in (17cm) Unis 301 child, all original. *H&J Foulke, Inc.*

Verlingue

Maker: J. Verlingue of Boulogne-sur-Mer, France
Date: 1914—1921
Material: Bisque head, composition body
Size: Various
Mark:

PETITE FRANÇAISE
FRANCE
J V
3/0 D
LIANE

Marked J. V. Child: Perfect bisque
head, good wig, glass eyes, open
mouth; jointed papier-mâché
body; nicely dressed.
15—17in (38—43cm) $525—575
22—24in (56—61cm)   800—900
Painted eyes
  14in (36cm)   450—475

Verlingue All-bisque Doll: Head
with wig, swivel neck, sleep eyes,
closed mouth; jointed shoulders
and hips; long painted hose, garters, black boots; undressed; mediocre quality.
7in (18cm) $250—300

14in (36cm) ***Petite Française Liane***, painted
eyes. *H&J Foulke, Inc.*

Vogue-Ginny®

Maker: Vogue Dolls, Inc.
Date: 1937—on
Material: 1937—1948 composition, 1948—1962 hard plastic
Size: 7—8in (18—20cm)
Creator: Jennie Graves
Clothes Designer: Virginia Graves Carlson
Clothes Label: "Vogue," "Vogue Dolls," or

> VOGUE DOLLS, INC.
> MEDFORD, MASS. USA
> ® REG U.S. PAT OFF

All-composition Toddles: Jointed neck, shoulders and hips; molded hair or mohair wig, painted eyes looking to side; original clothes; all in good condition.

Mark: "VOGUE" on head
"DOLL CO." on back
"TODDLES" stamped on sole of shoe

7—8in (18—20cm)	**$200—250**
Mint condition	**275—325**

Hard Plastic Ginny: All-hard plastic, jointed at neck, shoulders and hips (some have jointed knees and some walk); nice wig, sleep eyes (early ones have painted eyes, later dolls have molded eyelashes); original clothes; all in excellent condition with perfect hair and pretty coloring.

Mark: On strung dolls: "VOGUE DOLLS"
On walking dolls: "GINNY//VOGUE DOLLS"

7—8in (18—20cm):
1948—1949:

Painted eyes	**$250—350**
Separate outfits	**50—65**

1950—1953:

Painted eyelashes, strung,	**250—300**
Caracul wig*	**325—350**
Separate outfits	**50—65**

1954:

Painted eyelashes, walks	**200—250**
Separate outfits	**45—55**

1955—1957:

Molded eyelashes, walks	**150—175**
Separate outfits	**40—50**

1957—1962:

Molded eyelashes, walks, jointed knees	**125—150**
Separate outfits	**30—40**
Crib Crowd Baby, 1950	**550 up**

*See color photograph on page 220.

Ginny® is a registered trademark of Vogue Dolls, Inc.

Vogue-Ginny continued

Vogue **Toddles Alice in Wonderland**, all original. *H&J Foulke, Inc.*

Vogue **Ginny** skater, strung, all original. *H&J Foulke, Inc.*

Vogue **Ginny** walker, all original. *H&J Foulke, Inc.*

Wagner & Zetzsche

Maker: Wagner & Zetzsche, doll factory, Ilmenau, Thüringia, Germany. Bisque heads by porcelain factories including Gebrüder Heubach and Alt, Beck & Gottschalck

Date: 1875—on

Material: Bisque head, cloth, kid or composition body, celluloid-type heads

---

Closed-mouth Child: Ca. 1880s. Perfect turned bisque shoulder head with solid dome (mold *639*) or open crown (mold *698*), sometimes with plaster dome, mohair wig, paperweight eyes (a few with sleep eyes), flat eyebrows, closed mouth, small ears; kid or cloth body with bisque hands; appropriate clothes; all in good condition.

Mark: Blue paper body label with "W Z" initials entwined in fancy scroll.

15—17in (38—43cm)	**$550—650**
20—22in (51—56cm)	**750—850**
26in (66cm)	**1000—1100**

Character Baby or Child: Ca. 1910. Perfect bisque socket head, wig, sleep eyes, open mouth with upper teeth; dressed; all in good condition.

Mark:

#10586 made by Gebrüder Heubach.

Baby body, 16—18in (41—46cm)	**$550—600**
Kid and composition body,	
14—16in (36—41cm)	**450—550**
#10585 (shoulder head, kid body):	
16—18in (41—46cm)	**350—400**

Portrait Children: 1915—on. Celluloid-type head (*Haralit*) with molded hair, painted eyes. Portraits of the children of Max Zetzsche: *Harold, Hansi,* and *Inge*.

Mark: "Harald
    W.Z."
        (or name of child)

14in (36cm) *Harald*. (For photograph see *6th Blue Book*, page 363.)	
Fair condition	**$250****
8in (20cm) *Hansi*	**125****
Inge, 1924, 14in (36cm). For photograph see *8th Blue Book*, page 279.	
Excellent	**450****

**Not enough price samples to compute a reliable range.

Wagner & Zetzsche continued

22in (56cm) 698 made by Alt, Beck & Gottschalck for Wagner & Zetzsche. *H&J Foulke, Inc.*

15in (38cm) 10586 made by Gebrüder Heubach for Wagner & Zetzsche. *H&J Foulke, Inc.*

Izannah Walker

Maker: Izannah Walker, Central Falls, R.I., U.S.A.
Date: 1873, but probably made as early as 1840s
Material: All-cloth
Size: 15—30in (38—76cm)
Mark: Later dolls are marked: " *Patented Nov. 4th 1873* "

Izannah Walker Doll: Stockinette, pressed head, features and hair painted
   with oils, applied ears, treated limbs; muslin body; appropriate clothes; in
   good condition.

17—19in (43—48cm)   **$18,000—22,000**
Fair condition, 18in (46cm)   **10,000**

18in (46cm) Izannah Walker. *Private Collection.*

Wax Doll, Poured

Maker: Various firms in London, England, such as Montanari, Pierotti, Peck, Meech, Marsh, Morrell, Cremer and Edwards
Date: 1850s through the early 1900s
Material: Wax head, arms and legs, cloth body
Mark: Sometimes stamped on body with maker or store

Poured Wax Child: Head, lower arms and legs of wax; cloth body; set-in hair, glass eyes; original clothes or very well dressed; all in good condition.

17—19in (43—48cm)	**$1350—1650***
24—26in (61—66cm)	**1850—2100***
Lady, 22—24in (56—61cm)	**1650—1950**
Man, 18in (46cm) inset mustache	**1650—1750**
Pierotti, incised on shoulder 17—21in (43—53cm)	**1500—1800**
Morrell, 18in (46cm) child	**1800**

*Greatly depending upon appeal of face.

17¾in (45cm) signed Pierotti wax child, all original. *Private Collection.*

Wax (Reinforced)

Maker: Various firms in Germany
Date: 1860 to 1890
Material: Poured wax shoulder head lined on the inside with plaster composition to give strength and durability, (not to be confused with wax-over-composition which simply has a wax coating), muslin body usually with wax-over-composition lower arms and legs.
Mark: None

Reinforced Poured Wax Doll: Poured wax shoulder head lined on the inside with plaster composition, glass eyes (may sleep), closed mouth, open crown, pate, curly mohair or human hair wig nailed on (may be partially inset into the wax around the face); muslin body with wax-over-composition lower limbs (feet may have molded boots); appropriate clothes; all in good condition, but showing some knicks and scrapes.

11in (28cm)	**$250—300**
19—21in (48—53cm)	**550—650**
Lady, 23in (58cm)	**800**

21in (53cm) German "reinforced wax" child with sleep eyes and hair partially inset around her face. The rest is on a wig cap nailed to her head. *H&J Foulke, Inc.*

19in (48cm) German "reinforced wax" child with blue sleep eyes, curly blonde mohair wig nailed on, open crown covered by pate, cloth body with "wax over" arms and legs. She is wearing original clothing. *H&J Foulke, Inc.*

Wax-Over-Composition

Maker: Numerous firms in England, Germany or France
Date: During the 1800s
Material: Wax-over-shoulder head of some type of composition or papier-mâché, cloth body, wax-over-composition or wooden limbs
Mark: None

English Slit-head Wax: Ca. 1830—1860. Wax-over-shoulder head with round face, not rewaxed; human hair wig, glass eyes (may open and close by a wire), faintly smiling; original cloth body with leather arms; original or suitable old clothing; all in fair condition, showing wear.

12—14in (31—36cm)	**$350—400**
23—26in (58—66cm)	**650—750**
15in (38cm) all original and boxed, cracked face	**500**

Molded Hair Doll: Ca. 1860—on. German wax-over-shoulder head, not rewaxed; molded hair sometimes with bow, glass sleep or set eyes; original cloth body; wax-over or wooden extremities with molded boots or bare feet; nice old clothes; all in good condition, good quality.

14—16in (36—41cm)	**$250—300**
22—25in (56—64cm)	**450—500**

20in (51cm) early-type wax-over-composition, original hair wig. *Private Collection.*

12in (31cm) wax-over-composition girl with molded hair. *H&J Foulke, Inc.*

Wax-Over-Composition continued

Wax Doll With Wig: Ca. 1860s to 1900. German. Wax-over-shoulder head, not rewaxed; blonde or brown human hair or mohair wig, blue, brown or black glass eyes, sleep or set, open or closed mouth; original cloth body, any combination of extremities mentioned above, also arms may be made of china; original clothing or suitably dressed; entire doll in nice condition.

Standard quality:

11—12in (28—31cm)	**$125—150**
16—18in (41—46cm)	**300—325**
22—24in (56—61cm)	**400—450**

Superior quality (heavily waxed):

11—12in (28—31cm)	**200—250**
16—18in (41—46cm)	**400—450**
22—24in (56—61cm)	**600—650**

Bonnet Wax Doll: Ca. 1860 to 1880. Wax-over-shoulder head, with molded bonnet; molded hair may have some mohair or human hair attached, blue, brown or black set eyes; original cloth body and wooden extremities; nice old clothes; all in good condition.

16—17in (41—43cm) common model **$ 350—450**

21in (53cm) early round face with molded poke bonnet **2300**

Double-Faced Doll: 1880—on. Fritz Bartenstein. One face crying, one laughing, rotating on a vertical axis by pulling a string, one face hidden by a hood. Body stamped "Bartenstein."

15—16in (38—41cm) **$850**

17in (43cm) wax-over-composition with wig and sleep eyes, all original. *H&J Foulke, Inc.*

Norah Wellings

Maker: Victoria Toy Works, Wellington, Shropshire, England, for Norah Wellings
Date: 1926—Ca. 1960
Material: Fabric: Felt, velvet and velour, and other material, stuffed
Designer: Norah Wellings
Mark: On tag on foot: "Made in England by Norah Wellings"

Wellings Doll: All-fabric, stitch-jointed shoulders and hips; molded fabric face (also of papier-mâché, sometimes stockinette covered), painted features; all in excellent condition. Most commonly found are sailors, Canadian Mounties, Scots and Black Islanders.

Characters (floppy limbs):

8—10in (20—25cm)	**$ 50—85**
13—14in (33—36cm)	**125—150**
Glass eyes,	
14in (36cm) Black	**175—185**

Children:

12—13in (31—33cm)	**$325—375**
16—18in (41—46cm)	**500—600**
23in (58cm)	**900—1100**
Glass eyes,	
16—18in (41—46cm)	**600—700**

See additional photograph on page 7.

24in (61cm) Norah Wellings Dutch girl, all original. *Esther Schwartz Collection.*

12½in (32cm) Norah Wellings character girl. *H&J Foulke, Inc.*

Wislizenus

Maker: Adolf Wislizenus, doll factory, Waltershausen, Thüringia, Germany. Heads made by Bähr & Pröschild, Simon & Halbig and Ernst Heubach.
Date: 1851—on
Material: Bisque head, composition ball-jointed body
Trademarks: Old Glory, Special, Queen Quality
Mark:

Ge r m a n y

A.W.

□

Papier-mâché Shoulder Head: Molded and painted black or blonde hair, painted eyes, closed mouth; cloth body sometimes with leather arms; old or appropriate clothes; all in good condition, showing some wear. (For photograph see *7th Blue Book*, page 303.)
Mark:

14—16in (36—41cm)	A.W. Serial 3	$250—275
19—21in (48—53cm)		350—400
24—25in (61—64cm)		475—525
Glass eyes, 23in (58cm)		750**

Wislizenus Child Doll: Ca. 1890—on. Perfect bisque head, composition ball-jointed body; good wig; blue or brown sleep eyes, open mouth; dressed; all in good condition.

17—19in (43—48cm)	$350—400
23—25in (58—64cm)	500—550

Wislizenus Character Doll: Ca. 1910. Perfect bisque socket head, molded hair, painted or glass eyes, open/closed mouth with molded teeth; composition toddler body; dressed; all in good condition. (For photograph see *8th Blue Book*, page 394.)
#110 or *115:*

16—18in (41—46cm)	$900—1000

Marked A.W. Character: Ca. 1910. Perfect bisque socket head, good wig, sleep eyes, open/closed mouth with molded tongue and two separated porcelain teeth; bent-limb baby body. (For photograph see *7th Blue Book*, page 379.)

26in (66cm)	$1500**

**Not enough price samples to compute available range.

Wislizenus continued

25½in (65cm) A.W. Special. *H&J Foulke, Inc.*

Wood, English

Maker: English craftsmen
Date: Late 17th to mid 19th century
Material: All-wood or with leather or cloth arms
Mark: None

William & Mary Period: Ca. 1690. Carved wooden face, painted eyes, tiny lines comprising eyebrows and eyelashes, rouged cheeks, flax or hair wig; wood body, cloth arms, carved wood hands (fork shaped), wood-jointed legs. Appropriate clothes; all in fair condition.
12—17in (31—43cm)   **$50,000 up**

Queen Anne Period: Ca. early 1700s. Carved wooden face, dark glass eyes (sometimes painted), dotted eyebrows and eyelashes; jointed wood body, cloth upper arms; appropriate clothes; all in fair condition.
24in (61cm)   **$25,000 up**

Georgian Period: Mid to late 1700s. Round wooden head with gesso covering, inset glass eyes (later sometimes blue), dotted eyelashes and eyebrows, flax or hair wig; jointed wood body with pointed torso; appropriate clothes; all in fair condition.
12—13in (31—33cm)   **$2500—3000**
16—18in (41—46cm)   **4500—5000**
24in (61cm)   **6000—6500**

Early 19th Century: Wooden head, gessoed, painted eyes, pointed torso, flax or hair wig; old clothes (dress usually longer than legs); all in fair condition.
16—21in (41—53cm)   **$2000—3000**
For color photographs see pages 222 and 223.

Wood German
(Early)

Maker: Craftsmen of the Grodner Tal, Austria, and Sonneberg, Germany, such as Insam & Prinoth (1820—1830) Gorden Tirol and Nürnberg verlegers of peg-wood dolls and wood doll heads.
Date: Late 18th to 20th century
Material: All-wood, pegged or ball-jointed
Mark: None

Early to Mid 19th Century: Delicately carved head, varnished, carved and painted hair and features, with a yellow tuck comb in hair, painted spit curls, sometimes earrings; mortise and tenon peg joints; old clothes; all in fair condition.

6—7in (15—18cm)	$ **500—700**
12—13in (31—33cm)	**1150—1250**
17—18in (43—46cm)	**1600—1700**
22in (56cm) exceptional	**8000**
26in (66cm) ball and socket joints, exceptional	**12,000 up**

See color photograph on page 224.

Late 19th Century: Wooden head with painted hair, carving not so elaborate as previously, sometimes earrings, spit curls; dressed; all in good condition.

4in (10cm)	**$125**
7—8in (18—20cm)	**175—225**
12in (31cm)	**350**

Early 20th century: Turned wood head, carved nose, painted hair, peg-jointed, painted white lower legs, painted black shoes.

11—12in (28—31cm)	**$50—75**

Wood, German
(Later)

Maker: Various companies, such as Rudolf Schneider and Schilling, Sonneberg, Thüringia, Germany
Date: 1901—1914
Material: All-wood, fully jointed or wood head and limbs, cloth body
Mark: Usually none; sometimes Schilling "winged angel" trademark

---

"Bébé Tout en Bois" (Doll all of Wood): All of wood, fully jointed; wig, inset glass eyes, open mouth with teeth; appropriate clothes; all in fair to good condition.

10—13in (25—33cm)	$325—400
17—19in (43—48cm)	500—600
22—24in (56—61cm)	750

11—12in (28—31cm) German all-wood dolls. *Private Collection.*

Wood, Swiss

Maker: Various Swiss firms
Date: 20th century
Material: All-wood or wood head and limbs on cloth body
Size: Various, but smaller sizes are more commonly found
Mark: Usually a paper label on wrist or clothes

Swiss Wooden Doll: Wooden head with hand-carved features and hair with
  good detail (males sometimes have carved hats); all carved wood jointed
  body; original, usually regional attire; excellent condition.

9—10in (23—25cm)	**$225—250**
12in (31cm)	**350**
18in (46cm)	**650**

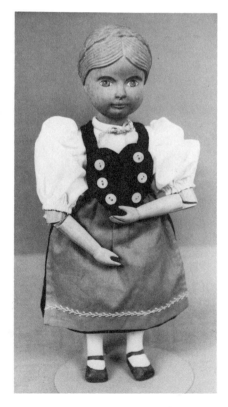

12in (31cm) Swiss wood girl, all original.
H&J Foulke, Inc.

Glossary

Applied Ears: Ear molded independently and affixed to the head. (On most dolls the ear is included as part of the head mold.)

Bald Head: Head with no crown opening, could be covered by a wig or have painted hair.

Ball-jointed Body: Usually a body of composition or papier-mâché with wooden balls at knees, elbows, hips and shoulders to make swivel joints; some parts of the limbs may be wood.

Bébé: French child doll with "dolly face."

Belton-type: A bald head with one, two or three small holes for attaching wig.

Bent-limb Baby Body: Composition body of five pieces with chubby torso and curved arms and legs.

Biscaloid: Ceramic or composition substance for making dolls; also called imitation bisque.

Biskoline: Celluloid-type of substance for making dolls.

Bisque: Unglazed porcelain, usually flesh tinted, used for dolls' heads or all-bisque dolls.

Breather: Dolls with an actual opening in each nostril; also called open nostrils.

Breveté (or Bté):   Used on French dolls to indicate that the patent is registered.

Character Doll: Dolls with bisque or composition heads, modeled to look likelike, such as infants, young or older children, young ladies and so on.

China: Glazed porcelain used for dolls' heads and *Frozen Charlottes.*

Child Dolls: Dolls with a typical "dolly face" which represents a child.

Composition: A material used for dolls' heads and bodies, consisting of such items as wood pulp, glue, sawdust, flour, rags and sundry other substances.

Contemporary Clothes: Clothes not original to the doll, but dating from the same period when the doll would have been a plaything.

Crown Opening: The cut-away part of a doll head.

DEP: Abbreviation used on German and French dolls claiming registration.

D.R.G.M.:   Abbreviation used on German dolls indicating a registered design or patent.

Dolly Face: Typical face used on bisque dolls before 1910 when the character face was developed; "dolly faces" were used also after 1910.

Embossed Mark: Raised letters, numbers or names on the backs of heads or bodies.

Feathered Eyebrows: Eyebrows composed of many tiny painted brush strokes to give a realistic look.

Fixed Eyes: Glass eyes which do not move or sleep.

Flange Neck: A doll's head with a ridge at the base of the neck which contains holes for sewing the head to a cloth body.

Flapper Dolls: Dolls of the 1920s period with bobbed wig or molded hair and slender arms and legs.

Flirting Eyes: Eyes which move from side to side as doll's head is tilted.

Frozen Charlotte: Doll molded all in one piece including arms and legs.

Ges. (Gesch.): Used on German dolls to indicate design is registered or patented.

Googly Eyes: Large, often round eyes looking to the side; also called roguish or goo goo eyes.

Hard Plastic: Hard material used for making dolls after 1948.

Incised Mark: Letters, numbers or names impressed into the bisque on the back of the head or on the shoulder plate.

Intaglio Eyes: Painted eyes with sunken pupil and iris.

JCB: Jointed composition body. See *ball-jointed body*.

Kid Body: Body of white or pink leather.

Lady Dolls: Dolls with an adult face and a body with adult proportions.

Mohair: Goat's hair widely used in making doll wigs.

Molded Hair: Curls, waves and comb marks which are actually part of the mold and not merely painted onto the head.

Motschmann-type Body: Doll body with cloth midsection and upper limbs with floating joints; hard lower torso and lower limbs.

Open-Mouth: Lips parted with an actual opening in the bisque, usually has teeth either molded in the bisque or set in separately and sometimes a tongue.

Open/Closed Mouth: A mouth molded to appear open, but having no actual slit in the bisque.

Original Clothes: Clothes belonging to a doll during the childhood of the original owner, either commercially or homemade.

Painted Bisque: Bisque covered with a layer of flesh-colored paint which has not been baked in, so will easily rub or wash off.

Paperweight Eyes: Blown glass eyes which have depth and look real, usually found in French dolls.

Papier-mâché: A material used for dolls' heads and bodies, consisting of paper pulp, sizing, glue, clay or flour.

Pate: A shaped piece of plaster, cork, cardboard or other material which covers the crown opening.

Pierced Ears: Little holes through the doll's earlobes to accommodate earrings.

Pierced-in Ears: A hole at the doll's earlobe which goes into the head to accommodate earrings.

Pink Bisque: A later bisque of about 1920 which was pre-colored pink.

Pink-toned China: China which has been given a pink tint to look more like real flesh color; also called lustered china.

Rembrandt Hair: Hair style parted in center with bangs at front, straight down sides and back and curled at ends.

S.G.D.G.: Used on French dolls to indicate that the patent is registered "without guarantee of the government."

Shoulder Head: A doll's head and shoulders all in one piece.

Shoulder Plate: The actual shoulder portion sometimes molded in one with the head, sometimes a separate piece with a socket in which a head is inserted.

Socket Head: Head and neck which fit into an opening in the shoulder plate or the body.

Solid-dome Head: Head with no crown opening, could have painted hair or be covered by wig.

Stationary Eyes: Glass eyes which do not move or sleep.

Stone Bisque: Coarse white bisque of a lesser quality.

Toddler Body: Usually a chubby ball-jointed composition body with chunky, shorter thighs and a diagonal hip joint; sometimes has curved instead of jointed arms; sometimes is of five pieces with straight chubby legs.

Topsy-Turvy: Doll with two heads, one usually concealed beneath a skirt.

Turned Shoulder Head: Head and shoulders are one piece, but the head is molded at an angle so that the doll is not looking straight ahead.

Vinyl: Soft plastic material used for making dolls after 1950s.

Watermelon Mouth: Closed line-type mouth curved up at each side in an impish expression.

Wax Over: A doll with head and/or limbs of papier-mâché or composition covered with a layer of wax to give a natural, lifelike finish.

Weighted Eyes: Eyes which can be made to sleep by means of a weight which is attached to the eyes.

Wire Eyes: Eyes which can be made to sleep by means of a wire which protrudes from doll's head.

Selected Bibliography

Anderton, Johana. *Twentieth Century Dolls*. North Kansas City, Missouri: Trojan Press, 1971.

_____. *More Twentieth Century Dolls*. North Kansas City, Missouri: Athena Publishing Co., 1974.

Angione, Genevieve. *All-Bisque & Half-Bisque Dolls*. Exton, Pennsylvania: Schiffer Publishing Ltd., 1969.

Borger, Mona. *Chinas, Dolls for Study and Admiration*. San Francisco: Borger Publications, 1983.

Buchholz, Shirley. *A Century of Celluloid Dolls*. Cumberland, Maryland: Hobby House Press, Inc., 1983.

Casper, Peggy Wiedman. *Fashionable Terri Lee Dolls*. Cumberland, Maryland: Hobby House Press, Inc., 1988.

Cieslik, Jürgen and Marianne. *German Doll Encyclopedia 1800-1939*. Cumberland, Maryland: Hobby House Press, Inc., 1985.

Coleman, Dorothy S., Elizabeth Ann and Evelyn Jane. *The Collector's Book of Dolls' Clothes*. New York: Crown Publishers, Inc., 1975.

_____. *The Collector's Encyclopedia of Dolls, Vol. I & II*. New York: Crown Publishers, Inc., 1968 & 1986.

Foulke, Jan. *Blue Books of Dolls & Values, Vol. I-VIII*. Cumberland, Maryland: Hobby House Press, Inc., 1974-1987.

_____. *Doll Classics*. Cumberland, Maryland: Hobby House Press, Inc., 1987.

_____. *Focusing on Dolls*. Cumberland, Maryland: Hobby House Press, Inc., 1988.

_____. *Focusing on Effanbee Composition Dolls*. Riverdale, Maryland: Hobby House Press, 1978.

_____. *Focusing on Gebrüder Heubach Dolls*. Cumberland, Maryland: Hobby House Press, 1980.

_____. *Kestner, King of Dollmakers*. Cumberland, Maryland: Hobby House Press, Inc., 1982.

_____. *Simon & Halbig Dolls, The Artful Aspect*. Cumberland, Maryland: Hobby House Press, Inc., 1984.

_____. *Treasury of Madame Alexander Dolls*. Riverdale, Maryland: Hobby House Press, 1979.

Gerken, Jo Elizabeth. *Wonderful Dolls of Papier-Mâché*. Lincoln, Nebraska: Doll Research Associates, 1970.

Hillier, Mary. *Dolls and Dollmakers*. New York: G. P. Putnam's Sons, 1968.

_____. *The History of Wax Dolls*. Cumberland, Maryland: Hobby House Press, Inc.; London: Justin Knowles, 1985.

King, Constance Eileen. *The Collector's History of Dolls*. London: Robert Hale, 1977; New York: St. Martin's Press, 1978.

Mathes, Ruth E. and Robert C. *Dolls, Toys and Childhood*. Cumberland, Maryland: Hobby House Press, Inc., 1987.

McGonagle, Dorothy A. *The Dolls of Jules Nicolas Steiner*. Cumberland, Maryland: Hobby House Press, Inc., 1988.

Merrill, Madeline O. *The Art of Dolls, 1700-1940*. Cumberland, Maryland: Hobby House Press, Inc., 1985.

Noble, John. *Treasury of Beautiful Dolls*. New York: Hawthorn Books, 1971.

Shoemaker, Rhoda. *Compo Dolls, Cute and Collectible, Vol. I-III*. Menlo Park, California: 1971, 1971 & 1979.

Tarnowska, Maree. *Fashion Dolls*. Cumberland, Maryland: Hobby House Press, Inc., 1986.

About the Author

The name Jan Foulke is synonymous with accurate information. As the author of the *Blue Book of Dolls & Values*®, she is the most quoted source on doll information and the most respected and recognized authority on dolls and doll prices in the world.

Born in Burlington, New Jersey, Jan Foulke has always had a fondness for dolls. She recalls, "Many happy hours of my childhood were spent with dolls as companions, since we lived on a quiet country road, and until I was ten, I was an only child." Jan received a B.A. from Columbia Union College, where she was named to the *Who's Who in American Colleges & Universities* and was graduated with high honors. Jan taught for twelve years in the Montgomery County school system in Maryland, and also supervised student teachers in English for the University of Maryland, where she did graduate work.

Jan and her husband, Howard, who photographs the dolls presented in the *Blue Book*, were both fond of antiquing as a hobby, and in 1972 they decided to open a small antique shop of their own. The interest of their daughter, Beth, in dolls sparked their curiosity about the history of old dolls — an interest that quite naturally grew out of their love of heirlooms. The stock in their antique shop gradually changed and evolved into an antique doll shop.

Early in the development of their antique doll shop, Jan and Howard realized that there was a critical need for an accurate and reliable doll identification and price guide resource. In the early 1970s, the Foulkes teamed up with Hobby House Press (publishers of *Doll Reader*® Magazine) to produce (along with Thelma Bateman) the first *Blue Book of Dolls & Values*, originally published in 1974. Since that time, the Foulkes have exclusively authored and illustrated the eight successive editions, and today the *Blue Book* is regarded by collectors and dealers as the definitive source for doll prices and values.

Jan and Howard Foulke now dedicate all of their professional time to the world of dolls, writing and illustrating books and articles, appraising collections, lecturing on antique dolls, acting as consultants to museums, auction houses and major collectors, and selling dolls both by mail order and through exhibits at major shows throughout the United States. Mrs. Foulke is a member of the United Federation of Doll Clubs, Doll Collectors of America, and the International Doll Academy.

Mrs. Foulke has appeared on numerous TV talk shows and is often quoted in newspaper and magazine articles as the ultimate source for doll pricing and trends in collecting. In 1985, both "USA Today" and "The Washington Post" observed that the *Blue Book of Dolls & Values* was "the bible of doll collecting."

In addition to her work on the nine editions of the *Blue Book of Dolls & Values*, Jan Foulke has also authored: *Focusing on Effanbee Composition Dolls; A Treasury of Madame Alexander Dolls; Kestner, King of Dollmakers; Simon & Halbig: The Artful Aspect; Focusing on Gebruder Heubach Dolls; Doll Classics;* and *Focusing on Dolls.*

Index

Text references are indicated in alphabetical and numerical order. Often there is a photograph to accompany the text reference. References to illustrations indicate that photographs appear on a different page.

Mold and Mark Numbers